Getting Started in
Options

The *Getting Started In* Series

Getting Started in
Options

FIFTH EDITION

Michael C. Thomsett

WILEY

John Wiley & Sons, Inc.

Published by John Wiley & Sons, Inc., Hoboken, New Jersey.
Published simultaneously in Canada.

For general information on our other products and services, or technical support, please contact our Customer Care Department within the United States at 800-762-2974, outside the United States at 317-572-3993 or fax 317-572-4002.

Wiley also publishes its books in a variety of electronic formats. Some content that appears in print may not be available in electronic books.

For more information about Wiley products, visit our web site at www.wiley.com.

Library of Congress Cataloging-in-Publication Data:
Thomsett, Michael C.
  Getting started in options / Michael C. Thomsett.—5th ed.
    p.   cm.
  ISBN 0-471-44493-6 (PAPER)
  1. Stock options.   2. Options (Finance)   I. Title.
  HG6042. T46   2003
  332.63'228—dc21   2003001702

Printed in the United States of America.

10   9   8   7   6   5   4   3   2

Contents

Chapter 10

Acknowledgments

Thanks to those readers of the previous four editions who were kind enough to write and offer their suggestions for improving this book. Their letters have been invaluable in clarifying explanations, definitions, and examples.

Thanks also to my editor at John Wiley & Sons, Debra Englander, for her encouragement through many editions of this and other books.

Finally, thanks go to my wife, Linda Rose Thomsett, for her understanding and belief in the value of this book, and for her enthusiasm and support of my writing career.

An Investment with Many Faces

―――――

The people who get on in this world are the people who get up and look for the circumstances they want, and if they can't find them, make them.
—George Bernard Shaw, *Mrs. Warren's Profession*, 1893

The market has changed dramatically in the past few years and, for those who profited in the past—perhaps significantly—more recent events have shown that investments in publicly traded companies are not always as safe as many had believed.

Of course, the experienced investor understands that knowledge and familiarity with trading risks spell the difference between confidence and worry. Even the experienced investor may need to adopt a more defensive stance given the changes in the market. With that in mind, the options market can play an important role in your portfolio in several ways: enhancing profits without a corresponding increase in risk, protecting investments with a form of insurance not otherwise available, and guarding against loss (at least to a degree). This book explains how these and other advantages can be achieved through the use of options.

You probably have heard people describe the options market as risky or complicated. Certainly, aspects of option investing fit these descriptions, but so do some aspects of virtually all forms of investing. The truth is, options can take many forms, some high risk and others extremely conservative.

The risk element does need to be examined and compared, however. Like the stock market, options are subject to their own special set of rules, including potential for gain and limits on the degree of profit; the risk and reward nature of options; timing considerations and the need for close monitoring of options positions; and the close connection between options values and the value of stocks associated with those options. You might ask, "If options are not as risky as I have heard, why don't more people take part in options trading?" The answer is twofold. First, the relatively brief existence of options for the general public has kept this market removed from the public eye for the most part. Second, while various options strategies are not as complex as many people believe, the language of options is highly specialized and, perhaps, exotic. When language is overly technical, the average person comes away with a sense of alienation—the language itself, while necessary, also creates a sense of fear. Unfortunately, the terminology of the options market is far from user friendly. One of the main features of this book is that it carefully presents *ideas* behind the terminology as each new term is introduced, supported further with examples, explanations, and graphics.

This book emphasizes the strategic use of stock options in several different ways. In order to determine the suitability of options in your own portfolio, you need to go through a four-step process of evaluation:

1. Master the terminology of this highly specialized market.
2. Study the options market in terms of risk.
3. Observe the market.
4. Set a risk standard for yourself.

For any strategy to work well, it needs to be appropriate, comfortable, and affordable. These ideas are not commonly expressed in books about investing but, in fact, they are of great importance to you when it comes to the decision point. So you need to keep in mind as you consider and make decisions about how and where to invest, that the ultimate test of whether or not to proceed should be to question whether it is appropriate, comfortable, and affordable. No one idea works for everyone, and options are no exception. No matter how easy, practical, or foolproof an idea seems in print, and no matter how well it works on paper, placing real money at risk changes everything. Your decision has to feel right to you. Investing in any manner should not only be profitable, but enjoyable as well. Too many would-be investors make their decisions on the basis of advice from others—friends, family members, brokers, or books—without researching on their own, and without studying the attributes and risks involved in that decision. They overlook the need to study information and analyze the risk/opportunity before going ahead.

Chapter 1

Calls and Puts

I know of no more encouraging fact than the unquestionable ability of man to elevate his life by a conscious endeavor.
— Henry David Thoreau, *Walden*, 1854

Most people are familiar with two forms of investment: equity and debt. There is a third method, however, and that third method is far more interesting than the other two. Its attributes are unlike any that most people understand—and these differences can be viewed as a troubling set of problems, or as a promising set of opportunities.

To begin by laying the groundwork: An *equity investment* is the purchase of ownership in a company. The best-known example of this is the purchase of stock in publicly listed companies, whose shares are sold through the stock exchanges. Each *share* of stock represents a portion of the total capital, or ownership, in the company.

When you buy 100 shares of stock, you are in complete control over that investment. You decide how long to hold the shares, and when to sell. Stocks provide you with tangible value, because they represent part ownership in the company. Owning stock entitles you to dividends if they are declared, and gives you the right to vote in matters before the board of directors. (Some special nonvoting stock lacks this right.) If the stock rises in value, you will gain a profit. If you wish, you can keep the stock for many years, even for your whole life. Stocks, be-

equity investment
an investment in the form of part ownership, such as the purchase of shares of stock in a corporation.

share
a unit of ownership in the capital of a corporation.

3

cause they have tangible value, can be traded to other investors over public exchanges, or they can be used as collateral to borrow money.

Example: You purchase 100 shares at $27 per share, and place $2,700 plus trading fees into your account. You receive notice that the purchase has been completed. This is an equity investment, and you are a stockholder in the corporation.

debt investment
an investment in the form of a loan made to earn interest, such as the purchase of a bond.

The second broadly understood form is a *debt investment*, also called a debt instrument. This is a loan made by the investor to the company, government, or government agency, which promises to repay the loan plus interest, as a contractual obligation. The best-known form of debt instrument is the bond. Corporations, cities and states, the federal government, agencies, and sub-divisions, finance their operations and projects through bond issues, and investors in bonds are lenders, not stockholders.

When you own a bond, you also own a tangible value—not in stock but in a contractual right with the lender. Your contract promises to pay you interest and to repay the amount loaned by a specific date. Like stocks, bonds can be used as collateral to borrow money. They also rise and fall in value based on the interest rate a bond pays compared to current rates in today's market. Bondholders usually are repaid before stockholders as part of their contract, so bonds have that advantage over stocks.

Example: You purchase a bond currently valued at $9,700 from the U.S. government. Although you invest your funds in the same manner as a stockholder, you have become a bondholder; this does not provide any equity interest to you. You are a lender and you own a debt instrument.

The two popular forms of investing are comfortable and widely understood. However, the third form of investing is less well known. Equity and debt contain a tangible value that we can grasp and visualize. Part ownership in a company or a contractual right for repayment are basic features of equity and debt investments. Not only are these tangible, but they have a specific life as well. Stock ownership lasts as long as you continue to own the stock and cannot be canceled; a bond has a contractual repayment schedule and ending date. The third form of investing does not contain these features; it disappears—expires—within a short period of time. Most investors, when first told of this attribute, hesitate at the idea of investing money in a product that evaporates and then ceases to have any value. In fact, there is no tangible value at all. So you would be investing money in something with no tangible value, that will be absolutely worthless within a few months. To make this even more perplexing, imagine that the value of this intangible is certain to decline just because time passes by.

These are some of the features of options. Taken by themselves (and out of context), these attributes certainly do not make this market seem very appealing. These attributes—lack of tangible value, worthlessness in the short term, and decline in value itself—make options seem far too risky for most people. However, there are good reasons for you to read on. Not all methods of investing in options are as risky as they might seem; some are quite conservative, because the features just mentioned can work to your advantage. In whatever way you might use options, the many strategies that can be applied make options one of the more interesting strategies for investors.

> **Smart Investor Tip** Option strategies range from high risk to extremely conservative. The risk features on one end of the spectrum work to your advantage on the other. Options provide you with a rich variety of choices.

option
the right to buy or to sell 100 shares of stock at a specified, fixed price and by a specified date in the future.

An *option* is a contract that provides you with the right to execute a stock transaction—that is, to buy or sell 100 shares of stock. (Each option always refers to a 100-share unit.) This right includes a specific stock and a specific fixed price per share that remains fixed until a specific date in the future. When you own an option, you do not have any equity in the stock, and neither do you have any debt position. You have only a contractual right to buy or to sell 100 shares of the stock at the fixed price.

Since you can always buy or sell 100 shares at the current market price, you might ask: "Why do I need to purchase an option to gain that right?" The answer is that the option fixes the price, and this is the key to an option's value. Stock prices may rise or fall, at times significantly. Price movement is unpredictable, which makes stock market investing interesting, and also defines the risk to the market itself. As an option owner, the stock price you *can* apply to buy or sell 100 shares is frozen for as long as the option remains in effect. So no matter how much price movement takes place, your price is fixed should you decide to purchase or sell 100 shares of that stock. Ultimately, an option's value is going to be determined by a comparison between the fixed price and the stock's current market price.

A few important restrictions come with options:

round lot
a lot of 100 shares of stock or of higher numbers divisible by 100, the usual trading unit on the public exchanges.

✔ The right to buy or to sell stock at the fixed price is never indefinite; in fact, time is the most critical factor because the option exists for only a few months. When the deadline has passed, the option becomes worthless and ceases to exist. Because of this, the option's value is going to fall as the deadline approaches, and in a predictable manner.

✔ Each option also applies only to one specific stock and cannot be transferred.

✔ Finally, each option applies to exactly 100 shares of stock, no more and no less.

odd lot
a lot of shares that is fewer than the more typical round lot trading unit of 100 shares.

Stock transactions commonly occur in blocks divisible by 100, called a *round lot*, and that has become a standard trading unit on the public exchanges. In the market, you have the right to buy or sell an unlimited number of shares, assuming that they are available for sale and that you are willing to pay the seller's price. However, if you buy fewer than 100 shares in a single transaction, you will be charged a higher trading fee. An odd-numbered grouping of shares is called an *odd lot*.

So each option applies to 100 shares, conforming to the commonly traded lot, whether you are operating as a buyer or as a seller. There are two types of options. First is the *call*, which grants its owner the right to buy 100 shares of stock in a company. When you buy a call, it is as though the seller is saying to you, "I will allow you to buy 100 shares of this company's stock, at a specified price, at any time between now and a specified date in the future. For that privilege, I expect you to pay me the current option price."

That price is determined by how attractive an offer is being made. If the price per share of stock specified in the option is attractive (based on the current price of the stock), then the price will be higher than if the opposite were true. The more attractive the fixed option price in comparison with the stock's current market price, the higher the cost of the option will be. Each option's value changes according to the changes in the price of the stock. If the stock's value rises, the value of the call option will follow suit and rise as well. And if the stock's market price falls, the option will react in the same manner. When an investor buys a call and the stock's market value rises after the purchase, the investor profits because the call becomes more valuable. The value of an option actually is quite predictable—it is affected by time as well as by the ever-changing value of the stock.

call
an option acquired by a buyer or granted by a seller to buy 100 shares of stock at a fixed price.

Smart Investor Tip Changes in the stock's value affect the value of the option directly, because while the stock's market price changes, the option's specified price per share remains the same. The changes in value are predictable; option valuation is no mystery.

The second type of option is the *put*. This is the opposite of a call in the sense that it grants a selling right instead of a purchasing right. The owner of a put contract has the right to sell 100 shares of stock. When you buy a put, it is as though the seller were saying to you, "I will

put
an option acquired by a buyer or granted by a seller to sell 100 shares of stock at a fixed price.

allow you to sell me 100 shares of a specific company's stock, at a specified price per share, at any time between now and a specific date in the future. For that privilege, I expect you to pay me a price."

The attributes of calls and puts can be clarified by remembering that either option can be bought or sold. This means there are four possible permutations to options transactions:

1. Buy a call (buy the right to buy 100 shares).
2. Sell a call (sell the right to someone else to buy 100 shares from you).
3. Buy a put (buy the right to sell 100 shares).
4. Sell a put (sell the right to someone else to sell 100 shares to you)

Another way to keep the distinction clear is to remember these qualifications: A call buyer believes and hopes that the stock's value will rise, but a put buyer is looking for the price per share to fall. If the belief is right in either case, then a profit will occur. A call seller hopes that the stock price will remain the same or fall, but a put seller hopes the price of the stock will rise. (The seller profits if value goes out of the option—more on this later.)

 market value
the value of an investment at any given time or date; the amount a buyer is willing to pay to acquire an investment and what a seller is also willing to receive to transfer the same investment.

 Smart Investor Tip   Option buyers can profit whether the market rises or falls; the difficult part is knowing ahead of time which direction the market will take.

If an option buyer—dealing either in calls or in puts—is correct in predicting the price movement in *market value*, then the action of buying the option will be profitable. Market value is the price value agreed upon by both buyer and seller, and is the common determining factor in the auction marketplace. However, when it comes to options, you have an additional obstacle besides estimating the direction of price movement: The change has to take place before the deadline that is attached to every option. You might be correct about a stock's long-term prospects and as a stockholder, you have the luxury of being able to wait out long-term change. However, options are always short term. This is the critical point. Options are finite and unlike stocks, they cease to exist and lose all of their value within a relatively short period, usually only a few months. Because of this daunting limitation to options trading, time may be the ultimate factor in determining whether or not an option buyer is able to earn a profit.

Smart Investor Tip   It is not enough to accurately predict the direction of a stock's price movement. For option buyers, that movement has to occur within a very short period.

Why does the option's market value change when the stock's price moves up or down? First of all, the option is an intangible right, a contract lacking the kind of value associated, for example, with shares of stock. The option is an agreement relating to 100 shares of a specific stock *and* to a specific price per share. Consequently, if the buyer's timing is poor—meaning the stock's movement doesn't occur or is not substantial enough by the dead line—then the buyer will not realize a profit.

When you buy a call, it is as though you are saying, "I am willing to pay the price being asked to acquire a contractual right. That right provides that I may *buy* 100 shares of stock at the specified fixed price per share, and this right exists to buy those shares at any time between my option purchase date and the specified deadline." If the stock's market price rises above the fixed price indicated in the option agreement, the call becomes more valuable. Imagine that you buy a call option granting you the right to buy 100 shares at the price of $80 per share. Before the deadline, though, the stock's market price rises to $95 per share. As the owner of a call option, you have the right to buy 100 shares at $80, or 15 points below the current market value. This is the purchaser's advantage in the scenario described, when market value exceeds the fixed and contractual price indicated in the call's contract. In that instance, you as buyer would have the right to buy 100 shares 15 points below the current market value.

The same scenario applies to buying puts, but with the stock moving in the opposite direction. When you buy a put, it is as though you are saying, "I am willing to pay the asked price to buy a contractual right. That right provides that I may *sell* 100 shares of the specified stock at the indicated price per share, at any time between my option purchase date and the specified deadline." If the stock's price falls below that level, you will be able to sell 100 shares *above* current market value. For example, let's say that you buy a put option providing you with the right to sell 100 shares at $80 per share. Before the deadline, the stock's market value falls to $70 per share. As the owner of a put, you have the right to sell 100 shares at the fixed price of $80, which is $10 per share above the current market value. As the buyer of a put, you can sell your 100 shares at 10 points above current market value. The potential advantage to options buyers is found in the contractual rights that they provide. This right is central to the nature of the option, and each option bought or sold is referred to as a *contract*.

THE CALL OPTION

A call is the right to buy 100 shares of stock at a fixed price per share, at any time between the purchase of the call and the specified future deadline. This time is limited. As a call *buyer*, you acquire the right, and as a call *seller*, you grant the right of the option to someone else. (See Figure 1.1.)

Let's walk through the illustration and apply both buying and selling as they relate to the call option:

✔ *Buyer of a call.* When you buy a call, you hope that the stock will rise in value, because that will result in a corresponding increase in value for the call. As a result, the call will have a higher market value. The call can be

contract
a single option, the agreement providing the buyer with the rights the option grants. (Those rights include identification of the stock, the cost of the option, the date the option will expire, and the fixed price per share of the stock to be bought or sold under the right of the option.)

buyer
an investor who purchases a call or a put option; the buyer realizes a profit if the value of stock moves above the specified price (call) or below the specified price (put).

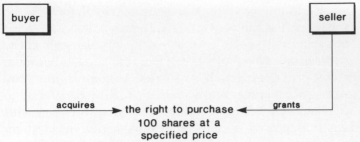

FIGURE 1.1   The call option.

sold and closed at a profit; or the stock can be bought at a fixed price below current market value.

✔ *Seller of a call.* When you sell a call, you hope that the stock will fall in value, because that will result in a corresponding decrease in value for the call. As a result, the call will have a lower market value. The call can be purchased and closed at a profit; or the stock can be sold to the buyer at a price above current market value. The order is the reverse for the better-known buyer's position. The call seller will first sell and then later on, will close the transaction with a buy order. (More information on selling calls is presented in Chapter 5.)

The backwards sequence used by call sellers often is difficult to grasp for many people accustomed to the more traditional buy-hold-sell pattern. The seller's approach is to sell-hold-buy. Remembering that time is running for every option contract, the seller, by reversing the sequence, has a distinct advantage over the buyer. Time is on the seller's side.

Smart Investor Tip   Option sellers reverse the sequence by selling first and buying later. This strategy has many advantages, especially considering the restriction of time unique to the option contract. Time benefits the seller.

supply and demand

the market forces that determine the current value for stocks. A growing number of buyers represent demand for shares, and a growing number of sellers represent supply. The price of stocks rises as demand increases, and falls as supply increases.

Prices of listed options—those traded publicly on exchanges like the New York, Chicago, and Philadelphia Stock exchanges—are established strictly through *supply and demand*. Those are the forces that dictate whether market prices rise or fall for stocks. As more buyers want stocks, prices are driven upward by their demand; and as more sellers want to sell shares of stock, prices decline due to increased supply. The supply and demand for stocks, in turn, affect the market value of options. The option itself has no direct fundamental value or underlying financial reasons for rising or falling; its market value is related entirely to the fundamental and technical changes in the stock.

Smart Investor Tip   The market forces affecting the value of stocks in turn affect market values of options. The option itself has no actual fundamental value; its market value is formulated based on the stock's fundamentals.

auction market

the public exchanges in which stocks, bonds, options, and other products are traded publicly; and in which values are established by ever-changing supply and demand on the part of buyers and sellers.

The orderly process of buying and selling stocks, which establishes stock price values, takes place on the exchanges through trading that is available to the general public. This overall public trading activity, in which prices are establishing through ever-changing supply and demand, is called the *auction market*, because value is not controlled by any forces other than the market itself. These forces include economic news and perceptions, earnings of listed companies, news and events affecting products and services, competitive forces, and Wall Street events, positive or negative. Individual stock prices also rise or fall based on index motion.

Options themselves have little or no direct supply and demand features because they are not finite. Stocks issued by corporations are limited in number, but the exchanges will allow investors to buy or sell as many options as they want. The *number* of active options is unlimited. However, the values in option contracts respond directly to changes in the stock's value. There are two primary factors affecting the option's value: First is time and second is the market value of the stock. As time passes, the option loses market desirability, because the time approaches after which that option will lose all of its value; and as market value of the stock changes, the option's market value follows suit.

Smart Investor Tip   Option value is affected by movement in the price of the stock, and by the passage of time. Supply and demand affects option valuation only indirectly.

The owner of a call enjoys an important benefit in the auction market. There is always a *ready market* for the option at the current market price. That means that the owner of an option never has a problem selling that option, although the price reflects its current market value.

This feature is of critical importance. For example, if there were constantly more buyers than sellers of options, then market value would be distorted beyond reason. To some degree, distortions do occur on the basis of rumor or speculation, usually in the short term. But by and large, option values are directly formulated on the basis of stock prices and time until the option will cease to exist. If buyers had to scramble to find a limited number of willing sellers, the market would not work efficiently. Demand between buyers and sellers in options is rarely equal, because options do not possess supply and demand features of their own; changes in market value are a function of time and stock market value. So the public exchanges place themselves in a position to make the market operate as efficiently as possible. They facilitate trading in options by acting as the seller to every buyer, and as the buyer to every seller.

ready market
a liquid market, one in which buyers can easily sell their holdings, or in which sellers can easily find buyers, at current market prices.

How Call Buying Works

When you buy a call, you are not obligated to buy the 100 shares of stock. You have the *right*, but not the obligation.

expiration date

the date on which an option becomes worthless, which is specified in the option contract.

underlying stock

the stock on which the option grants the right to buy or sell, which is specified in every option contract.

exercise

the act of buying stock under the terms of the call option or selling stock under the terms of the put option, at the specified price per share in the option contract.

In fact, the vast majority of call buyers do not actually buy 100 shares of stock. Most buyers are speculating on the price movement of the stock, hoping to sell their options at a profit rather than buying 100 shares of stock. As a buyer, you have until the *expiration date* to decide what action to take, if any. You have several choices, and the best one to make depends entirely on what happens to the market price of the *underlying stock*, and on how much time remains in the option period.

There will be three scenarios relating to the price of the underlying stock, and several choices for action within each:

1. *The market value of the underlying stock rises.* In the event of an increase in the price of the underlying stock, you can take one of two actions. First, you can *exercise* the option and buy the 100 shares of stock below current market value. Second, if you do not want to own 100 shares of that stock, you can sell the option for a profit.

The value in the option is there because the option fixes the price of the stock, even when current market value is higher. This fixed price in every option contract is called the *striking price* of the option. Striking price is expressed as a numerical equivalent of the dollar price per share, without dollar signs. The striking price is normally divisible by five, as options are established with striking prices at five-dollar price intervals. (Exceptions are found in some instances, such as after stock splits.)

Example: You decided two months ago to buy a call. You paid the price of $200, which entitled you to buy 100 shares of a particular stock at $55 per share. The striking price is 55. The option will expire later this month. The stock currently is selling for $60 per share, and the option's current value is 6 ($600). You have a choice to make: You may exercise the call and buy 100 shares at the contractual price of $55 per share, which is $5 per share below current market value; or you may sell the call and realize a profit of $400 on the investment (current market value of the option of $600, less the original price of $200).

Smart Investor Tip In setting standards for yourself to determine when or if to take profits in an option, be sure to factor in the cost of the transaction. Brokerage fees and charges vary widely, so shop around for the best option deal based on the volume of trading you undertake.

striking price
the fixed price to be paid for 100 shares of stock specified in the option contract, which will be paid or received by the owner of the option contract upon exercise, regardless of the current market value of the stock.

2. *The market value of the underlying stock does not change.* It often happens that within the relatively short life span of an option, the stock's market value does not change, or changes are too insignificant to create the profit scenario you hope for in buying calls. You have two alternatives in this situation. First, you may sell the call before its expiration date (after which the call becomes worthless). Second, you may hold onto the option, hoping that the stock's market value will rise before expiration, resulting in a rise in the call's value as well, at the last minute. The first choice, selling at a loss, is advisable when it appears there is no hope of a last-minute surge in the stock's market value. Taking some money out and reducing your loss may be wiser than waiting for the option to lose even more value. Remember, after expiration date, the option is worthless. An option is a *wasting asset*, because it is designed to lose value after expiration. By its limited life attribute, it is expected to lose value as time goes by. If the market value of the stock remains at or below the striking price all the way to expiration, then the *premium* value—the current market value of the option—will be much less near expiration than it was at the time you purchased it, even if the stock's market value remains the same. The difference reflects the value of time itself. The longer the time until expiration, the more opportunity there is for the stock (and the option) to change in value.

wasting asset
any asset that declines in value over time. (An option is an example of a wasting asset because it exists only until expiration, after which it becomes worthless.)

Example: You purchased a call a few months ago "at 5." (This means you paid a premium of $500). You hoped that the underlying stock would increase in market value, causing the option to also rise in value. The call will expire later this month, but contrary to your expectations,

premium
the current price
of an option,
which a buyer
pays and a seller
receives at the
time of the
transaction.
(The amount of
premium is ex-
pressed as the
dollar value of
the option, but
without dollar
signs; for exam-
ple, stating that
an option is "at 3"
means its current
market value is
$300.)

the stock's price has not changed. The option's value has declined to $100. You have the choice of selling it now and taking a $400 loss; or you may hold the option hoping for a last-minute increase in the stock's value. Either way, you will need to sell the option before expiration, after which it will become worthless.

Smart Investor Tip   The options market is characterized by a series of choices, some more difficult than others. It requires discipline to apply a formula so that you make the "smart" decision given the circumstances, rather than acting on impulse. That is the key to succeeding with options.

3. *The market value of the underlying stock falls.* As the underlying stock's market value falls, the value of all related calls will fall as well. The value of the option is always related to the value of the underlying stock. If the stock's market price falls significantly, your call will show very little in the way of market value. You may sell and accept the loss or, if the option is worth nearly nothing, you may simply allow it to expire and take a full loss on the transaction.

Example: You bought a call four months ago and paid 3 (a premium of $300). You were hoping that the stock's market value would rise, also causing a rise in the value of the call. Instead, the stock's market value fell, and the option followed suit. It is now worth only 1 ($100). You have a choice: You may sell the call for 1 and accept a loss of $200; or you may hold onto the call until near expiration. The stock could rise in value at the last minute, which has been known to happen. However, by continuing to hold the call, you risk further deterioration in the call premium value. If you wait until expiration occurs, the call will be worthless.

This example demonstrates that buying calls is risky. The last-minute rescue of an option by sudden increases in the value of the underlying stock can and does happen, but usually, it does not. The limited life of the option works against the call buyer. The entire amount invested could be lost. The most significant advantage in speculating in calls is that instead of losing a larger sum in buying 100 shares of stock, the loss is limited to the relatively small premium value. At the same time, you could profit significantly as a call buyer because less money is at risk. The stockholder, in comparison, has the advantage of being able to hold stock indefinitely, without having to worry about expiration date. For stockholders, patience is always possible, and it might take many months or even years for growth in value to occur. The stockholder is under no pressure to act, because stock does not expire as options do.

Example: You bought a call last month for 1 (premium of $100). The current price of the stock is $80 per share. For your $100 investment, you have a degree of control over 100 shares, without having to invest $8,000. Your risk is limited to the $100 investment; if the stock's market value falls, you cannot lose more than the $100, no matter what. In comparison, if you paid $8,000 to acquire 100 shares of stock, you could afford to wait indefinitely for a profit to appear, but you would have to tie up $8,000. You could also lose much more; if the stock's market value falls to $50 per share, your investment will have lost $3,000 in market value.

Smart Investor Tip For anyone speculating over the short term, option buying is an excellent method of controlling large blocks of stock with minor commitments of capital.

In some respects, the preceding example defines the difference between investing and speculating. The very idea of investing usually indicates a long-term mentality and perspective. Because stock does not expire, investors enjoy the luxury of being able to wait out short-term market conditions, hoping that over several years that company's fortunes will lead to profits—not to mention continuing dividends and ever-higher market value for the stock. There is no denying that stockholders enjoy clear advantages by owning stock. They can wait indefinitely for the market to go their way. They earn dividend income. And stock can be used as collateral for buying or financing other assets. Speculators, in comparison, risk losing all of their investment, while also being exposed to the opportunity for spectacular gains. Rather than considering one method as being better than the other, think of options as yet another way to use investment capital. Options buyers know that their risk/reward scenario is characterized by the ever-looming expiration date. To understand how the speculative nature of call buying affects you, consider the following two examples.

> **Smart Investor Tip**   The limited life of options defines the risk/reward scenario and option players recognize this as part of their strategic approach. The risk is accepted because the opportunity is there, too.

Example when the stock price rises: You buy a call for 2 ($200), which provides you with the right to buy 100 shares of stock for $80 per share. If the stock's value rises above $80, your call will rise in value dollar-for-dollar along with the stock. So if the stock goes up $4 per share to $84, the option will also rise four points, or $400 in value. You would earn a profit of $200 if you were to sell the call at that point (four points of value less the purchase price of 2). That would be the same amount of profit you would realize by purchasing 100 shares of stock at $8,000 and selling those shares for $8,200. (Again, this example does not take into account any brokerage and trading costs. Chances are that fees for the stock trade would be higher than for an options trade because more money is being exchanged.)

Example when the stock price falls: You buy a call for 2 ($200), which gives you the right to buy 100 shares of stock at $80 per share. By the call's expiration date, the stock has fallen to $68 per share. You lose the entire $200 investment as the call becomes worthless. However, if you had purchased 100 shares of stock and paid $8,000, your loss at this point would be $1,200 ($80 per share at purchase, less current market value of $68 per share). Your choice, then, would be to sell the stock and take the loss or continue to keep your capital tied up, hoping its value will eventually rebound. Compared to buying stock directly, the option risks are more limited. Stockholders can wait out a temporary drop in price even indefinitely. However, the stockholder has no way of knowing when the stock's price will rebound, or even if it ever will do so. As an option buyer, you are at risk for only a few months at the most. One of the risks in buying stock is the "lost opportunity" risk—capital is committed in a loss situation while other opportunities come and go.

In situations where an investment in stock loses value, stockholders can wait for a rebound. During that time, they are entitled to continue receiving dividends, so their investment is not entirely in limbo. If you are interested in long-term gains, then a temporary drop in market value is not catastrophic as long as you continue to believe that the company remains a viable long-term "hold" candidate; market fluctuations might even be expected. Some investors would see such a drop as a buying opportunity, and pick up even more shares. The effect of this move is to lower the overall basis in the stock, so that a rebound creates even greater returns later on.

Smart Investor Tip   A long-term investor can hold stock indefinitely and does not have to worry about expiration. If that is of primary importance to someone, then that person probably will not want to buy options.

Anyone who desires long-term gains such as this should not be buying options, which are short term in nature, and which do not fit the risk profile for long-term investing. The long-term investor is aware of the permanence of stock.

The real advantage in buying calls is that you are not required to tie up a large sum of capital nor to keep it at risk for a long time. Yet, you are able to control 100 shares of stock for each option purchased as though you had bought those shares outright. Losses are limited to the amount of premium you pay.

Investment Standards for Call Buyers

People who work in the stock market—including brokers who help investors to decide what to buy and sell—regularly offer advice on stocks. If a stockbroker, analyst, or financial planner is qualified, he or she may also offer advice on dealing in options. Several important points should be kept in mind when you are working with a broker, especially where option buying is involved:

1. *You need to develop your own expertise.* The broker might not know as much about the market as you do. Just because someone has a license does not mean that he or she is an expert on all types of investments.

2. *You cannot expect on-the-job training as an options investor.* Don't expect a broker to train you. Remember, brokers earn their living on commissions and placement of orders. That means their primary motive is to get investors to buy and to sell.

3. *There are no guarantees.* Risk is found everywhere and in all markets. While it is true that call buying comes with some specific risk characteristics, that does not mean that buying stock is safe in comparison.

Smart Investor Tip   Anyone who wants to be involved with options will eventually realize that a broker's advice is unnecessary and could even get in the way of a well-designed program.

Brokers are required by law to ensure that you are qualified to invest in options. That means that you should have at least a minimal understanding of market risks, procedures, and terminology, and that you understand what you will be doing with options. Brokers are required to apply a rule called *know your customer*. The brokerage firm has to ask new investors to complete a form that documents the investor's knowledge and experience with options; the firms also give out a *prospectus*, which is a document explaining all of the risks of option investing.

know your customer a rule for brokers requiring the broker to be aware of the risk and capital profile of each client, designed to ensure that recommendations are suitable for each individual.

> **Smart Investor Tip** You can get a copy of the options prospectus, called "Characteristics and Risks of Standardized Options," online at http://www.cboe.com/Resources/Intro.asp.

The investment standard for buying calls includes the requirement that you know how the market works, and that you invest only funds that you can afford to have at risk. Beyond that, you have every right to decide for yourself how much risk you want to take. Ultimately, you are responsible for your own profits and losses in the market. The role of the broker is to document the fact that the right questions were asked before your money was taken and placed into the option. One of the most common mistakes made, especially by inexperienced investors, is to believe that a broker is responsible for providing guidance.

prospectus a document designed to disclose all of the risk characteristics associated with a particular investment.

How Call Selling Works

Buying calls is similar to buying stock, at least regarding the sequence of events. You invest money and, after some time has passed, you make the decision to sell. The transaction takes place in a predictable order. Call selling doesn't work that way. A seller begins by selling a call, and later on buys the same call to close out the transaction.

Many people have trouble grasping the idea of selling *before* buying. A common reaction is, "Are you sure?

short selling
a strategy in the stock market in which shares of stock are first sold, creating a short position for the investor; and later bought in a closing purchase transaction.

Is that legal?" or "How can you sell something that you don't own?" It is legal, and you can sell something before you buy it. This is done all the time in the stock market through a strategy known as *short selling*. An investor sells stock that he or she does not own; and later places a "buy" order, which closes the position.

The same technique is used in the options market, and is far less complicated than selling stock short. Because options have no tangible value, becoming an option seller is fairly easy. A call seller grants the right to someone else—a buyer—to buy 100 shares of stock, at a fixed price per share and by a specified expiration date. For granting this right, the call seller is paid a premium. As a call seller, you are paid for the sale but you must also be willing to deliver 100 shares of stock if the call buyer exercises the option. This strategy, the exact opposite of buying calls, has a different array of risks from those experienced by the call buyer. The greatest risk is that the option you sell could be exercised, and you would be required to sell 100 shares of stock far below the current market value.

When you operate as an option buyer, the decision to exercise or not is entirely up to you. But as a seller, that decision is always made by someone else. As an option seller, you can make or lose money in three different ways:

1. *The market value of the underlying stock rises.* In this instance, the value of the call rises as well. For a buyer, this is good news. But for the seller, the opposite is true. If the buyer exercises the call, the 100 shares of stock have to be delivered by the option seller. In practice, this means you are required to pay the difference between the option's striking price and the stock's current market value. As a seller, this means you lose money. Remember, the option will be exercised only if the stock's current market value is higher than the striking price of the option.

Example: You sell a call which specifies a striking price of $40 per share. You happen to own 100 shares of the subject stock, so you consider your risks to be minimal in selling a call. In addition, the call is worth $200, and that amount is paid to you for selling a call. One month later, the stock's market value has risen to $46 per share and the buyer exercises the call. You are obligated to deliver the 100 shares of stock at $40 per share. This is $6 per share below current market value. Although you received a premium of $200 for selling the call, you lose the increased market value in the stock, which is $600. Your net loss in this case is $400.

Example: Given the same conditions as before, let's now assume that you did not own 100 shares of stock. What happens if the option is exercised? In this case, you are still required to deliver 100 shares at $40 per share. Current market value is $46, so you are required to buy the shares at that price and then sell them at $40, a net loss of $600. (In practice, you would be required to pay the difference rather than physically buying and then selling 100 shares.)

> **Smart Investor Tip**   Call sellers have much less risk when they already own their 100 shares. They can select calls in such a way that In the event of exercise, the stock investment will still be profitable.

The difference between these two examples is that in the first case, you owned the shares and could deliver them if the option were exercised. There is even the possibility that you originally purchased those shares below the $40 per share value. So the loss exists only regarding the call transaction; in effect, you exchanged potential gain in the stock for the value of the call premium you received. In the second example, it is all loss because you have to buy the shares at current market value and sell them for less.

2. *The market value of the stock does not change.* In the case where the stock's value remains at or near its value at the time the call is sold, the value of the call will fall over time. Remember, the call is a wasting asset. While that is a problem for the call buyer, it is a great advantage for the call seller. Time works against the buyer, but it works for the call seller. You have the right to close out your sold call at any time before expiration date. So you can sell a call and see it fall in value; and then buy it at a lower premium, with the difference representing your profit.

Example: You sell a call for a premium of 4 ($400). Two months later, the stock's market value is about the same as it was when you sold the call. The option's premium value has fallen to 1 ($100). You cancel your position by buying the call at 1, realizing a profit of $300.

   3. *The market value of the stock falls.* In this case, the option will also fall in value. This provides you with an advantage as a call seller. Remember, you are paid a premium at the time you sell the call. You want to close out your position at a later date, or wait for the call to expire worthless. You can do either in this case. Because time works against the seller, it would take a considerable change in the stock's market value to change your profitable position in the sold option.

Example: You sell a call and receive a premium of 5 ($500). The stock's market value later falls far below the striking price of the option and, in your opinion, a recovery is not likely. As long as the market value of the stock is at or below the striking price at expiration, the option will not be exercised. By allowing the option to expire in this situation, the entire $500 received is a profit.

short position
the status assumed by investors when they enter a sell order in advance of entering a buy order. (The short position is closed by later entering a buy order, or through expiration.)

   Remember three key points as a call seller. First, the transaction takes place in reverse order, with sale occurring before the purchase. Second, when you sell a call, you are paid a premium; in comparison, a call buyer pays the premium at the point of purchase. And third, what is good news for the buyer is bad news for the seller, and vice versa.

   When you sell a call option, you are a short seller and that places you into what is called a *short position*. The sale is the opening transaction, and it can be closed in one of two ways. First, a buy order can be entered, and that closes out the position. Second, you can wait until expiration, after which the option ceases to exist and the position closes automatically. In comparison, the better-known "buy first, sell later" approach is called a *long position*. The long position is also closed in one of two ways. Either the buyer enters a sell order, closing the position; or the option expires worthless, so that the buyer loses the entire premium value.

> **long position**
> the status assumed by investors when they enter a buy order in advance of entering a sell order. (The long position is closed by later entering a sell order, or through expiration.)

THE PUT OPTION

A put is the opposite of a call. It is a contract granting the right to sell 100 shares of stock at a fixed price per share and by a specified expiration date in the future. As a put buyer, you acquire the right to sell 100 shares of stock; and as a put seller, you grant that right to the buyer. (See Figure 1.2.)

Buying and Selling Puts

As a buyer of a put, you hope the underlying stock's value will fall. A put is the opposite of a call and so it acts in the opposite manner as the stock's market value changes. If the stock's market value falls, the put's value rises; and if the stock's market value rises, then the put's value falls. There are three possible outcomes when you buy puts.

1. *The market value of the stock rises.* In this case, the put's value falls in response. Thus, you can sell the put for a price below the price you paid and take a loss; or you

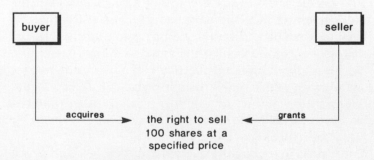

FIGURE 1.2   The put option.

can hold onto the put, hoping that the stock's market value will fall before the expiration date.

Example: You bought a put two months ago, paying a premium of 2 ($200). You expected the stock's market price to fall, in which case the value of the put would have risen. Instead, the stock's market value rose, so that the put's value fell. It is now worth only $25. You have a choice: Sell the put and take a $175 loss, or hold onto the put, hoping the stock will fall before the expiration date. If you hold the put beyond expiration, it will be worthless.

This example demonstrates the need to assess risks. For example, with the put currently worth only $25— nearly nothing—there is very little value remaining, so you might consider it too late to cut your losses in this case. Considering that there is only $25 at stake, it might be worth the long shot of holding the put until expiration. If the stock's price does fall between now and then, you stand the chance of recovering your investment and, perhaps, even a profit.

Smart Investor Tip   Options traders constantly calculate risk and reward, and often make decisions based not upon how they hoped prices would change, but upon how an unexpected change has affected their position.

2. *The market value of the stock does not change.* If the stock does not move in value enough to alter the value of the put, then the put's value will still fall. The put, like the call, is a wasting asset; so the more time that passes and the closer expiration date becomes, the less value will remain in the put. In this situation, you can sell the put and accept a loss, or hold onto it, hoping that the stock's market price will fall before the put's expiration.

Example: You bought a put three months ago and paid a premium of 4 ($400). You had expected the stock's market value to fall, in which case the put's value would have risen. Expiration comes up later this month. Unfortunately, the stock's market value is about the same as it was when you bought the put, which now is worth only $100. Your choices: Sell the put for $100 and accept the $300 loss; or hold onto the put on the chance that the stock's value will fall before expiration.

The choice comes down to a matter of timing and an awareness of how much price change is required. In the preceding example, the stock would have to fall at least four points below the put's striking price just to create a breakeven outcome (before trading costs). Of course, if you have more time, your choice is easier because you can defer your decision. You can afford to adopt a wait-and-see attitude, with a long time to go, because the value falls out of the option slowly at first, and then more rapidly as expiration approaches.

3. *The market value of the stock falls.* In this case, the put's value will rise. You have three alternatives in this case: First, you may hold the put in the hope that the stock's market value will decline even more, increasing your profit. Second, you may sell the put and take your profit now. Third, you may exercise the put and sell 100 shares of the underlying stock at the striking price. That price will be above current market value, so you will profit from exercise by selling at the higher striking price.

Example: You own 100 shares of stock that you bought last year for $38 per share. You are worried about the threat of a falling market; however, you would also like to hold onto your stock as a long-term investment. To protect yourself against the possibility of a price decline in your stock, you recently bought a put, paying a premium of $50. This guarantees you the right to sell 100 shares for $40 per share. Recently, the price of your stock fell to $33 per share. The value of the put increased to $750, offsetting your loss in the stock.

You can make a choice given this example. You can sell the option and realize a profit of $700, which offsets the loss in the stock. This choice is appealing because you can take a profit in the option, but you continue to own the stock. So if the stock's price rebounds, you will benefit twice.

A second alternative is to exercise the option and sell the 100 shares at $40 per share (the striking price of the option), which is $7 per share above current market value (but only $2 per share above the price you paid originally for the stock). This choice could be appealing if you believe that circumstances have changed and that it was a mistake to buy the stock as a long-term investment. By getting out now with a profit instead of a loss, you recover your full investment even though the stock's market value has fallen.

A third choice is to hold off taking any immediate action, at least for the moment. The put acts as a form of insurance to protect your investment in the stock, protecting you against further price declines. That's because at this point, for every drop in the stock's price, the option's value will offset that drop point for point. If the stock's value increases, the option's value will decline dollar for dollar. So the two positions offset one another. As long as you take action before the put's expiration, your risk is virtually eliminated.

Smart Investor Tip   At times, inaction is the smartest choice. Depending on the circumstances, you could be better off patiently waiting out price movements until the day before expiration.

While some investors buy puts believing the stock's market value will fall, or to protect their stock position, other investors sell puts. As a put seller, you grant someone else the right to sell 100 shares of stock to you at a fixed price. If the put is exercised, you will be required to buy 100 shares of the stock at the striking price, which would be above the market value of the stock. For taking this risk, you are paid a premium when you sell the put. Like the call seller, put sellers do not control the outcomes of their positions as much as buyers do, since it is the buyer who has the right to exercise at any time.

Example: Last month, you sold a put with a striking price of $50 per share. The premium was $250, which was paid to you at the time of the sale. Since then, the stock's market value has remained in a narrow range between $48 and $53 per share. Currently, the price is at $51. You do not expect the stock's price to fall below the striking price of 50. As long as the market value of the underlying stock remains at or above that level, the put will not be exercised. (The buyer will not exercise, meaning that you will not be required to buy 100 shares of stock.) If your opinion turns out to be correct, you will make a profit by selling the put.

Your risk in this example is that the stock's market price could decline below $50 per share before expiration, meaning that upon exercise you would be required to buy 100 shares at $50 per share. To avoid that risk, you have the right to cancel the position by buying the put at current market value. The closer you are to expiration (and as long as the stock's market value is above the striking price), the lower the market value of the put—and the more your profit.

Put selling also makes sense if you believe that the striking price represents a fair price for the stock. In the worst case, you will be required to buy 100 shares at a price above current market value. If you are right, though, and the striking price is a fair price, then the stock's market value will eventually rebound to that price or above. In addition, to calculate the real loss on buying, an overpriced stock has to be discounted for the premium you received.

Selling puts is a vastly different strategy from buying puts, because it places you on the opposite side of the transaction. The risk profile is different as well. If the put you sell is exercised, then you end up with overpriced stock, so you need to establish a logical standard for yourself if you sell puts. Never sell a put unless you would be willing to acquire 100 shares of the underlying stock, at the striking price.

One advantage for put sellers is that time works for you and against the buyer. As expiration approaches, the put loses value. However, if movement in the underlying stock is opposite the movement you expected, you could end up taking a loss or having to buy 100 shares of stock for each put you sell. Sudden and unexpected changes in the stock's market value can occur at any time. The more inclined a stock is to volatile price movement, the greater your risk as a seller. You might also notice as you observe the pricing of options that, due to higher risks, options on volatile stocks tend to hold higher premium value than those on more predictable, lower volatility issues.

> **Smart Investor Tip** Option price behavior is directly affected by the underlying stock and its attributes. So volatile (higher risk) stocks demand higher option premium and tend to experience faster, more severe price changes.

As a put seller, your risk is also limited to how far a stock is likely to fall, the absolute worst case being zero. The risk of exercise is not absolute, either. A put buyer will exercise only if the gap between market value and striking price justifies the action. For example, let's say a stock is two points below its striking price, but the put buyer paid 3 for the put. Exercise would produce a loss of a dollar per share, so that particular buyer will not exercise. At the point of exercise by any buyer, the option exchange assigns the exercise to a put seller. Remember, the exchange facilitates the market by acting as seller to all buyers, and as buyer to all sellers. So when a put is exercised, you have a random chance of its being assigned to you. If your gap between market price and striking price is significant, the chances of being assigned an exercise at or before expiration are increasingly high.

OPTION VALUATION

Option values change in direct proportion to the changing market value of the underlying stock. Every option is married to the stock of a specific company and cannot be interchanged with others. How you fare in your option positions depends on how the stock's value changes in the immediate future.

The selection of options cannot be made without also reviewing the attributes of the stock, both fundamental and technical. Whether you treat options only as a form of speculative side bet or as an important aspect associated with being in the market, the judgment you use in selection has to apply both to the option and stock characteristics and values. Criteria for the selection of good-value stocks are at the heart of smart stock market investing. The need for careful, thorough, and continuing analysis cannot be emphasized too much. So attributes such as financial strength, price stability and volatility, dividend and profit history, and other tests are important, not only to stockholders but to options traders as well.

The fundamentals—everything related to the financial value of a company—are considered by most investors as the foundation for sound stock selection. Troubling scandals and revelations among many large corporations and the resulting loss of investor confidence bring this point into focus as well. Even more troubling than the discovery that some company finances have been mismanaged and even fraudulently exaggerated, is the discovery that even so-called independent auditing firms might not be entirely trustworthy, either. Obviously, big changes need to be made in federal oversight and enforcement, industry self-regulation, the entire accounting and auditing industry, and standards for corporate executives. Before any investor—whether stockholder or options trader—can feel entirely confident, a lot of change will be needed to ensure that the fraud and misrepresentations of the recent past will not happen again.

The fundamental analysis you perform or rely upon—assuming that you can take confidence in the numbers as they are reported—should serve as a starting point. In Chapter 6, you will be given specific ideas for ways to test fundamental trends to spot any questionable results, and to minimize the chances that you will be proceeding based on results that are misleading or inaccurate. For now the point to be made is this: The numbers are a starting point for identifying value stocks and options in over- or undervalued options.

Of equal importance are some technical indicators, those nonfinancial tests applied by investors and analysts. The price of stock is entirely separate from the company's fundamentals, especially in the short term. By their nature, options are short-term instruments. So picking worthwhile options trades depends on fundamental and technical indicators, even while you are recognizing that short-term indicators may not be reliable. The two major market theories are the Dow Theory and the Random Walk Hypothesis. The Dow Theory contends that certain signals are confirmed independently and indicate a change in market directions. The Random Walk Hypothesis is based on the idea that market movements are not predictable based on specific tests, and that given the presumed efficiency of the auction marketplace, there is an equal chance that future prices of stocks will rise or they will fall. The one point that both of these theories agree upon is that short-term indicators are of no value in determining whether to buy or sell in the market.

 Smart Investor Tip In the stock market, the perception of value is far more important to stock prices than actual fundamental value. This is especially true in the short term, which by definition means the entire options market.

The analysis of stock values for the purpose of determining whether or not to buy stock is a complex science. When options are added to the equation, it becomes even more complicated. As shown in Table 1.1, you would consider stock price movement to be either a plus or a minus depending on whether you are planning to work as a seller or buyer, and whether you plan to utilize calls or puts.

at the money
the status of an option when the underlying stock's value is identical to the option's striking price.

Example: Two months ago, you bought a call and paid a premium of $300. The striking price was $40 per share. At that time, the underlying stock's price was at $40 per share. In this condition—when the option's striking price is identical to the current market value of the stock—the option is said to be *at the money*. If the market value per share of stock increases so that the per-share value is

TABLE 1.1 Price Movement in the Underlying Security		
	Increase in Price	*Decrease in Price*
Call buyer	Positive	Negative
Call seller	Negative	Positive
Put buyer	Negative	Positive
Put seller	Positive	Negative

above the call's striking price, then the call is said to be *in the money*. When the price of the stock decreases so that the per-share value is below the option's striking price, then the call is said to be *out of the money*.

These definitions are reversed for puts. "In" and "out of" the money occurs in the opposite direction. Figure 1.3 shows the price ranges that represent in the money, at the money, and out of the money for a call.

 in the money
the status of a call option when the underlying stock's market value is higher than the option's striking price, or of a put option when the underlying stock's market value is lower than the option's striking price.

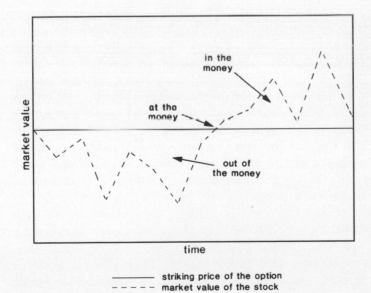

 out of the money
the status of a call option when the underlying stock's market value is lower than the option's striking price, or of a put option when the underlying stock's market value is higher than the option's striking price.

FIGURE 1.3 Market value of the underlying stock in relation to striking price of a call.

The dollar-for-dollar price movement of an option's value occurs whenever an option is in the money. The tendency will be for the option's value to mirror price movement in the stock, going up or down to the same degree as the stock's market price. This will not always be identical because, as expiration nears, the time factor also affects the option's value.

When the option is out of the money, changes in value relate primarily to the time element, and very little of price change reflects changes in the stock's value.

Example: You bought a put last month with a striking price of 30 and you paid 2. (The striking price is $30 per share and you paid $200 for the put.) At that time, the stock's market value was $34 per share, so the option was four points out of the money. More recently, the stock price has fallen to $31 per share; however, the put's premium remains at 2. Because the put remains out of the money, its premium value cannot be expected to change just because of stock movement—at least not until or unless the stock's market value falls so that the put is in the money.

In the preceding example, a significant change would occur if the stock's market price continues to fall below the striking price. Once in the money, the put's value would rise one dollar for each dollar of decline in the stock's market value (not considering the time factor).

The value of options that are in the money relates to the underlying stock's current market value. But in the stock market, value also depends on two additional factors. First is the stock's *volatility*, the tendency to trade within a narrow range (low volatility) or a broad range (high volatility). The degree of volatility will, of course, also affect valuation of the option. Second is the time element. In additional to volatility and time, value is also affected by *volume*—the level of trading activity in the stock *and* in the option, or in the market as a whole. The level of volume in a stock might have a similar effect in options, or option volume could be affected by entirely different factors. Options traders look for clues to explain circumstances when option volume increases but no corresponding increase is seen in the stock. That could indicate that

volatility
a measure of the degree of change in a stock's market value, measured over a 12-month period and stated as a percentage. (To measure volatility, subtract the lowest 12-month price from the highest 12-month price, and divide the answer by the 12-month lowest price.)

volume
the level of trading activity in a stock, an option, or the market as a whole.

other factors, not yet widely appreciated in the market, are distorting the option's value or the stock's value, or other factors (such as unfounded rumors) are causing distortions in option values.

How to Pick a Stock

The question of selecting stocks is more involved and complex than the method of picking an option. For options, the selection has to do with risk assessment, current value, time until expiration, and your own risk tolerance level; in addition, numerous strategies you may employ will affect the ultimate decision. But option selection is formulated predictably. In comparison, stock selection involves no precise formula that works in every case. Price movement in the stock is itself not known, whereas the reaction of option premium value is completely predictable, based on the way the stock's price changes.

The selection of a stock is the critical decision point that determines whether you will succeed with options. This observation applies for buying or selling stock, and also applies when you never intend to own the stock at all, but want only to deal with options themselves. It is a mistake to pick options based only on current value and time, hoping to succeed without also thinking about the particulars of the stock—volatility, relation to striking price of the option, and much more. Of course, to some degree, the features of the option can be used to calculate likely outcomes, but that is only a part of the whole picture. Because option value is tied to stock price and volatility, you also need to develop a dependable method for evaluation of the underlying stock.

Some investors pick stocks strictly on the basis of *fundamental analysis*. This includes a study of financial statements, dividends paid to stockholders, management, the company's position within its industry, capitalization, product or service, and other financial information.

The importance of the fundamentals cannot be emphasized too much, as they define a company's long-term growth prospects, ability to produce consistent profits, and to demonstrate market strength over time. However, remember that the fundamentals are historical and have little to do with short-term price changes in the company's

fundamental analysis
a study of financial information and attributes of a company's management and competitive position, as a means for selecting stocks.

stock. It is that very thing—short-term price change—that determines whether a particular option strategy will succeed or fail. While the fundamentals are essential for long-term stock selection, short-term price movement is affected more by perception of value. Indicators involving market price and perception are broadly classified under the umbrella of *technical analysis.*

technical analysis
a study of trends and patterns of price movement in stocks, including price per share, the shape of price movement on charts, high and low ranges, and trends in pricing over time.

Both fundamental and technical indicators have something to offer, and you can use elements of both to study and identify stocks for option trading. The distinctions should be kept in mind, however, including both advantages and disadvantages of each method.

The usual assumption in using any form of analysis is to identify stocks that you would want to buy or hold, and when the news turns bad, the investor would then want to sell shares. With options, however, a stock that shows inherent weaknesses can also signal the time to use options in a different way. For example, if you are convinced that a stock is overpriced and susceptible to price decline, one reaction would be to buy puts. If you're right and the price falls, your puts will gain in value. Thus, the difference between stock investors and options traders is the reaction to news. Stock investors tend to view bad news—weakness, negative economic news, overpricing of shares, corporate scandals, and so on—as just bad news. An options trader, though, can use any form of news to make a profitable move in options, even when the news is negative for the company and its stockholders.

Smart Investor Tip Selecting options wisely depends on also identifying or picking stocks using logical criteria. Using options without also analyzing stocks is a big mistake.

Investors can get current information about any listed company from a number of sources on the Internet. These include several free services allowing downloads of corporate annual reports in addition to direct contact with the companies themselves.

Smart Investor Tip Get free annual reports for any listed company from one of three online sources: reportgallery.com, www.annualreportservice.com, and www.prars.com.

Another source for information concerning stocks is one of several subscription services. Using either online or mail-oriented services, check out Value Line and Standard & Poors, both of which offer nicely detailed analytical services for investors.

Smart Investor Tip Check websites for online subscription services at www.valueline.com and www.standardandpoors.com.

Intrinsic Value and Time Value

Once you become comfortable with methods of stock selection, you will be ready to use that knowledge to select and decide how to use options. Remember that options themselves change in value based on movement in the underlying stock. Because option valuation is inescapably tied to stock value and market conditions, options do not possess any fundamental value of their own. By definition, the fundamentals are the financial condition and results of the corporation; an option is related to the stock's market value and exists only for a brief period of time. Every *listed option*—those tied to listed stocks—and its pricing structure are more easily comprehended by a study of valuation, which has two parts.

The first of the two segments of value is called *intrinsic value*, which is that part of an option's premium equal to the number of points in the money. Intrinsic value, for example, is three points for a call that is three points above striking price; or for a put that is three points lower than the striking price.

listed option
an option traded on a public exchange and listed in the published reports in the financial press.

intrinsic value
that portion of an option's current value equal to the number of points that it is in the money. ("Points" equals the number of dollars of value per share, so 35 points equals $35 per share.)

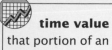

time value
that portion of an
option's current
value above in-
trinsic value.

Any value above the intrinsic value is known as *time value*. This will decline predictably over time, as expiration nears. With many months before expiration, time value can be substantial; if the option is at the money or out of the money, the entire premium is time value. As expiration approaches, time value evaporates at a quickening pace, and at the point of expiration, no time value remains. Time value also tends to fall away when the option is substantially out of the money. In other words, an option that is 2 points out of the money will be likely to have greater time value than one with the same time until expiration, but 15 points out of the money. Option valuation can be summed up in the statement:

> The relative degree of intrinsic value and time value is determined by the distance between striking price and current market value of stock, adjusted by the time remaining until expiration of the option.

Example: A 45 call is valued currently at 3 ($300 premium value on a $45 striking price). The underlying stock's market value currently resides at $45 per share. Because the option is at the money, it has no intrinsic value. The entire premium represents time value alone. You know that by expiration, the time value will disappear completely, so it will be necessary for the stock to increase in value at least three points just in order for you to break even were you to buy the call (and without also considering transaction fees). The stock will need to rise beyond the three-point level before expiration if you are to earn a profit.

A comparison between option premium and market value of the underlying stock is presented in Table 1.2. This reveals the direct relationship between intrinsic value (using a call as an example), market value of the underlying stock, and time value of the option. If the option were a put, intrinsic value would be represented by the degree to which the stock's market value was *below* striking price.

Another helpful illustration is shown in Figure 1.4. This summarizes movement in the underlying stock (top

		Option Premium (Striking Price of $45)		
Month	Stock Price	Total Value	Intrinsic Value[1]	Time Value[2]
1	$45	$3	$0	$3
2	47	5	2	3
3	46	4	1	3
4	46	3	1	2
5	47	4	2	2
6	44	2	0	2
7	46	2	1	1
8	45	1	0	1
9	46	1	1	0

TABLE 1.2 The Declining Time Value of an Option

[1]Intrinsic value reflects the price difference between the stock's current market value and the option's striking price.
[2]Time value is greatest when the expiration date is furthest away and declines as expiration approaches.

graph) and option values (bottom graph). Note that intrinsic value (black portion) is identical to stock price movement in the money; and that time value moves independently, gradually dissolving as expiration approaches. From this illustration, you can see how the two types of value act independently from one another, because different influences—stock price versus time—affect the two segments of the option premium.

The total amount of the option premium can be expected to vary greatly between two different stocks at the same price level and identical option features, due to other influences. These include the perception of value by investors, the stock's price history and volatility, financial status and trends, interest in options among buyers and sellers, and dozens of other possible influences. For example, two stocks may have options at 35 and identical expiration dates, with both stocks currently valued at the same price. But even given identical features, the option premium could be different for each.

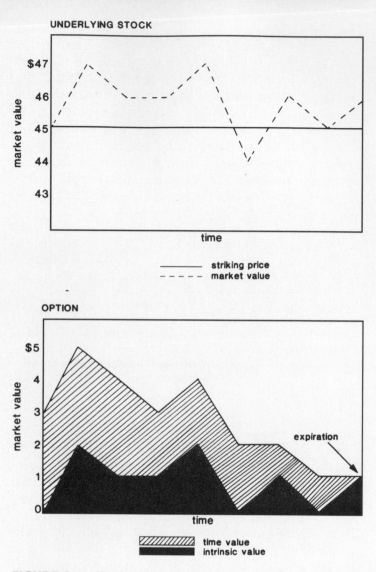

FIGURE 1.4 Time and intrinsic values of underlying stock and options.

It is important to note that the differences will exist solely in time value, even though time until expiration is identical. Intrinsic value is always a factor of the number of in-the-money points in the option, so effectively, time value is affected by many elements other than just the time until expiration. Perception of value among different stocks will vary, often to a significant degree, and those differences are going to be reflected in option valuation.

Options buyers, as a rule, will be willing to pay more for options when they perceive a greater than normal potential for price movement. Higher levels of volatility increase risks all around, but also increase potential for bigger profits in option speculation. Of course, low-volatility stocks are going to be far less interesting to would-be options buyers, because little price change is expected in the stock. The same arguments apply to sellers; higher-volatility stocks are accompanied by options with higher time value, and more potential for profits from selling options (as well as greater risks for exercise).

You can recognize time value easily by comparing the stock's current value to the option's premium. For example, a stock currently priced at $47 per share may have an option valued at 3 and a striking price of 45. To break down the total option premium, subtract striking price from total premium value. If premium value is at or below striking price (for a call) or above striking price (for a put), there is no intrinsic value. In the preceding example:

Stock Price

Current market value of the stock	$47
Less: Striking price of the option	−45
Intrinsic value	$ 2

Option premium

Total premium	$ 3
Less: intrinsic value	− 2
Time value	$ 1

In the next chapter, several important features of options—striking price, expiration date, and exercise—are more fully explored, especially in light of how these features affect your personal options strategy.

Chapter 2

Opening, Closing, and Tracking the Option

I was brought up to believe that the only thing worth doing was to add to the sum of accurate information in the world.
—Margaret Mead, *New York Times*, August 9, 1964

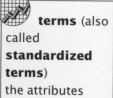

terms (also called **standardized terms**) the attributes that describe an option, including the striking price, expiration month, type of option (call or or put), and the underlying security.

Every option is characterized by four specific attributes, collectively called the *terms* of the option. These are striking price, expiration month, type of option (call or put), and the underlying security. These are also alternatively referred to as *standardized terms*.

These are the four essential pieces you need to see the whole picture, to know which option is being discussed, and to distinguish it from all other options. In evaluating risk and potential gain, and even to discuss an option, every buyer and every seller needs to have these four essential pieces of information in hand. Of course, because point of view between buyer and seller is going to be opposite (as it often will be between investors involved with calls versus those involved with puts), an advantageous situation to one person may well be disadvantageous to another. That is the nature of investing in options: You can take a position on one side or the other for any particular option, depending upon where you believe the advantage lies.

To review the four terms briefly:

1. *Striking price.* The striking price is the fixed price at which the option can be exercised. It is the pivotal piece of information that determines the relative value of options based on the proximity of a stock's market value to the option's striking price; it is the price per share to be paid or received in the event of exercise. The striking price normally is divisible by 5 points. The exception: Some very low-priced shares may be sold in increments divisible by 2.50 and other issues end up with fractional values after a stock split. High-priced stocks may have options selling at intervals divisible by 10 points. The striking price remains unchanged during the entire life of each option, no matter how much change occurs in the market value of the underlying stock.

For the buyer, striking price identifies the price at which 100 shares of stock can be bought (with a call) or sold (with a put). For a seller, striking price is the opposite: It is the price at which 100 shares of stock can be sold (with a call) or bought (with a put) in the event that the buyer decides to exercise.

2. *Expiration month.* Every option exists for only a limited number of months. That is a problem or an opportunity, depending upon whether you are acting as a buyer or as a seller; and upon the specific strategies you employ. Every option has three possible outcomes. It will eventually be canceled through a closing transaction, exercised, or it will expire, but it never just goes on forever. Because the option is not tangible, the number of potential active options is unlimited except by market demand. A company issues only so many shares of stock, so buyers and sellers need to adjust prices according to supply and demand. This is not the same with options, which have no specific limitations such as numbers issued.

Options active at any given time are limited by the risks involved. An option far out of the money will naturally draw little interest, and those with impending expiration will similarly lose market interest as their time value evaporates. Buyers need to believe there is enough time for a profit to materialize, and that the market price is close enough to the striking price that a profit is realistic; or if in the money, that it is not so expensive that risks are too great. The same considerations that create disadvantages for buyers represent opportunities for sellers.

Pending expiration reduces the likelihood of out-of-the-money options being exercised, and distance between market price of the stock and striking price of the call means the seller's profits are more likely to materialize than are the hopes of the buyer.

3. *Type of option.* The distinction between calls and puts is essential to success in the options market; even so, some first-time investors are confused in trying to understand how and why calls and puts are different and must be considered as opposites. Identical strategies cannot be used for calls and puts, for reasons beyond the obvious fact that they are opposites. Calls are by definition the right to buy 100 shares, whereas puts are the right to sell 100 shares. But comprehending the essential opposite nature of the two contracts is not enough.

It might seem at first glance that, given the behavior of calls and puts when in the money or out of the money, it would make no difference to buy a put or to sell a call. As long as expiration and striking price were identical, what is the difference? In practice, however, significant differences do make these two ideas vastly different in terms of risk profile. When you buy a put, your risk is limited to the amount you pay for premium. When you sell a call, your risk can be far greater because the stock may rise many points, requiring the call seller to deliver 100 shares at a price far below current market value. Each specific strategy has to be reviewed in terms not only of likely price movement given a set of market price changes in the underlying stock, but also how one's position is affected by exposure to varying degrees of risk. Some of the more exotic strategies involving the use of calls and puts at the same time, or buying and selling of the same option with different striking prices are examples of advanced strategic approaches, which will be explored in detail in later chapters.

4. *Underlying stock.* Every option is identified with a specific company's stock, and this cannot be changed. Listed options are not offered on all stocks traded, nor are they available on every stock exchange. (Some options trade on only one exchange, while others trade on several.) Options can exist only when a specific underlying stock has been identified, since it is the stock's market value that determines the option's related premium value. All options traded on a specific underlying stock are referred to as a single *class* of options. Thus, a single stock might be associated with a wide variety of calls and puts with different striking prices and expiration months, but they all belong to the same class. In comparison, all of those options with the same combination of terms—identical striking prices, expiration month, type (call or put), and underlying stock—are considered a single *series* of options.

class
all options traded on a single underlying security, including different striking prices and expiration dates.

A Note on the Expiration Cycle

Expiration dates for options of a single underlying stock expire on a predictable *cycle*. Every stock with listed options can be identified by the cycle to which it belongs and these remain unchanged. There are three cycles:

series
a group of options sharing identical terms.

1. January, April, July, and October (JAJO).
2. February, May, August, and November (FMAN).
3. March, June, September, and December (MJSD).

In addition to these fixed expiration cycle dates, active options are available for expiration in the upcoming month and at any time, and perhaps in the month following that, regardless of expiration cycle. For example, let's suppose that a particular stock has options expiring in the cycle month of April. In February, you may be able to trade in short-term options expiring in March (even though that is not a part of the normal cyclical expiration).

cycle
the pattern of expiration dates of options for a particular underlying stock. (The three cycles occur in four-month intervals and are described by month abbreviations. They are (1) January, April, July, and October, or JAJO; (2) February, May, August, and November, or FMAN; and (3) March, June, September, and December, or MJSD.)

Smart Investor Tip Some options traders use the short-term options as speculative devices. Because they come and go more rapidly than the cyclical options, they often are overlooked as opportunities. For example, they can be used to temporarily protect longer-term short option positions.

last trading day
the Friday preceding the third Saturday of the expiration month of an option.

expiration time
the latest possible time to place an order for cancellation or exercise of an option, which may vary depending on the brokerage firm executing the order and on the option itself.

An option's expiration takes place on the third Saturday of the expiration month. An order to close an open position has to be placed and executed no later than the *last trading day* before expiration day; and before the indicated *expiration time* for the option. As a general rule, this means that the trade has to be executed before the close of business on the Friday immediately before the Saturday of expiration; however, a specific cutoff time could be missed on an exceptionally busy Friday, so you need to ensure that your brokerage is going to be able to execute your trade under the rules.

The last-minute order that you place can be one of three types of transactions. It can be an order to buy in order to close an open (previously sold) position; an order to sell a long position option to close it; or an exercise order to buy or to sell 100 shares of stock for each option involved.

Example: You bought a call scheduled to expire in the month of July. Its expiration occurs on the third Saturday in that month. You need to place a sell order or an order to exercise the call (to buy 100 shares of stock at the striking price) before expiration time on the preceding Friday, which is the last trading day prior to expiration. If you fail to place your order by that time, the option will expire worthless and you will receive no benefit.

With the crucial deadline in mind and the unknown potential for a busy Friday in the market—which can occur on the floor or over the Internet—you need to place that order with adequate time for execution. You can place the order far in advance with instructions to execute it by the end of business on Friday. If the brokerage accepts that order, then you will be protected if they fail to execute—as long as you placed the order well in advance of the deadline.

OPENING AND CLOSING OPTION TRADES

Every option trade you make must specify the four terms: striking price, expiration month, call or put, and the underlying stock. If any of these terms changes, it represents an entirely different option.

There are two ways to open a position in an option: by buying and by selling. And there are three ways to close an option: by cancellation (selling a previously bought option, or buying a previously sold option), by exercise, and by expiration.

Whenever you have opened an option by buying or selling, the status is called an *open position*. When you buy, it is described as an *opening purchase transaction*. And if you start out by selling an option, that is called an *opening sale transaction*.

Example: You bought a call two months ago. When you entered your order, that was an opening purchase transaction. That status remains the same as long as you take no further action. The position will be closed when you enter a *closing sale transaction* to sell the call; you may also exercise the option; if you do not take either of these actions, the option will expire.

Example: You sold a call last month, placing yourself in a short position. As long as you take no further action, the position remains open. You can choose to wait out the expiration period; or you may execute a *closing purchase transaction*, and cancel the option before expiration. As long as the short position remains open, it is also possible that the call will be exercised and you will have 100 shares called away at the striking price.

DEFINING POSSIBLE OUTCOMES OF CLOSING OPTIONS

Every option will be canceled by an offsetting closing transaction, by exercise, or by expiration. The results of each affects buyers and sellers in different ways.

Results for the Buyer

1. If you cancel your open long position with a closing sale transaction, you will receive payment. If the closing

open position
the status of a transaction when a purchase (a long position) or a sale (a short position) has been made, and before cancellation, exercise, or expiration.

opening purchase transaction
an initial transaction to buy, also known as the action of "going long."

opening sale transaction
an initial transaction to sell, also known as the action of "going short."

closing sale transaction
a transaction to close a long position, executed by selling an option previously bought, closing it out.

closing purchase transaction
a transaction to close a short position, executed by buying an option previously sold, canceling it out.

price is higher than the original purchase amount, you realize a profit; if lower, you suffer a loss.

2. If you exercise the option, you will receive 100 shares (if a call) or sell 100 shares (if a put) at the striking price. You will exercise only when that action is advantageous based on current market value of the underlying stock. To justify exercise, market value has to be higher than the striking price (of a call) or lower than the striking price (of a put).

3. If you allow the option to expire, you will lose the entire amount of premium paid at the time of purchase. It will be a complete loss.

Results for the Seller

1. If you cancel your open position with a closing purchase transaction, you pay the premium, which is due on the business day following your order. If the price you pay to close is lower than the amount you received when you opened the position, you realize a profit; if it is higher, you suffer a loss.

2. If your option is exercised by the buyer, you are required to deliver 100 shares of the underlying stock at the specified striking price (of a call); or to purchase 100 shares of stock at the specified striking price (of a put).

3. If the option expires worthless, you earn a profit. Your open position is canceled through expiration, and the premium you received at the time that you sold the option is yours to keep.

These outcomes are summarized in Figure 2.1. Notice that buyers and sellers have opposite results for each outcome upon close. The investor who opened the position through buying receives payment upon sale; and the investor who opened the position through selling makes payment upon a later purchase. The buyer elects to exercise, whereas the seller has no choice as to the decision, nor timing of exercise. If the option expires worthless, the buyer suffers a total loss, and the seller realizes a total profit.

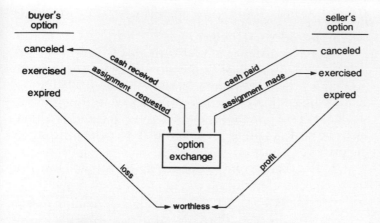

buyer's option

seller's option

canceled

exercised

expired

cash received

assignment requested

cash paid

assignment made

canceled

exercised

expired

option exchange

loss

profit

worthless

FIGURE 2.1 Outcomes of closing the position.

Smart Investor Tip Analysis of the possible outcomes is the key to identifying opportunities in the options market. Risk and opportunity evaluation is imperative. Successful options traders need to be shrewd analysts.

EXERCISING THE OPTION

Options transactions occur through the exchange on which an option has been listed. While several different exchanges handle options trading, and automated trading has become widespread on the Internet (especially in options), there is but one registered clearing agency for all listed options trades in the United States. The Options Clearing Corporation (OCC) has the broad responsibility for *orderly settlement* of all option contracts, which takes place through contact between brokerage houses and customers working with the exchange. Orderly settlement means, generally, that buyer and seller both trade in confidence knowing that they will be able to execute their orders when they want, finding a ready market and not having to worry about uncertainty. It also means that all terms of the contract are ironclad; exercise price, expira-

orderly settlement
the smooth process of buying and selling, in full confidence that the terms and conditions of options contracts will be honored in a timely manner.

tion date, and availability of shares upon exercise are all a part of the orderly settlement.

When a customer notifies a broker and places an order for execution of an option trade, the OCC ensures that the terms of the contract will be honored. Under this system, buyer and seller do not need to depend upon the goodwill of one another; the transaction goes through the OCC, which depends upon member brokerage firms to enforce *assignment*. Remember that buyers and sellers are not matched together one-on-one. A disparate number of open buy and sell options are likely to exist at any given time, so that exercise will be meted out at random to options in the money—thus the term "assignment." Since buyers and sellers are not matched to one another as in other types of transactions, how does a seller know whether or not a specific option will be exercised? There is no way to know. If your sold option is in the money, exercise could occur at any time. It might not happen at all, or it might take place on the last trading day.

When exercise occurs long before expiration date, that exercise is assigned to any of the sellers with open positions in that option. This takes place either on a random basis or on the basis of first-in, first-out (the earliest sellers are the first ones exercised). Upon exercise, 100 shares *must* be delivered. The idea of *delivery* is in relation to the movement of 100 shares of stock from the seller of the option to the exercising buyer. The buyer makes payment and receives registration of the shares, and the seller receives payment and relinquishes ownership of the shares.

assignment
the act of exercise against a seller, done on a random basis or in accordance with orderly procedures developed by the Options Clearing Corporation and brokerage firms.

delivery
the movement of stock ownership from one owner to another. (In the case of exercised options, shares are registered to the new owner upon receipt of payment.)

> **Smart Investor Tip**   The seller often can avoid exercise through a series of steps—picking out-of-the-money options, taking short-term profits, and exchanging short-term options for longer-term ones. Avoiding exercise makes sense when stock price movement justifies it.

What happens if the seller does not deliver shares as demanded by the terms of the option contract? Remember that the OCC "facilitates" the market and enforces assignment. The buyer is given timely possession of 100 shares of stock, even when the seller is unwilling or unable to comply. The broker will deal with the seller by attaching other assets as necessary, or taking legal action, as well as suspending the seller's trading privileges. The buyer would have no awareness of these problems in the event this occurs, because the problem is between the violating seller and the "system" of broker, exchange, and the OCC. So orderly settlement ensures that everyone trading in options in good faith experiences a smooth, dependable system in which terms of the option contract are honored automatically and without fail.

When a buyer decides to exercise, 100 shares are either purchased ("called from") or sold ("put to") the option seller. When you have sold a call, exercise means your 100 shares could be called away and transferred to the buyer; and when you sell a put, exercise means that 100 shares of stock can be "put to" you upon exercise, meaning you are required to buy. The entire process of calling and putting shares of stock upon exercise is broadly referred to as *conversion*. Stock is assigned at the time of exercise, a necessity because the number of buyers and sellers in a particular option will rarely, if ever, match. The assignment of an option's exercise, by definition, means that 100 shares of stock are *called away*.

Is exercise always seen as a negative to the seller? At first glance, it would appear that being exercised is undesirable, and it often is seen that way; many sellers take steps to minimize the risk of exercise, or to avoid it altogether. However, the question really depends upon the seller's intentions at the time he or she entered the short position. For example, a seller might recognize that being

conversion
the process of moving assigned stock from the seller of a call option or to the seller of a put option.

called away
the result of having stock assigned. (Upon exercise, 100 shares of the seller's stock are called away at the striking price.)

Smart Investor Tip Some sellers enter into a short position in the hopes that exercise will occur, recognizing that the combination of capital gain on the stock and option premium would represent a worthwhile profit.

exercised at a specific price is desirable, and will be willing to take exercise with the benefit of also keeping the premium as a profit.

It is logical that most sellers will close out their short positions or pick options the least likely to be exercised. Sellers have to be aware that exercise is one possible outcome and that it can occur at any time that the option is in the money. The majority of exercise actions are most likely to occur at or near expiration, so the risk of *early exercise* is minimal, although it can and does occur.

Exercise is not always generated by a buyer's action, either. The Options Clearing Corporation can order an *automatic exercise* policy acting through the exchange. Remember, the exchange acts as buyer to every seller, and as seller to every buyer. Exercise orders will be assigned as they are made by owners of option contracts. But if, at the point of expiration, there are more open short positions than exercising long positions, those open short positions that are in the money will be exercised.

The decision to avoid exercise is made based on current market value as well as the time remaining until expiration. Many options sellers spend a great deal of time and effort avoiding exercise and trying also to avoid taking losses in open option positions. A skilled options trader can achieve this by exchanging one option for another, and by timing actions to maximize deteriorating time value while still avoiding exercise. As long as options remain out of the money, there is no practical risk of exercise. But once an option goes in the money, sellers have to decide whether to risk exercise or cancel the position with an offsetting transaction.

Example: You bought 100 shares of stock several months ago for $57 per share. You invested $5,700 plus transaction fees. Last month, the stock's market value was $62 per share. At that time, you sold a call with a striking price of 60 ($60 per share). You were paid a premium of 7 ($700). You were willing to assume this short position. Your reasoning: If the call were exercised, your profit would be $1,000 before transaction fees. That would consist of three points per share of profit in the stock plus the $700 you were paid for selling the option.

early exercise
the act of exercising an option prior to expiration date.

automatic exercise
action taken by the Options Clearing Corporation at the time of expiration, when an in-the-money option has not been otherwise exercised or canceled.

Striking price	$60
Less: Your cost per share	–57
Stock profit	$ 3
Option premium	7
Total profit per share	$10

This example shows that it is possible for an investor to sell a call in the money, hoping for exercise. The key is in the profit made combining high option premium with a profit on the stock. The premium on the option effectively discounts your basis in the stock, so that exercise creates a nice profit. If the stock's market value falls below striking price and remains there until exercise the profit in the above example is still $700 from option premium; and you would be free to wait out price movement and repeat the process again.

Example: You bought 100 shares of stock several months ago for $57 per share. You invested $5,700 plus transaction fees. Last month, the stock's market value was $62 per share. At that time, you sold a call with a striking price of 60, and you were paid a premium of 7 ($700). By expiration, the stock had fallen to $58 per share, and the call expired worthless. At this point, your basis in the stock is $50 per share ($57 per share paid at purchase less your profit from selling a call and receiving a premium of $700). After the call expires, you sell another call with a striking price of 55 and receive 6. If this option were to be exercised, you would realize an adjusted profit of $1,100 ($500 profit on stock plus $600 profit from selling the call). If the option's time value declines, you can sell the option and realize the difference as profit. If the option expires worthless, you can repeat the process a *third* time, realizing yet more profit.

The decision to act or to wait depends upon the amount of time value involved, and upon the proximity of striking price to market value of the stock. As a general rule, the greater the time until expiration, the higher the time value will be; and the closer the striking price is to market value of the stock, the more important the time value becomes, both to buyer and to seller. For the buyer, time value is a negative, so the higher the time value, the greater the risk. For the seller, the opposite is true. Buyers pay the time value, which can also be considered the amount above intrinsic value—the difference between the stock's *current market value* and the option's striking price—knowing that the time value will disappear by expiration. The seller picks options to sell with the same thing in mind, but recognizing that more time value means more potential profit.

> **current market value**
> the market value of stock at any given time.

Example: You have decided to buy a call with a striking price of 30. The underlying stock's current market value is $32 per share and the option premium is 5 ($500). Your premium includes two points of intrinsic value and three points of time value. If the stock's market value does not increase enough by expiration to offset your cost, then you will not be able to earn a profit. One of two things needs to happen in this situation. Either the stock's current market value needs to rise quickly so that your call premium will be greater than the 5 you paid; or the stock's market value has to rise enough points by expiration to offset time value (three points) plus grow beyond the intrinsic value level. If this occurs, at the point of expiration, you would need the stock's current market value to increase six points just to break even (three points of disappeared time value added to three additional points for intrinsic value).

The previous example shows how option buyers need to evaluate risk. In this example, time value represents three-fifths of the total premium. If expiration comes up quickly, the stock will need to increase significantly in a short period of time to produce a profit. In thinking about whether it makes sense to buy such a call, some alternatives might also be considered, especially if you believe that the stock will rise in value. These include:

✔ Buy 100 shares of the stock. If you believe it has potential to increase in value, owning the shares without the built-in deadline of expiration makes ownership more desirable.

✔ Sell a put instead of buying a call. Put sellers have limited exposure compared to call sellers; and if the stock's market price rises, the entire premium will represent profit. Compared to buying a call, the selling of a put often is an overlooked strategy that could make a lot of sense.

A third opportunity could present itself in taking the opposite approach to buying. Given the previous example, in which significant increase in value would be required to make a profit, it might be an opportunity to sell a call instead of buying one—as long as you remember the relatively higher risks that are involved.

Example: Given the same circumstances as those in the previous example, you decide to *sell* a call instead of buying one. Instead of paying the $500 premium, you receive $500 as a seller. Of this, $300 represents time value, which now is an advantage rather than a problem. As far as looming expiration, as a seller that presents you with an advantage as well. The pending expiration places pressure for time value to evaporate, meaning greater profits for you as a seller. As long as the stock's current market value does not increase more than three points between now and expiration, the transaction will be profitable.

By the time of expiration, all of the time value will have disappeared from the premium value, and all remaining premium will represent intrinsic value only. This condition is known as *parity*.

Using the Daily Options Listings

Online trading is a natural for options traders. The ability to monitor a changing market on the basis of only a 20-minute delay is a significant advantage over telephone calls to a broker, and for an extra charge you can get real-time quotations (or as close as possible to real time) online. The Internet is also likely to be far more responsive than a broker, who may be on another line, with another client, or away from the desk when you call. For you as an options trader, even a few minutes of inaccessibility can

parity
the condition of an option at expiration, when the total premium consists of intrinsic value and no time value.

have the consequence of a lost opportunity. Of course, exceptionally heavy volume market periods translate to slowdowns, even on the Internet.

In the past, options traders depended on alert brokers, hoping they would be able to telephone them if price changes made fast decisions necessary. Some placed stop limit orders, a cumbersome and limiting method for managing an options portfolio. And in the worst of all cases, some investors used to wait until the day after to review options listings in the newspaper. None of these antiquated methods are adequate for the modern options trader, who should be able to find a dependable online source for rapid options quotations.

Smart Investor Tip   You can find brokerage sites that offer free daily options quotes by performing online searches. Two sites that have especially easily accessible quotation services are Harris*direct* at http://www.csfbdirect.com and Schwab at http://www.schwab.com.

Not only should options investors work on their own through discount service brokers and without expensive and unneeded broker advice; they also need to be online to maximize their market advantage. Option pricing can change from minute to minute in many situations, and you need to be able to keep an eye on the market.

Whether you use an automated system or published options listings, you also need to learn how to read options listings. A typical daily options listing is summarized in Figure 2.2.

The details of what this shows are:

First column: The underlying stock and the current market value of the stock. In this example, Motorola closed at $37 per share.

Second column: This shows the striking price for each available option. As a general rule, stocks valued at $100 or less will have options available at

		CALLS			PUTS		
		JAN	APR	JUL	JAN	APR	JUL
Motorola	25	12	14	17.50	.62	—	—
37	30	7.50	8.37	9	—	.12	—
37	35	2.62	5.12	7	.37	2	3.50
37	40	.12	1.50	—	3.25	5	—
37	45	—	—	—	8.50	11	14.12

FIGURE 2.2 Example of daily options listing.

5-point intervals; and stocks with market value above $100 at 10-point intervals.

Third, fourth, and fifth columns: These report current premium levels for calls.

Sixth, seventh, and eighth columns: These report current premium levels for puts.

In this example, Motorola is on the January, April, July, October (JAJO) cycle, so those three monthly expiration dates are reported. Since options exist only for up to nine months or so, the furthest reported month in the cycle is not shown in this reporting format. In this illustration, no October calls or puts are shown; they will appear only after expiration of the January options. In some other reporting formats, it is possible that more options are reported.

Understanding Option Abbreviations

Option values are expressed in abbreviated form, both in listings and in communication between brokers and customers. The abbreviated expressions in the options market go far beyond current premium. Both expiration month and striking price are expressed in shorthand form as well. For example, an October option with a striking price of 35 per share is referred to as an OCT 35 option. And a January option with a 50 striking price is called a JAN 50. Like the premium value, striking price is expressed without dollar signs.

The complete option description must include all four terms plus value: underlying stock, expiration month, striking price, type of option (call or put), and current premium. Following is a sample of this. Here, all of the required elements are expressed. The terms, remember, must all be present to distinguish one option from another. In the example, the single expression gives you the underlying stock, expiration month, striking price, type of option, and current premium. The Motorola Call expiring in October with a striking price of $35 per share currently is valued at 3 (premium is $300):

Motorola OCT 35 Call at 3

When you call a broker on the telephone or sign onto a web site and place a trade, an additional coding system is used to specify the expiration month and striking price, and to distinguish calls from puts. This helps to avoid misunderstandings and to classify options properly. A large number of options can exist on a single stock, so the coding system used for trading purposes is very helpful and efficient. After trading options actively, you might memorize these codes; however, it also helps to make a chart and keep it handy for quick reference. Figure 2.3 summarizes the symbols used for buying and selling options. You will need these for typing in correct option designations online or, if you trade by telephone, for communication with a broker.

The expiration month is always expressed first, followed immediately by the striking price. Note that striking prices of 5, 105, and 205 have identical symbols. This works because the market value of the underlying stock quickly determines which range of pricing applies.

Example: You want to trade in calls with October expiration and 35 striking price. The symbols to use are J for the month (October is the tenth month and J is the tenth letter); and G for the striking price. In this case, a call would have the designation JG and a put would be coded as VG.

The complete option quote also includes the abbreviated symbol for the underlying stock. Every listed stock on every stock exchange has a unique abbrevia-

expiration month symbols		
MONTH	CALLS	PUTS
January	A	M
February	B	N
March	C	O
April	D	P
May	E	Q
June	F	R
July	G	S
August	H	T
September	I	U
October	J	V
November	K	W
December	L	X

striking price symbols			
STRIKING PRICE			SYMBOL
5	105	205	A
10	110	210	B
15	115	215	C
20	120	220	D
25	125	225	E
30	130	230	F
35	135	235	G
40	140	240	H
45	145	245	I
50	150	250	J
55	155	255	K
60	160	260	L
65	165	265	M
70	170	270	N
75	175	275	O
80	180	280	P
85	185	285	Q
90	190	290	R
95	195	295	S
100	200	300	T
7½	–	–	U
12½	–	–	V
17½	–	–	W
22½	–	–	X

FIGURE 2.3 Option trading symbols.

tion that distinguishes it from all other listed stocks. Motorola, for example, is abbreviated MOT. So a Motorola option code consists of two sections. First is the symbol for the stock (in this case, three letters). This is followed by a period and then a two-letter code indicating month and striking price. Distinction between call and put is part of the month code. A Motorola October 35 call with a striking price of 35 is designated as: MOT.JG

A put for the same striking price and month is designated as: MOT.VG

Smart Investor Tip If you know the name of the company but not its abbreviated symbol, most online sites offering free quotations also offer cross-reference services. One example is found at http://finance.lycos.com. From this page, go to "find symbol" and type in the company name. This is also a free service.

rate of return
the yield from investing, calculated by dividing net cash profit upon sale by the amount spent at purchase.

annualized basis
a method for comparing rates of return for holdings of varying periods, in which all returns are expressed as though investments had been held over a full year. (It involves dividing the holding period by the number of months the positions were open, and multiplying the result by 12.)

CALCULATING THE RATE OF RETURN FOR SELLERS

Investors guide themselves and judge their success by their *rate of return*. In a single transaction involving one buy and one sell, rate of return is easily calculated. Simply divide the net profit (after trading fees) by the total purchase amount (including trading fees), and the resulting percentage is the rate of return. When you sell options, though, the rate of return is more complicated. The sale precedes the purchase, so rate of return is not as straightforward as it is in the more traditional investment.

Rate of return can be looked at only in comparative form. In other words, comparing one short position outcome to another, given dissimilar holding periods, makes the comparison invalid. The calculation should be adjusted so that all short position outcomes are reviewed and compared on an *annualized basis*. Because different lengths of time can be involved in a short position—from a few hours up to several months—it is not realistic to compare calculated rates of return without making the adjustment. A 50 percent return in two months is far more significant than the same rate of return held for 10 months.

To annualize a rate of return, follow these steps:

1. Calculate the rate of return. Divide the net profit by the amount of purchase.
2. Divide the rate of return by the number of months the investment position was open.
3. Multiply the result above by 12 (months).

Example: You realize a net profit of 12 percent on an investment. The annualized rate of return will vary depending upon the holding period:

1. *Three months:*
   net profit 12%
   holding period = 3 months
   12 ÷ 3 = 4%
   4% × 12 months = 48% annualized

2. *Eight months:*
   net profit 12%
   holding period = 8 months
   12 ÷ 8 = 1.5%
   1.5% × 12 months – 18% annualized

3. *Fifteen months:*
   net profit 12%
   holding period = 15 months
   12 ÷ 15 = .8%
   .8% ÷ 12 = 9.6% annualized

As these examples demonstrate, annualized rate of return differs dramatically depending upon the period the position remained open. Annualizing applies for periods above one year, as in example 3. A short period is properly extended through annualizing, just as a period beyond one year should be contracted to reflect rate of return *as though* the investment were held for exactly 12 months. By making all returns comparable, it becomes possible to study the outcomes realistically.

Example: You recently sold a call at 3 and, only two weeks later, closed the position by buying at 1. The profit, $200, is 4,800 percent on an annualized basis. This is impressive, but it is of little use in your comparative analysis. Not only is it untypical of the returns you earn from options trading; it also reflects an exceptionally brief period that you were at risk. For analytical purposes, this rate of return has to be ignored.

Smart Investor Tip   Annualized basis is helpful in judging the success of a series of transactions employing a particular strategy. It is less useful in looking at individual outcomes, especially those with very short holding periods.

return if exercised
the estimated rate of return options sellers will earn in the event the buyer exercises the option. (The calculation includes profit or loss on the underlying stock, dividends earned, and premium received for selling the option.)

return if unchanged
the estimated rate of return options sellers will earn in the event the buyer does not exercise the option. (The calculation includes dividends earned on the underlying stock, and the premium received for selling the option.)

The calculation of return is made even more complex when it involves more than return on the option premium. When you sell calls against stock you own, you need to adjust the comparative analysis to study the possible outcome based on two possible events. The first is called *return if exercised*. This is the rate of return you will earn if the call you have sold is exercised and 100 shares of stock are called away. It includes both the profit on your option and profit or loss on the stock as well as any dividends you received during the period you owned the stock.

The second calculation is called *return if unchanged*. This is a calculation of the return to be realized if the stock is not called away, and the option is allowed to expire worthless (or it is closed out through a closing purchase transaction).

In both types of return, the calculations take into account all forms of income. The major difference between the two rates has to do with profit or loss on the underlying stock. These factors complicate the previous observation that comparisons should be made on an annualized rate. It is extremely difficult to account for each dividend payment, especially if the stock has been held over many years. In addition, how do you account for the return on stock held but not sold? There is a valid return involved in the paper profit, and the stock's market value affects option return directly, but this is not a legitimate return because the profit has not been realized.

Neither of these analytical tools lend themselves to annualized return. That is a good tool for the study of relatively simple transactions involving only one source of income. The return if exercised and return if unchanged are far more valuable as a method for determining the wisdom of a decision to sell a call *in advance* of actually taking that step. By comparing these potential rates of return, you can determine which options are more likely to yield profits adequate to justify tying up 100 shares of stock with a short call position.

The actual steps involved in calculation should always be net of brokerage fees, both for sale and purchase. Remember that no attempt should be made to make comparisons on an annualized basis, however, because a complex transaction with differing types of profit, and generated over different lengths of time, make annualized return inappropriate. While the following examples use single option contracts, in practice options traders often use multiple options and involve more than 100 shares of stock.

Example: You own 100 shares of stock that you purchased originally at $58 per share. Current market value is $63 per share. You sell a call with a striking price of 60 and receive a premium of 7. Between the date the option is sold and expiration, you also receive two dividend payments, totaling $68.

Return If Exercised:

Striking price	$6,000
Less: Original cost of stock	-5,800
Profit on stock	$ 200
Dividends received	68
Call premium received	700
Total profit	$ 968

Return if exercised: ($968 ÷ $5,800) = 16.69%

Return If Unchanged

Call premium received	$ 700
Dividends received	68
Total profit	$ 768

Return if unchanged: ($768 ÷ $5,800) = 13.24%

Annualizing these returns is not recommended because the transactions involve three different time periods:

stock holding period, dividend income, and short position in the call. In addition, the purpose here is not to compare results after the transaction has been completed, but to make a comparison in advance to determine whether the transaction would be worthwhile. You can use these calculations not only to compare the two outcomes, but also to compare outcomes between two or more possible option short positions.

Smart Investor Tip   The purpose in comparing returns on option selling is not to decide which outcome is more desirable, but to decide whether or not to enter into the transaction in the first place.

Succeeding in options trading means entering open positions with complete awareness of all possible outcomes and their consequences or benefits. You need to know when it makes sense to close out a position with a closing transaction; avoid exercise with subsequent trades; or just wait for expiration. You also need to be aware of market conditions and the timing of options trades, as well as the relative degree of risk to which you are exposed by entering into open options positions. Knowledge about potential profit is only part of a more complex picture. The more you study options and participate in the market, the more skill you develop in making an overall assessment and comparison.

Chapter 3

Buying Calls

When written in Chinese, the word crisis *is composed of two characters.
One represents danger and the other represents opportunity.*
— John F. Kennedy, speech, April 12, 1959

If you embark upon a program of buying calls, you take the most speculative position that is possible with options. Since time works against you, substantial change in the underlying stock is required in order to produce a profit. Remember, a call grants the *buyer* the right to purchase 100 shares of the underlying stock, at an established striking price per share, and before a firm expiration date in the near-term future. The buyer acquires that right in exchange for paying a premium. As a call buyer, you face three alternatives: First, you can sell the call before it expires; second, you can exercise the call and purchase 100 shares of the underlying stock; or third, you can allow the call to expire worthless.

As a call buyer, you are never obligated to buy 100 shares. In comparison, the seller *must* deliver 100 shares upon exercise of a call. The buyer has the right to determine which of the three outcomes will occur. The decision depends upon:

✔ Price movement of the underlying stock and the resulting effect on the call's premium value.

✔ Your reasons for buying the call in the first place, and how related strategies are affected through ownership of the call.

65

✔ Your risk posture and willingness to wait for future price movement of both stock and the call, as opposed to taking a profit or cutting a loss today. (This is where setting and following standards come into play.)

UNDERSTANDING THE LIMITED LIFE OF THE CALL

You can become a call buyer simply for the potential profit you could earn within a limited period of time—in other words, buying purely on the chance of earning a profit in the short term. That profit will be realized if the premium value increases, so that the call can be sold for more than it cost; or by exercising the call and buying 100 shares of stock below current market value. The call also can be used to offset losses in a short position held in the underlying stock. These uses of calls are explored in more detail later in this chapter.

Every investor experiences risk in many forms, but risks for buyers are not the same as those for sellers; in fact, they often are the exact opposite. Before becoming an options buyer, examine all of the risks and become familiar with potential losses as well as potential gains. Since the purchased option exists for a very limited time, you probably will need to achieve your objective quickly. Time value evaporates with ever-increasing speed, and that is a significant factor that should affect your decision about *when* to close out your long position in the option. Because time value disappears by the point of expiration, the time factor should dictate which options you can afford to buy. More time value usually means more time until expiration and more price movement you need to make a profit. In fact, even when the stock price movement goes the way you want, you still might not make a profit; price

speculation
the use of money to assume risks for short-term profit, in the knowledge that substantial or total losses are one possible outcome. (Buying calls for leverage is one form of speculation. The buyer may earn a very large profit in a matter of days, or could lose the entire amount invested.)

Smart Investor Tip   Time works against you as a buyer, so the more time value in the option you buy, the more difficult it will be to make a profit.

movement has to exceed the number of points of time value *and* more to produce a profit.

Anyone who has purchased stock knows that time is a luxury. In fact, market wisdom dictates that the wise investor knows how to be patient. It takes time for stock prices to move, and to the inexperienced investor, nothing happens quickly enough. Stockholders who look for long-term growth settle for very small price increases each year, but collectively this adds up to a good return on the investment. The stockholder decides when or if to sell, and can time that decision based on personal requirements, stock price movement, and tax considerations. Call buyers, however, cannot afford to wait too long. To the stockholder, time means long-term profit. To the call buyer, time means short-term loss. Time is the enemy.

A simple comparison between purchasing stock as a long-term investment, and purchasing calls for short-term profit, points out the difference between investment and *speculation*. Typically, speculators accept the risk of loss in exchange for the potential for profit, and they take their positions in short-term instruments such as options for the exposure to that potential. Because a relatively small amount of money can be used to tie up 100 shares of stock, call buying is one form of *leverage*, a popular strategy for making investment capital go further. Of course, the greater the degree of leverage, the greater the associated risk.

Knowing exactly what you are getting into, determining the best strategy, and full comprehension of risk, add up to the definition of your own *suitability* for a particular investment or strategy. Suitability identifies what is appropriate, given your income, sophistication, experience, understanding of markets and risks, and capital resources. All too often, investors understand the profit potential of a strategy, but not the full extent of risk.

leverage
the use of investment capital in a way that a relatively small amount of money enables the investor to control a relatively large value. (This is achieved through borrowing—for example, using borrowed money to purchase stocks or bonds—or through the purchase of options, which exist for only a short period of time but enable the option buyer to control 100 shares of stock. As a general rule, the use of leverage increases the potential for profit as well as for loss.)

Example: An investor has no experience in the market, having never owned stock; he also does not understand how the market works. He has $1,000 available to invest today, and decides that he wants to earn a profit as quickly as possible. A friend told him that big profits can be made buying calls. He wants to buy three calls at 3 each, requiring $900, plus trading fees. He expects to double his money within one month.

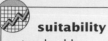

suitability
a standard by which a particular investment or market strategy is judged. (The investor's knowledge and experience with options represent important suitability standards. Strategies are appropriate only if the investor understands the market and can afford to take the risks involved.)

This investor does not meet the minimum suitability standards for buying calls. He does not understand the market, know the risks, or understand the workings of options. He probably does not know anything about time value and the chance of the option going down in value. He is aware only of the profit potential, based only on information he received from a friend. In this situation, the broker is responsible for recognizing that option buying is not appropriate. One of the broker's duties is to ensure that investors know what they are doing and understand all of the risks. The broker should discourage this investor from buying calls and to first read up on options to fully understand them. Given the circumstances, the broker's duty is to refuse to execute the transaction.

Suitability refers not only to your ability to afford losses, but also to your understanding of the many forms of risk in the options market. If the investor in the preceding example worked with an experienced broker at the onset, it would also make sense to listen to that broker's advice about a proposed option position. Every would-be options investor should recognize that not every broker understands options, and the less knowledgeable ones might even have a bias against that market, based on misconceptions of high risk combined with relatively low commissions available to brokers for options trading by their clients. So an unexplained rejection of a proposed strategy could indicate the broker's lack of knowledge rather than an informed position. Make sure a broker knows *more* than you do about options before taking his or her advice.

JUDGING THE CALL

Most call buyers lose money. Even with a thorough understanding of the market and trading experience, this fact cannot be overlooked. In many situations, an underlying stock's value rises, but not enough to offset the declining time value in the option's time value premium. So if the stock rises, but not enough, then the call buyer will not be able to earn a profit. A simple rise in stock price is not adequate in every case, and call buyers have to recognize the need for not just price change, but *adequate* price change to offset declining time value.

Example: You recently bought a call for 4 when it was at $45, at the money (the current market value of the underlying stock was identical to the call's striking price). By expiration, the stock had risen to $47 per share, but the call was worth only 2. Why? The entire $400 premium originally paid consisted of time value, and it contained no intrinsic value. The time value was gone by expiration. The $200 value at closing represents the $2 of intrinsic value. In this case, the best action would be to sell the call and get half your money back. The only alternative is to allow the call to expire and lose the entire $400.

It is a mistake to assume that a call's premium value will rise with the stock in every case, even when in the money. The time value declines as expiration nears, so a rise in the option's premium is seen only in intrinsic value. It is likely that even a rising stock price will not reflect dollar-for-dollar gains in the option until the time value has been used up. That's because time value has to be viewed as "soft" and is likely to evaporate quickly, as opposed to the "hard" intrinsic value that is specifically predictable.

Smart Investor Tip The increase in premium value of an in-the-money option takes place only in intrinsic value. Time value has to be absorbed, too, and as expiration approaches, time value evaporates with increasing speed.

This means that if you buy a call with several dollars of time value, you cannot earn a profit unless the stock rises enough to (1) offset the time value premium and (2) create enough growth above striking price. This double requirement is easy to overlook, but worth remembering.

Example: You bought a call two months ago and paid 1. At the time, the stock was seven points out of the money. Now the expiration date has arrived. The stock's market value has increased an impressive six points. However, the option is worthless because, with expiration pending, there is no intrinsic value. The call is still out of the money, even though the underlying stock's market value has increased six points.

Call buyers will lose money if they fail to recognize the requirement for the underlying stock to increase in value. A mere increase is not enough if time value needs to be offset as well. For this reason, the call buyer needs to establish a bailout point, so that losses can be minimized when the situation appears hopeless. This is of equal importance with knowing when to take profits. Today's momentary profit will disappear quickly if time value remains in the call, and the opportunity might not repeat itself.

> **Smart Investor Tip**   Knowing when to take a profit is only a part of the option trader's goal. It is equally important to know when to take a loss.

Example: You are the type of investor who believes in setting goals for yourself. So when you bought a call at 4, you promised yourself you would sell if the premium value fell to 2 or rose to 7. This standard reduces losses in the event that the transaction declined in value, while also providing a point at which the profit would be realized. You recognize that when it comes to options, time is the enemy and an opportunity might not return. Options buyers often do not get a second chance.

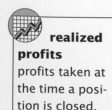

realized profits
profits taken at the time a position is closed.

Goal setting is important because *realized profits* can occur only when you actually close the position. For buyers, that means executing a closing sale; and for sellers, it requires an offsetting closing purchase. As an options trader, you need to set a standard and then stick to it. Otherwise, you can only watch the potential for realized profits come and go. Your *paper profits* (also known as *unrealized profits*) would end up as losses.

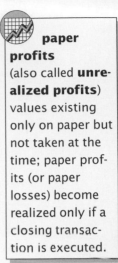

Most call buyers study four attributes: current premium value, the portion representing time value, time until expiration, and perception of the underlying stock (including the price proximity to striking price). For example, you might look through listings in the financial press, seeking a call that can be bought at 2 or less, that is in the money or close to it, with at least three months until expiration. Furthermore, you limit your search to options on a specific list of stocks you consider to be strong prospects for short-term price appreciation. This method encompasses all of the attributes, but it is flawed. The lowest premiums do not necessarily represent the best values.

Bargain options are identified by all of the circumstances, but limiting the search to premiums of 2 or less might be unrealistic. For example, let's say the striking price of one option is 40 and the stock is currently selling at $35. In this case, with five points out of the money, you can expect a six-month option to be a low-priced bargain. Of course, with five points to go just to reach striking price, the stock will have to grow significantly by expiration.

The real bargain depends on the immediate circumstances. However, time to go until expiration, combined with the distance between current market value of the stock and striking price, determine what is a bargain, more than the premium of the call.

Trading on time value is a very poor strategy for buyers, often doomed from the start. It is possible for time value to increase, but that is rare. It is more likely that out-of-the-money options will be unresponsive to price movement in the underlying stock, as long as its price remains below striking price. So if striking price is 40 and the option is trading between $34 and $39 per share, don't expect time value to grow as the stock's price rises. While price changes are taking place, time is passing, and that means a decline in the premium value.

Example: You bought a call with a striking price of 40 and paid a premium of 1. The call expires in four months.

The stock's market value is $34 per share, six points below striking price. In order for you to break even, the stock's price needs to rise seven points (before considering trading costs), to $41 per share.

In the previous example, time works against you as a buyer. If you review only the relationship between the option's premium and time until expiration, it is easy to mislead yourself. It might seem reasonable that there is plenty of time to create a profit, but in fact if a large gap exists between the stock's market value and the striking price, then your expectations could be unrealistic.

If you buy a call and the stock experiences an unexpected jump in market value, it is possible that the time value will increase as well; but this will be temporary. The wider your out-of-the-money range, the slimmer your chances for realizing a profit. Remember that the real leverage value of options takes place when the option is in the money. Then the intrinsic value will change point-for-point with the stock. As shown in Figure 3.1, whenever a

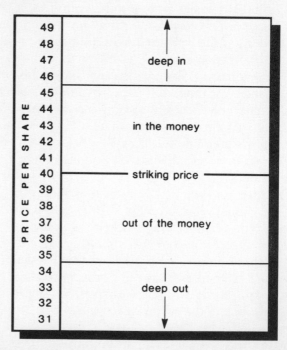

FIGURE 3.1   Deep in/deep out stock prices for calls.

stock is five points or more below the call's striking price, it is described as being *deep out* of the money. For puts, the number of points is the same, but the stock's market value would be five points or more above striking price. If the stock's market value is five points or more above striking price, it is said to be *deep in* the money.

These definitions are significant to call buyers. A deep out-of-the-money option, because it requires significant price movement just to get to a breakeven point, is a long shot; and a deep in-the-money call is going to demand at least five points of premium just for intrinsic value, in addition to its time value. So the majority of calls buyers will buy within the five point range on either side of the striking price.

deep out condition when the underlying stock's current market value is five points or more below the striking price of the call or above the striking price of the put.

CALL BUYING STRATEGIES

Most people think of buying options as purely a speculative activity. If the stock's market value increases, you make a profit; if it falls, you lose. While there is an element of truth in this observation, it is far from the entire picture. As you saw in the previous section, it is not enough for the stock's price to rise. That does not ensure a profit, given the nature of time value. And while movement in the underlying stock's market value is essential to the call buyer, movement alone does not ensure that the option premium will move as well. It is only when the call is in the money that the premium values begin to change in important ways. Calls can also be used, though, for reasons beyond mere speculation.

deep in condition when the underlying stock's current market value is five points or more above the striking price of the call or below the striking price of the put.

Strategy 1: Calls for Leverage

Leverage, you recall, is using a small amount of capital to control a larger investment. While the term usually is applied to borrowing money to invest, it also perfectly describes call buying. For a few hundred dollars placed at risk, you control 100 shares of stock. By "control," we mean that the option buyer has the right to buy the 100 shares at any time prior to expiration, with the price frozen by contract. Leverage is a common and popular reason for buying calls. It enables you to establish the potential for profit with a limited amount of at-risk capital. This is why so many call buyers willingly assume the risks, even knowing that the odds of making money on the call itself are against them.

Example: You are familiar with a pharmaceutical company's management, profit history, and product line. The company has recently announced that it has received approval for the release of a new drug. The release date is three months away. However, the market has not yet responded to the news. You expect that the stock's market price will rise substantially once the market realizes the significance of the new drug. But you are not sure. By buying a call with six months until expiration, you expose yourself to a limited risk; but the opportunity for gain is also worth that risk, in your opinion. In this case, you have not risked the price of 100 shares, only the relatively small cost of the option.

Profits can take place rapidly in an option's value. In the preceding example, if the price of the stock were to take off, you would have a choice: You could sell the call at a profit, or exercise it and pick up 100 shares at a fixed price below market value. That is a wise use of leverage, given the circumstances described. Things can change quickly. This can be demonstrated by comparing the risks between the purchase of 100 shares of stock, versus the purchase of a call that will expire in four months. See Figure 3.2.

In this example, the stock was selling at $62 per share. You could invest $6,200 and buy 100 shares, or you could purchase a call at 5 and invest only $500. In this example, the premium consists of two points of intrinsic value and three points of time value.

If you buy 100 shares, you are required to pay for the purchase within three business days. If you buy the call, you make payment the following day. The payment deadline for any transaction is called the *settlement date*.

As a call buyer, you may plan to sell the call prior to expiration. Most call buyers are speculating on price movement in the underlying stock and do not intend to

settlement date

the date on which a buyer is required to pay for purchases, or on which a seller is entitled to receive payment. (For stocks, settlement date is three business days after the transaction. For options, settlement date is one business day from the date of the transaction.)

	STOCK (1)		CALL (2)	
	PROFIT OR LOSS	RATE OF RETURN	PROFIT OR LOSS	RATE OF RETURN
price increase of 5 points	$500	8.1%	$500	100%
price increase of 1 point	$100	1.6%	$100	20%
no price change	0	0	0	0
price decrease of 1 point	–$100	–1.6%	–$100	–20%
price decrease of 5 points	–$500	–8.1%	–$500	–100%

(1) purchased at $62 per share ($6,200)

(2) striking price 60, premium 5 ($500)

FIGURE 3.2 Rate of return: buying stocks versus calls.

actually exercise the call; rather, their plan is to sell the call at a profit. In the example, a $500 investment gives you control over 100 shares of stock. That's leverage. You do not need to invest and place at risk $6,200 to gain that control. (The stock buyer, in comparison, is entitled to receive dividends and does not have to work against the time deadline.) Without considering trading costs associated with buying and selling calls, what might happen in the immediate future?

If the stock were to rise five points in market value, the stockholder's $500 profit would represent an 8.1 percent return. Because option premium will rise dollar-for-dollar (considering intrinsic value only) the call buyer realizes a 100 percent return in the same situation. (This could be modified by declining time value, if applicable. In other words, the rise of five points could be offset by a loss in some or all of the three points of time value premium.) Conceivably, if the five-point gain occurred only at the point of expiration, it would translate to only a two-point net gain:

Original cost	$500
Less: evaporated time value	−300
Original intrinsic value	$200
Plus: increased intrinsic value	+500
Value at expiration	$700
Profit	$200

A point-for-point change in option premium value would be substantial. An in-the-money increase of one point yields 1.6 percent to the stockholder in this example, but a full 20 percent to the option buyer. If there were to be no price change between purchase and expiration, three-fifths of the option premium would evaporate due to the disappearance of time value. The call buyer risks losses in this situation even without a change in the stock's market value.

As a call buyer, you are under pressure of time for two reasons. First, the option will expire at a specified date in the future. Second, as expiration approaches, the rate of decline in time value increases, making it even more difficult for options traders to get to even or profit status as expiration nears. At that point, increase in market value of the underlying stock will not be sufficient. The increase must be adequate to offset time value *and* to yield a profit above striking price in excess of the premium price you paid.

It is possible to buy calls with little or no time value. To do so, you will have to select calls that are relatively close to expiration, so that only a short time remains for the stock's value to increase; and fairly close to striking price to reduce the premium cost. The short time period increases risk in one respect; the lack of time value reduces risk in another respect.

Example: In the second week of May, the May 50 call is selling for 2 and the underlying stock is worth 51.50 ($1\frac{1}{2}$ points in the money). You buy one call. By the third Friday (the following week), you are hoping for an increase in the market value of the underlying stock. If the stock were to rise one point, the option would be minimally profitable. With only one-half point time value, only a small amount of price movement is required to offset time value and produce in-the-money profits (before considering trading fees). Because time is short, your chances for realizing a profit are limited. But profits—if they do materialize—will be very close to a dollar-for-dollar movement with the stock, given the small amount of time value remaining. If the stock were to increase three points, you could double your money in a day or two. And of course, were the stock to drop two points or more, the option would become worthless.

> **Smart Investor Tip** Short-term call buyers hope for price movement, and they need only a few points. The risk, of course, is that price movement could go in the wrong direction.

The greater the time until expiration, the greater the time value premium—and the greater the increase you will require in the market value of the underlying stock, just to maintain the call's value. For the buyer, the interaction between time and time value is the key. This is summarized in Figure 3.3.

Example: You buy a call at 5 at a time when the stock's market value is at or near the striking price of 30. Your advantage is that you have six months until expiration. For four months, the underlying stock's market value remains fairly close to the striking price, and the option's premium value—all or most time value—declines over the same period. Then the stock's market value increases to $33 per share. However, because most of the time value has disappeared, the call is worth only 3, the intrinsic value. You have lost $200.

Buying calls is one form of leverage—controlling 100 shares of stock for a relatively small investment of capital—and it offers the potential for substantial gain (or loss). But because time value is invariably a factor, the requirements for a successful experience are high. Even with the best timing and analysis of the option and the

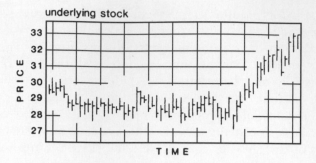

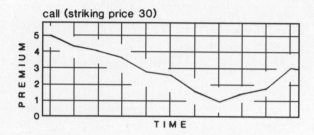

FIGURE 3.3 Diminishing time value of the call relative to the underlying stock.

underlying stock, it is very difficult to earn profits consistently by buying calls.

Strategy 2: Limiting Risks

In one respect, the relatively small investment of capital required to buy a call *reduces* your risk. A stockholder stands to lose a lot more if and when the market value of stock declines.

Example: You bought a call two months ago for a premium of 5. It expires later this month and is worth nearly nothing, since the stock's market value has fallen 12 points, well below striking price. You will lose your $500 investment or most of it, whereas a stockholder would have lost $1,200 in the same situation. You controlled the same number of shares for less exposure to risk, and for a smaller capital investment. Your loss is always limited to the amount of call premium paid. This comparison is not entirely valid, however. The stockholder receives dividends, if paid, and has the luxury of being able to hold stock indefinitely. The stock's market value could rebound. Options traders cannot afford to wait, because they face expiration in the near future.

The time factor impedes the value of risk limitation. You enjoy the benefits only as long as the option exists. The stockholder has more money at risk, but does not have to worry about expiration. It would make no sense to buy calls *only* to limit risks, rather than taking the risks of buying shares of stock. A call buyer has to believe that the stock will increase in value by expiration date. The point here is only that risks are limited in the event that the estimate of near-term price movement proves to be wrong.

Strategy 3: Planning Future Purchases

When you own a call, you fix the price of a future purchase of stock in the event you exercise that call prior to expiration. This use of calls goes far beyond pure speculation.

Example: The market had a large point drop recently, and one company you have been following experienced a drop in market value. It had been trading in the $50 to $60 range, and you would like to buy 100 shares at the current depressed price of $39 per share. You are convinced that market value will soon rebound. However, you do not have $3,900 available to invest at the moment. You will be able to raise this money within six months, but you believe that by then, the stock's market value will have returned to its higher range level. Not knowing exactly what will happen, one alternative is to buy a call. To fix the price, you can buy calls while the market is low with the intention of exercising each call once you have the capital available. The 40 call currently is selling for 3, and you purchase one contract at that price. Six months later, the stock's market price has risen to $58 per share. The option is worth 18 just before expiration.

In this case, you would have two choices. First, you could sell the call at 18 and realize a profit of $1,500.

Second, you could exercise the call and buy 100 shares of stock at $40 per share. If you seek long-term growth and believe the stock is a good value, you can use options to freeze the current price, with the idea of buying 100 shares later.

The advantage to this strategy is that your investment is limited. So if you are wrong and the stock continues to fall, you lose only the option premium. If you are right, you pick up 100 shares below market value upon exercise.

Some options speculators recognize that large drops in overall market value are temporary. There is a tendency for individual stock prices to follow the trend. So a large drop could represent a buying opportunity, especially in those stocks that fall more than the average. In this situation, many investors are afraid of further price drops, so they hold off and miss the opportunity. An options trader, however, can afford to speculate on the probability of a price rebound, and buy calls. When the market does bounce back, those calls gain value and can be sold at a profit.

Strategy 4: Insuring Profits

Another reason for buying calls is to protect a short position in the underlying stock. Calls can be used as a form of insurance. If you have sold short 100 shares of stock, you were hoping that the market value would fall so that you could close out the position by buying 100 shares at a lower market price. The risk, of course, is that the stock will rise in market value, creating a loss for you as a short seller.

Example: An investor sells short 100 shares of stock when market value is $58 per share. One month later, the stock's market value has fallen to $52 per share. The investor enters a closing purchase transaction—buys 100 shares—and realizes a profit of $600 before trading costs.

A short seller's risks are unlimited in the sense that a stock's market value, in theory at least, could rise to any level. If the market value does rise above the initial sale price, each point represents a point of loss for the short seller. To protect themselves against the potential loss in that event, sellers can buy calls for insurance.

Example: An investor sells short 100 shares when market value is $58 per share. At the same time, the investor buys one call, with a striking price of $65, paying a premium of $1/2$, or $50. The risk is no longer unlimited. If market value rises above $65 per share, the call protects the investor; each dollar lost in the stock will be offset by a dollar gained in the call. Risk, then, is limited to seven points (the difference between the short sale price of $58 and the call's striking price of 65).

In this example, a deep out-of-the-money call was fairly inexpensive, yet it provided valuable insurance for the short seller. The protection lasts only until expiration of the call, so if the short sellers wants to protect the position, the short position has to be closed, or the insurance has to be replaced with another call. Short sellers reduce their potential loss through buying offsetting calls, but this also erodes a portion of their profits. Short sellers, like anyone else buying insurance, need to assess the cost of insurance, versus the potential risk.

Example: A short seller pays a premium of 2 and buys a call that expires in five months. If the value of the stock decreases two points, the short seller might take the profit and close the position; however, with the added cost of the call, a two-point rise represents a breakeven point (before calculating the trading costs). The short seller needs more decrease in market value to create a profit.

Calls serve an important function when used by short sellers to limit risks. They also take part of their potential profit for insurance, hoping that the short position will be profitable enough to justify the added expense.

Example: An investor sold short 100 shares of stock at $58 per share. At the same time, he bought a call with a striking price of 65 and paid a premium of 2. A few weeks later, the underlying stock's market price rose on rumors of a pending merger, to a price of $75 per share. The short seller is down $1,700 in the stock (shares were sold at $58, and currently are valued at $75). However, the call is worth 10 in intrinsic value plus whatever time value remains. To close the position, the investor can exercise the call and reduce the loss to $700—the sales price of the stock ($58), versus the striking price of the exercised call ($65 per share).

Strategy 5: Premium Buying

A final strategy involves buying calls to average out the cost of stock held in the portfolio. This is an alternative to dollar cost averaging. Stockholders who desire to hold shares of a company's stock for the long term may wish to buy stock while prices are stable or falling, on the idea that lower prices represent an averaging-down of net price per share. However, the dollar cost averaging strategy, as effective as it is for a declining market situation, is not as desirable when future stock prices rise. In that case, hindsight shows that you would have been better off to buy more shares at the original price.

This is a dilemma for all investors. You never know what is going to happen, especially in short-term prices changes. So if you plan to keep a company's stock as an investment over the long term, but you do not want to put all of your capital into the stock right now (fearing possible decline in value), one alternative is premium buying. When you purchase a call using this strategy, you seek longer-term out-of-the-money calls for relatively low premium levels. Then, if the stock's value does rise you can purchase additional shares below market value.

breakeven price (also called the **breakeven point**) the price of the underlying stock at which the option investor breaks even. (For call buyers, this price is the number of points above the striking price equal to the call premium cost; for put buyers, this price is the number of points below the striking price equal to the put premium cost.)

Example: You own 400 shares of a particular company and you want to buy another 200 to 400 shares in coming months. You originally planned to buy more shares any time the stock's price dropped, creating a lower average cost with each subsequent purchase. However, at the same time you are concerned about losing the opportunity to buy at today's price in the event the stock's price were to rise. You purchase two calls, one two points out of the money expiring in three months, the other five points out expiring in six months.

By undertaking this strategy, you can have it both ways. If the stock's market value falls, you buy additional shares and reduce your overall basis in stock; if the stock's market value rises, you can exercise your calls and fix the price at the striking price, even if the stock's market value goes far above those levels.

For dollar-cost averaging, the strategy of purchasing when market value of stock falls is a smart idea because it does reduce basis—assuming that the drop is temporary and the stock does rebound. Of course, if the company's stock does not return to previous levels, then the strategy is ill advised.

Given the potential problems of buying *more* shares of a company whose prospects are increasingly poor is never sensible. However, in discussing an option strategy such as premium buying in conjunction with downward dollar cost averaging, we would assume that the investor has performed the required level of fundamental analysis to be confident in the company's long-term value.

DEFINING PROFIT ZONES

Whatever strategy you employ in your investment portfolio, always be keenly aware of how much price movement is required to create a profit; the risks involved in the strategy required to achieve that profit; and the range of potential losses to which you expose yourself. Throughout the rest of this book, we use illustrations to define the *breakeven price* as well as *profit zone* and *loss zone* for each strategy. See Figure 3.4 for a sample. Note that prices per share are listed at the left in a column, and the various zones are divided according to price levels. (As with all other examples, these zones are simplified for illustration purposes, and do not allow for the cost of trading. Be sure to add brokerage fees to the cost of all transactions in calculating your own breakeven, profit, and loss zones.)

Example: You buy a call and pay a premium of 3 and with a striking price of 50. What must the stock's price become by point of expiration, in order for you to break even (not considering trading costs)? What price must the stock achieve in order for a profit to be gained, assuming that only intrinsic value will remain at the time? And at what price will you suffer a loss?

 profit zone the price range of the underlying stock in which the option investor realizes a profit. (For the call buyer, the profit zone extends upward from the breakeven price. For the put buyer, the profit zone extends downward from the breakeven price.)

 loss zone the price range of the underlying stock in which the option investor loses. (A limited loss exists for options buyers, since the premium cost is the maximum loss that can be realized.)

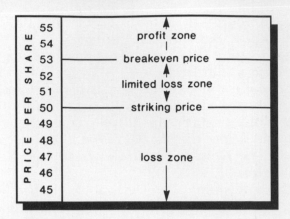

FIGURE 3.4 A call's profit and loss zones.

In this example, a loss occurs if the option expires out of the money, as is always the case. Because you paid a premium of 3, when the underlying stock's market value was three points or less above striking price, the loss will be limited. (Striking price was 50, so if the stock reaches 52, there will be two points of intrinsic value at point of expiration, for example.) With limited intrinsic value between striking price and 53, there is not enough increase in market value to produce a profit. Once the stock reaches $53 per share, you are at breakeven, because you are three points in the money, and you paid 3 for the option. When the stock rises above the $53 per share level, you enter the profit zone.

Defining breakeven price and profit and loss zones helps you to develop a strategy with complete awareness of the range for potential profit or loss. It also helps to define the range of limited loss in cases such as options buying, so that risk can be quantified more easily. An example of a call purchase with defined profit zone and loss zone, is shown in Figure 3.5. In this example, the investor bought one May 40 call for 2. In order to profit from this strategy, the stock's value must increase to a point greater than the striking price of the call plus two points (based on the assumption that all time value will have disappeared). So $42 per share is the breakeven price. Even when buying a call scheduled to expire within a few

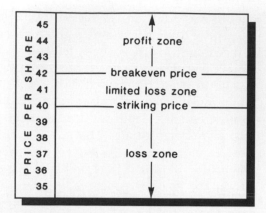

FIGURE 3.5 Example of call purchase with profit and loss zones.

months, you need to know in advance what risks you are taking, and how much price movement is needed to yield a profit.

Example: You have been tracking a stock with the idea of buying calls. Right now, you could buy a call with a striking price of 40 for a premium of 2. The stock's market value is $38 per share, two points out of the money. In deciding whether or not to buy this call, you understand that between the time of purchase and expiration, the stock will need to rise by no less than four points: two points to get to the striking price plus two more points to cover your cost. If this does occur, the option will be worth exactly what you paid for it, and represents a breakeven level (before trading costs). Because the entire premium consists of time value, the stock needs to surpass striking price and develop enough intrinsic value to cover your cost.

Example: Another stock you have been following has an option available for a premium of 1, and currently is at the money. Expiration is two months away and the stock is only one point below breakeven (because of your premium cost). Considering these circumstances, this option has greater potential to become profitable.

In the first example, a breakeven price was four points above current market value of the stock, and the option premium was $200. In the second example, only two points of price movement are required to create a profit, and the option can be bought for half the price. The lower premium also means you are exposed to less potential loss in the event the stock does not rise.

You could make as much profit from a $100 investment as from an equally viable $200 investment, as the previous examples demonstrate. The size of the initial premium cost cannot be used to judge potential profit, whereas they can be used to define potential losses. Premium level can be deceptive, and a more thoughtful risk/reward analysis often is required to truly compare one option choice to another.

> **Smart Investor Tip**   The option's premium level cannot be used reliably to judge the viability of a buy decision. It can be used to define potential losses, however.

after-tax breakeven point
the point level at which you will break even on an option trade, considering the taxes due on short-term capital gains you will be required to pay for trading options.

Yet one additional factor to consider when evaluating potential profit is the tax effect of buying options. By definition, option profits and losses are always short term because listed stock options expire within one year or less. So you should consider the tax consequences of profits as part of the breakeven analysis. The transaction cost has to be calculated on both sides of the transaction, of course. In addition, you probably need to calculate the *after-tax breakeven point*, which is the profit required to break even when also allowing for the federal, state, and (if applicable) local taxes you will owe.

Option profits are taxed in the year a transaction is closed. So option sellers receive payment in one year, but the option expires or is closed in the following year. In that situation, the option profit is taxed in the latter year, when the option has been closed or expires.

Example: You bought a call two months ago and you want to identify the after-tax breakeven point. Your effective tax rate (combining federal and state) is 50 percent, so your breakeven cannot simply be restricted to the calculation of pre-tax profit. Even though the true breakeven point is variable because as you earn more, a higher amount of taxes will be due, you should build in a 50 percent cushion to the breakeven point. So your after-tax breakeven point has to be raised enough to provide a cushion. If you were to make $200 on an option transaction, $100 would have to go to the combined tax bill, so you would have to raise the breakeven by one point to allow for that.

Before buying any option, you need to evaluate the attributes of the underlying stock in addition to the profit or loss potential of the option. The analysis of the underlying stock should include, at a minimum, a study of market price, dividend rate, volatility, P/E ratio, earnings history, and numerous other fundamental and technical features that define a stock's safety and stability. There is no point in selecting an option that has price appeal, when the underlying stock has undesirable qualities, such as price unpredictability, troubling financial problems, weak position within a sector or industry, or inconsistent earnings and dividend history. At the very least, you need to determine from recent history how responsive the stock's market price is likely to be to the general movement of the market. In a greater sense, options cannot be evaluated apart from their underlying stock. The real value and profit potential in your options strategy grows from first selecting likely stock candidates. It is the wise selection of a range of "good" stocks (by the definition you use of what constitutes that value) that determines viable option selection.

You may also evaluate the entire stock market before deciding whether your timing is good for buying calls. For example, do you believe that the market has been on an upward climb that may require a short-term correction? If so, it is possible that buying options, even on the best stock choices, could be ill timed. A second question worth asking is how you define the "market." The Dow Jones Industrial Averages considers only a few companies, whereas the S&P 500 is more representative. You might also judge the market in terms of changes in the NYSE Composite Index. The best method for defining the market as a whole is to look at all of the popular indicators, and then develop a sense of overall price movement. A strong signal in one direction by a majority of the popular indices is a good indicator for identifying overall market movement.

The problem with an opinion you develop about the market, no matter how well supported through analysis, is that in the end, it is still only an opinion. No one truly knows how markets move, nor why they behave as they do. The process of buying and selling is based, invariably, upon timing and opinion. See Chapter 6 for a more in-depth and expanded study and discussion of stock selection.

Beyond the point of stock and option analysis, you need to carefully observe the time factor, and how the passage of time affects the option premium. Time value changes predictably, but in different degrees by stock and from one period to another. Your call expires within a short period of time, so you have only limited time to accumulate value. Changes in time value can be elusive and unpredictable in the degree and timing of their changes. The only certainty is that at expiration, no time value will remain in the option premium.

In the next chapter, strategies for buying puts are examined in depth.

Buying Puts

The optimist proclaims that we live in the best of all possible worlds; and the pessimist fears this is true.
—James Branch Cabell, *The Silver Stallion*, 1926

You will recall that call buyers acquire the right to *buy* 100 shares of an underlying stock. In contrast, a put grants the buyer the opposite right: to *sell* 100 shares of an underlying stock. The premium paid to acquire a put grants the right to the buyer. Upon exercise of a put, the buyer sells 100 shares at the specified price, even if the stock's current market value has fallen below that level.

As a put buyer, you have a choice to make in the near future. You may sell the put before it expires; you may exercise the put and sell 100 shares of the underlying stock at the fixed striking price; or you may let the put expire worthless.

You are not obligated to sell 100 shares by virtue of owning the put. That decision is entirely up to you, and is a right but not an obligation. The seller, however, would

Smart Investor Tip The buyer of an option always has the right, but not the obligation to exercise. The seller has no choice in the event of exercise.

be obligated to buy 100 shares if the buyer did decide to exercise the put.

As a put buyer, your decisions will depend on the same features that affect and motivate call buyers. These are:

- ✔ Price movement in the underlying stock and how that affects the put's premium value.
- ✔ Your motives for buying the put, and how today's market conditions meet or fail that purpose.
- ✔ Your willingness to wait out a series of events between purchase date and expiration and see what develops, versus your desire for a sure profit in the short term.

THE LIMITED LIFE OF THE PUT

Puts can be bought purely on speculation. If you believe the underlying stock's market value will decline in the near future, you can take one of three actions in the market: Sell short on shares of the stock, sell calls, or buy puts. When you buy a put, your desire is that the underlying stock's value will fall below the striking price; the more it falls, the higher your profit. Your belief and hope is opposite that of a call buyer. In that respect, many people view call buyers as optimists and put buyers as pessimists. It is more reasonable to define put buyers as investors who recognize the cyclical nature of prices in the market; when they believe that a stock is overvalued, put buying is sensible for two reasons. First, if the put buyer is correct, it may be a profitable decision. Second, buying puts contains much lower risks than short selling or call selling.

Short Selling

Short selling is a risky strategy. It involves opening a position by selling stock in the belief that its market value will fall. At some point in the future, the short seller will close the position by buying those shares of stock, hopefully at a lower price. Short sellers borrow the stock from the bro-

kerage firm and then sell it short. The brokerage firm requires a deposit equal to a portion of the stock's value as
collateral at the time of the short sale. So short selling is
not only risky; it also requires a commitment of capital. If
the short seller is mistaken and the stock's market value
rises, the brokerage firm will require that more collateral
be placed on deposit; ultimately, the ill-timed short sale
would be closed at a loss.

The short seller risks the entire amount of a stock's
market value. Interest has to be paid on the borrowed
stock's value, meaning that the price of the stock has to
fall far enough to cover the interest *and* produce a profit.
Risk is high because the stock's value could rise, in theory
to any level. The short seller's only advantage over the put
buyer is that they do not have to be concerned with expiration. Of course, the longer the short seller keeps the position open, the higher the interest cost—not to mention
the lost opportunity cost involved with keeping collateral
on deposit with the brokerage firm. Even if that collateral
is in the form of securities, the investor cannot remove it
until the short position has been closed.

Call Selling

A second strategy when investors believe that a stock's
market value is going to fall involves selling calls. At first
glance, selling a call or buying a put is the same strategy. If
the stock's market value falls, either strategy produces the
same profit; and if the stock's market price rises, both
strategies produce the same loss. An important difference,
though, is that the put buyer is not exposed to the high
risks of the call seller.

Remember that the seller has no say in the decision
to exercise an option; that is up to the buyer. A call seller
receives a premium at the time the call is sold, which mitigates the risk to a degree. The call seller can also eliminate the market risk if he or she owns 100 shares of the
underlying stock at the time the call is sold. Upon exercise, those 100 shares can be delivered in satisfaction of
the call. In effect, this covers the short position and allows the call seller the luxury of receiving call premium.
If the call is not exercised, the investor may then sell another call and continue that process indefinitely. Selling

calls is a similar strategy to selling stock short, but the risks are much lower if the investor has covered the call with 100 shares of stock. Call selling when you also own 100 shares of stock for each call sold—the lowest-risk use of options—is described in much more detail in the next chapter.

Selling calls when you do not own 100 shares of stock is a far higher risk. Because share value might rise instead of fall, the call seller risks the possibility of exercise by the buyer. In that situation, the seller would be required to deliver 100 shares at the striking price, which would be lower than current market value. (In practice, the seller does not actually buy shares at market price and then sell them at strike price; they would have to pay the difference to settle the exercise.) So in theory, selling calls without owning 100 shares of stock for each call sold can lead to potentially large losses.

Buying Puts

The third strategy available to those who believe a stock's market price will fall is that of buying puts. The buyer has risks limited to the premium paid to acquire the put. In that regard, the put buyer faces identical risks to those experienced by the call buyer. But when compared to selling short 100 shares of stock, put buyers have far less risk *and* much less capital requirement. The put buyer does not have to deposit collateral or pay interest on borrowed stock, is not exposed to exercise as a seller would be, and does not face the same risks as the short seller; yet the put buyer can make as much profit. The only disadvantage is the expiration date that comes up in the short term. Time works against the put buyer, and time value premium evaporates with increasing speed as expiration approaches. If the stock's market value declines, but not enough to offset lost time value, you could experience a loss or only break even. The strategy requires price drops adequate to produce a profit. But still, your risk is limited to the price paid for the premium. Unlike short selling or call selling, put buying provides you with the right to exercise while limiting your overall risks.

Compare the various strategies you can employ using shares of stock or options, depending upon what you believe will happen in the near-term future to the market value of the underlying stock:

If You Believe that the Market Will

	Rise	*Fall*
Stock strategy	Buy shares (long)	Sell shares (short)
Option strategy (long)	Buy calls	Buy puts
Option strategy (short)	Sell puts	Sell calls

Example: You have been watching a stock over the past few months. You believe it is overpriced today, and you expect market value to decline in the near-term. Originally, you had planned to buy shares, but now you think the timing is wrong. Instead, you borrow 100 shares from your brokerage firm and sell them short. A few weeks later, the stock has fallen eight points. You close the position by buying 100 shares. Your profit is $800, less trading costs and interest.

Example: You sold short a stock last month that was selling at $59 per share. At the time, you believed the stock was overpriced and that its market value was going to fall. However, a few days ago the company announced a tender offer for the company's stock at $75 per share. The stock jumped to $73 and trading was halted. If it re-opens at $73 and you close your position, you will lose $1,400, the difference between your original sale price and current market value. If the tender offer is accepted and the stock continues to rise, you suffer in three ways. First, your market loss will become higher. Second, the brokerage firm will require more collateral. And third, your interest cost for the borrowed stock will continue as well.

Example: You believe that a particular stock is going to decline in value, so you sell a call, receiving a premium of 4. If you are right and the stock's market value falls, the value of the call will fall as well. Even if the stock remains at the same level, time value will decline, reducing the overall premium value of the call. In either case, you will be able to close the position and buy the call at a lower premium than you paid (as long as the stock's market price does not rise substantially). Or you can wait for the call to expire worthless.

Example: You believe that a particular stock's market value will decline, but you do not want to sell short on the shares, recognizing that the risks and costs are too high. You also do not want to sell a call. You do not own 100 shares, and you recognize the high risks in selling calls; if the stock's market value goes up, you could lose a lot of money. That leaves you with a third choice, buying a put. You identify a put with several months until expiration, whose premium is 3. If you are right and the stock's market value falls, you could make a profit. But if you are wrong and market value remains the same or rises (or falls, but not enough to produce a profit), your maximum risk exposure is only $300.

As a put buyer, you benefit from a stock's declining market value when you buy puts, and at the same time you avoid the cost and risk associated with short positions. Selling short or selling calls exposes you to significant market risks, often for small profit potential. These strategies often do not justify the risk, whereas the limited risk of put buying makes more sense.

The limited loss is a positive feature to put buying. However, the put—like the call—exists for only a limited amount of time. To profit from the strategy, you need to have adequate downward price movement in the stock to offset time value, and to exceed your initial premium cost. So as a put buyer, you trade limited risk for limited life.

Smart Investor Tip As a put buyer, you eliminate risks associated with going short, and in exchange, you accept the time restrictions associated with option long positions.

Understanding the potential benefit to a particular strategy is only half of the formula. The other half is the element of risk. For example, as a buyer, you need to know exactly how much price movement is needed to break even and to make a profit. Given time until expiration, is it realistic to expect that much price movement? There will be greater risks if your strategy requires a six-point movement in two weeks, and relatively small risks if you need only three points of price movement over two months. Too many speculators buy puts with high time value, believing that in-the-money situations can produce fast profits with minimal price movement. That is true, of course, if the stock's price behaves as the speculator expects it to. But if it does not happen quickly enough, then time value begins to disappear and the requirement for a small price movement becomes a need for a much larger one.

Put buying is suitable for you only if you understand the risks and are familiar with price history in the underlying stock, not to mention the other fundamental and technical aspects that make a particular stock a good prospect for your option strategy. You need to be willing to live with the potential loss of your entire premium. Without a doubt, buying puts is a risky strategy, and the smart put buyer knows this from the start.

Example: An investor has $600 available and believes that the market as a whole is overpriced. He expects it to fall in the near future. He buys two puts at 3 each. The market does fall as expected; but the underlying stock involved with the two puts remains unchanged and the puts begin to lose their time value. At expiration, they are worth only 1, and he sells, receiving only $200.

This investor's perception of the market was correct: Prices fell. But put buyers cannot afford to depend on overall impressions. The strategy lost money because the particular stock did not behave in the same way as the market in general. The problem with broad market indicators is that there are so many, and none are completely reliable. Each stock has its own attributes and reacts differently in changing markets. Many issues tend to follow an upward or downward price movement in the larger market, and others do not react to markets as a whole. It is important to study the attributes of the individual stock.

In the preceding example, it appears that the strategy was inappropriate for the investor. First of all, the entire amount of capital was invested in a high-risk strategy. Second, the whole thing was placed into puts on the same stock. It could be that this investor did not have enough capital to be involved in buying options in the first place; but by basing a decision on the entire market without considering the indicators for the specific company, the investor lost money. It is likely, too, that this investor did not understand the degree of price change that would be required to produce a profit. If you do not know how much risk a strategy involves, then it is not an appropriate strategy. More study and analysis is required.

Smart Investor Tip When it comes to market risk, the unasked question can lead to unexpected losses. Whatever strategy you employ, you need to first explore and understand all of the risks involved.

It is typical for investors to concentrate on potential gain without also considering the potential loss, especially in the options market. In the previous example, one reason the investor lost was due to a failure to study the individual stock. One aspect not considered was the company's strength in a declining market, its ability to hold its price. This information might have been revealed with more focused analysis and a study of the stock's price history in previous markets. Options traders may lose not because their perception of the market is wrong, but because there was not enough time for their strategy to work—in other words, because the investor did not fully understand the implications of buying options.

Once you understand the risks and are convinced that you can afford the losses that could occur, you might conclude that it is appropriate to buy puts in some circumstances. Remember, though, that the evaluation has to involve not only the option—premium level, time value, and time until expiration—but also the attributes of the underlying stock.

Example: An experienced investor has a well-diversified investment portfolio. He owns shares in companies in different market sectors and also owns shares in two mutual funds, plus some real estate. He has been investing for several years and fully understands the risks in various markets, considering himself a long-term and conservative investor. He has always selected stocks, with long-term price appreciation and stability in earnings the primary selection criteria. Short-term price movement does not concern him with these longer-term aspects in mind. Outside of this portfolio, the investor has several hundred dollars available, which he uses for occasional speculation. He believes the market will fall in the short-term, including shares of stock that he owns. He buys puts with this in mind. His theory: Any short-term losses in his permanent portfolio will be offset by gains in his put speculation. And if he is wrong, he can afford to lose the money he uses to speculate.

This investor understands the difference between long-term investment and short-term speculation He has established a base in his portfolio, and thoroughly understands how the market works. He knows that long-term appreciation is a separate matter from short-term price fluctuation. He can afford some minor losses with capital set aside purely for speculation. Buying puts is an appropriate strategy given the investor's belief about the market, particularly since he understands that stocks in his portfolio are likely to fall along with larger market trends. Not wanting to sell shares held for the long term, he uses his speculation funds to anticipate a temporary price drop. The ability to afford losses, the investor's understanding of the market, and the proper selection of stocks on which to buy puts, all add up to a greater chance of success.

JUDGING THE PUT

Time works against all options buyers. Not only will your option expire within a few months, but time value will decline even if the stock's price does not change. Buyers need to offset lost time value with price movement that creates intrinsic value in its place.

You can select low-priced puts—ones that are out of the money—but that means you require many points just to produce a profit. In other words, those puts are low-priced for a good reason. The likelihood of gain is lower than it is for higher-priced puts. When you buy in-the-money puts, you will experience a point-for-point change; but that can happen in either direction. For put buyers, a downward movement in the stock's market value is offset point-for-point with gains in the put's premium; but each upward movement in the stock's market value is also offset, by a decline in the put's premium value.

Example: You bought a put and paid a premium of 5. At the time, the stock's market value was four points below the striking price. It was four points in the money. (You will recall that for calls, "in the money" means the stock's market value is higher than striking price, but the opposite for puts.) However, by expiration, the stock has risen 4.50 points and the option is worth only 0.50 ($50). The time value has disappeared and you sell on the day of expiration, losing $450.

Example: You bought a put several months ago, paying a premium of 0.50 ($50). At that time, the stock's market value was five points out of the money. By expiration, the stock's market value has declined 5.50 points, so that the put is 0.50 point in the money. When you bought the put, it had no intrinsic value and only 0.50 point of time value. At expiration, the time value is gone and there remains only 0.50 point of intrinsic value. Overall, the premium value is the same; but no profit is possible because the stock's market value did not fall enough.

The problem is not limited to picking the right direction a stock's market value might change, although many novice options traders fall into the trap of believing that this is true. Rather, the *degree* of movement within a limited period of time must be adequate to produce profits that exceed premium cost and offset time value (and to cover trading costs on both sides).

Some speculators attempt to bargain hunt in the options market. The belief is that it is always better to pick up a cheap option than to put more money into a high-priced one. This is not always the case; many cheap options are cheap because they are *not* good bargains, and this is widely recognized by the market overall. The question of quality has to be remembered at all times when you are choosing options and comparing prices. The idea of value is constantly being adjusted for information about the underlying stock, but these adjustments are obscured by the double effect of (1) time to go until expiration and the effect on time value, and (2) distance between current market value of the stock and the striking price of the option. Obviously, when the market value of the stock is close to the striking price, it creates a situation in which profits (or losses) can materialize rapidly. At such times, the proximity between market and striking price will also be reflected in price, given time until expiration.

Smart Investor Tip   A bargain price might reflect a bargain, or it might reflect a lack of value in the option. Sometimes, real bargains are found in higher-priced options.

Example: You bought a put last week when it was in the money, paying a premium of 6. You believed the stock was overpriced and was likely to fall. Two days after your purchase, the stock's market value fell one point. You sold the put and received $700. This represents a return on your investment of 16.7 percent in two days (not considering trading costs).

In this example, the investor turned the position around rapidly and walked away with a profit. So the bargain existed in this put because the investor was right. The return was substantial, but that does not mean that it can be repeated consistently. Remember, when you buy puts on speculation, you are gambling that you are right about short-term price changes. You might be right about the general trend in a stock, but not have enough time for your prediction to become true before expiration. With this in mind, it is critical to set goals for yourself, knowing in advance when you will sell a put—based on profit goals as well as loss bailout points.

Example: You bought a put last month, paying a premium of 4. At that time, you decided to set a few goals for yourself. First, you decided that if the put's value fell by two points, you would sell and accept a loss of $200. Second, you promised yourself that if the put's value rose by three points, you would sell and take a profit. You decided you would be willing to accept either a 50 percent loss or a 75 percent gain. And failing either of these outcomes, you decided you would hold the put until just before expiration.

Setting goals is the only way to succeed if you plan to speculate by buying options. Too many speculators fall into a no-win trap because they program themselves to lose; they do not set standards, so they do not know when or how to make smart decisions.

Example: An investor bought a put last month and paid 5. His plan was to sell if the value went up two points. A week after his purchase, the stock's market value fell and the put's value went up to 8, an increase of three points. The investor did not sell, however, because he thought the stock's market value might continue to fall. If that happened and the put's value increased, he did not want to lose out on future profits. But the following week, the stock's value rebounded four points, and the put followed, also losing four points. The opportunity was lost.

This example demonstrates the absolute need for firm goals. This common trap shows that inexperienced options speculators do not recognize the need to take profits when they are there, or to cut losses—either decision based upon a predetermined standard. When the put becomes more valuable, human nature tempts us by saying, "I could make even more money if I wait." When the put's value falls, the same voice says, "I can't sell now. I have to get back to where I started."

Ask yourself: If you listen to that voice, when do you sell? The answer, of course, is that you can never sell. Whether your option is more valuable or less valuable, the voice tells you to wait and see. Lost opportunities are unlikely to repeat themselves, given the time factor associated with options. The old stock market advice Buy in a rising market cannot be applied to options, because options expire. Not only that, but time value declines over time, which means that profits you gain in intrinsic value could be offset by lost time value if you wait too long. You need to take profits or cut losses at the right moment.

Example: You bought a put last month for 6, and resolved that you would sell if its value rose or fell by two points. Two weeks ago, the stock's market value rose two points and the put declined to your bailout level of 4. You hesitated, hoping for a recovery. Today, the stock has risen a total of five points since you bought the put, which is now worth 1.

In this example, you would lose $300 by not following your own standard and bailing out at 4. Even if the subject stock did fall later on, time is working against you. The longer it takes for a turnaround in the price of the underlying stock, the more time value loss you need to overcome. The stock might fall a point or two over a three-month period, so that you merely trade time value for intrinsic value, with the net effect of zero; it is even likely that the overall premium value will decline if intrinsic value is not enough to offset the lost time value.

The problem of time value deterioration is the same problem experienced by call buyers. It does not matter whether price movement is required to go up (for call buyers) or down (for put buyers); time is the enemy, and price movement has to be adequate to offset time value as well as producing a profit through more intrinsic value. Those buyers who seek bargains several points away from the striking price often fail to recognize this reality. They need a substantial change in the stock's market value just to arrive at the price level where intrinsic value will begin to accumulate. The relationship between the underlying stock and time value premium is illustrated in Figure 4.1.

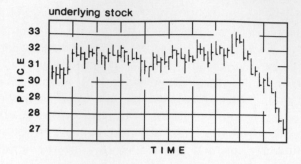

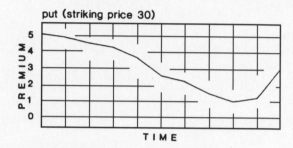

FIGURE 4.1   Diminishing time value of the put relative to the underlying stock.

Example: You buy a put for 5 with a striking price of 30. Between purchase date and expiration, the underlying stock rises above striking price, but then falls to 27, which is three points in the money. At expiration, the put is worth 3, meaning you lose $200 upon sale. Time value has evaporated. Even though you are three points in the money, it is not enough to match or beat your investment of $500.

The further out of the money, the cheaper the premium for the option—*and* the lower the potential to ever realize a profit. Inexperienced options traders fail to recognize that time value rarely increases, so deep out-of-the-money options are poor choices for buyers. The relationship between option premium and the gap between striking price and current market price demonstrates the problem. It is not coincidental; it is predictable. Likewise, the further in the money the option, the more expensive it becomes. You are paying one point for each point in the money, plus time value.

If you buy an in-the-money put and the underlying stock increases in value, you lose one point for each dollar of increase in the stock's market value—as long as it remains in the money—and, of course, for each dollar lost in the stock's market value, your put gains a point in premium value. Once the stock's market value rises above striking price, your put is out of the money and the premium value becomes less responsive to price movement in the underlying stock. While all of this is going on, time value is evaporating as well.

Smart Investor Tip   For options buyers, profits are realized primarily when the option is in the money. Out-of-the-money options are poor candidates for appreciation, because time value rarely increases.

Whether you prefer lower-premium puts that are out of the money, or higher-premium puts that are in the money, always be keenly aware of the point gap between the stock's current market value and striking price of the put. The further out of the money, the less likely it is that your put will produce a profit.

To minimize your exposure to risk, limit your speculation to options on stocks whose market value is within five points of the striking price. In other words, if you buy out-of-the-money puts, avoid those that are deep out of the money. What might seem like a relatively small price gap can become quite large when you consider that *all* of the out-of-the-money premium is time value, and that no intrinsic value can be accumulated until your put goes in the money. Added to this problem is the time factor. As shown in Figure 4.2, you should avoid speculating in puts that are either deep in the money or deep out of the money. Deep in-the-money puts are going to be expensive—one point for each dollar below striking price, plus time value—and deep out-of-the-money puts are too far from the striking price to have any realistic chances for producing profits.

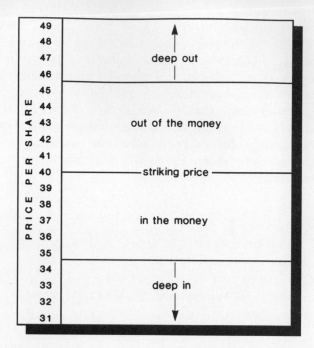

FIGURE 4.2 Deep in/deep out stock prices for puts.

PUT BUYING STRATEGIES

There are three reasons to buy puts. The first is purely speculative: the hope of realizing a profit in a short period of time, with relatively small risk exposure. This leveraged approach is appealing but contains higher risks along with the potential for short-term profits. The second reason to buy puts is as an alternative to short selling of stock. And third, you may buy puts to provide yourself with a form of insurance against price declines in a long position of stock.

Strategy 1: Gaining Leverage

Many put buyers recognize the value of leverage gained with the put. With a limited amount of capital, the potential for profits is greater for put buyers than through short selling of stock, and with considerably less risk. Here is how leverage works in the case of puts:

Example: A stock currently is valued at $60 per share. If you sell short 100 shares and the stock drops five points, you can close the position and take a profit of $500. However, rather than selling short, you could buy 12 puts at 5, for a total investment of $6,000. A five-point drop in this case would produce a profit of $6,000, a 100 percent gain (assuming no change in time value). So by investing the same amount in puts, you could earn a 100 percent profit, compared to an 8.3 percent profit through short selling.

This example demonstrates the value in leverage, but the risk element for each strategy is not comparable. The short seller faces risks not experienced by the put buyer, and has to put up collateral and pay interest; in comparison, the put buyer has to fight against time. Risking $6,000 by buying puts is highly speculative and, while short selling is risky as well, the two strategies have vastly different attributes. The greater profit potential through leverage in buying puts is accompanied by equally higher risk of loss. However, even without a large sum of capital to speculate with, you can still use leverage to your advantage.

Example: You buy a put for 5 with a striking price of 60. The stock currently is selling at $60 per share; your option is at the money. Aware of the potential profit or loss potential in your strategy, your decision to buy puts was, in your opinion, preferable over selling short the stock. As shown in Figure 4.3, a drop of five points in the stock's market value would produce a $500 gain with either strategy (assuming no change in time value premium).

The short seller, like the put buyer, has a time problem. The short seller has to place collateral on deposit equal to a part of the borrowed stock's value, and pay interest on the borrowed amount. Thus, the more time the short position is left open, the higher the interest cost—and the more decline in the stock's value the short seller requires to make a profit. While the put buyer is concerned with diminishing time value and

	STOCK (1)		PUT (2)	
	PROFIT OR LOSS	RATE OF RETURN	PROFIT OR LOSS	RATE OF RETURN
price decrease of 5 points	$500	8.1%	$500	100%
price decrease of 1 point	$100	1.6%	$100	20%
no price change	0	0	0	0
price increase of 1 point	-$100	-1.6%	-$100	-20%
price increase of 5 points	-$500	-8.1%	-$500	-100%

(1) sold short at $62 per share ($6,200)

(2) striking price 60, premium 5 ($500)

FIGURE 4.3 Rates of return: selling short versus buying puts.

experience, the short seller pays interest, which erodes future profits, if they ever materialize; or which increases losses.

A decline of five points in the preceding example produces an 8.1 percent profit for the short seller and a 100 percent profit for the put buyer. Compare the risks with this yield difference in mind. Short selling risks are unlimited in the sense that a stock's value could rise indefinitely. The put buyer's risk is limited to the $500 investment. A drop of $1 per share in the stock's value creates a 1.6 percent profit for the short seller, and a 20 percent profit for the put buyer.

Losses can be compared in the same way as one form of risk evaluation. When a short seller's stock rises in value, the loss could be substantial. It combines market losses with continuing interest expense and tied up collateral (creating a lost opportunity). The put buyer's losses can never exceed the premium cost of the put. Most put buyers do not intend to exercise; the more likely action in the event of a profit would be to sell the put and take the profit.

Strategy 2: Limiting Risks

It is possible to double your money in a very short period of time by speculating in puts. Leverage increases even a modest investment's overall potential (and risk). Risks increase through leverage due to the potential for loss. Like all other forms of investing or speculating, greater opportunity also means great risk.

Example: You recently bought a put for 4. However, the expiration date is coming up soon and the stock's market value has risen above striking price. When the put expires, you face the prospect of losing the entire $400 premium. Time has worked against you. Knowing that the stock's market value might eventually fall below striking price, but not necessarily before expiration, you realize it is unlikely that you will be able to earn a profit.

Risks are lower for puts in comparison to short selling. A short seller in a loss position is required to pay the difference between short-sold price and current market value if the stock has risen in value, not to mention the interest cost. The limited risk of buying puts is a considerable advantage.

Example: An investor sold short 200 shares of stock with market value of $45 per share; he was required to borrow $9,000 worth of stock, put up a portion as collateral, and pay interest to the brokerage company. The stock later rose to $52 per share and the investor sold. His loss on the stock was $1,400 plus interest expense. If the same investor had bought puts instead, the maximum loss would have been limited to the premium paid for the two puts. The fear of further stock price increases that would concern the short seller would not be a problem for the put buyer.

The advantage enjoyed by the put buyer typifies the long position over the short position. Losses are invariably limited in this situation. Although both strategies have the identical goal, risks make the long and short positions much different. Some investors may prefer short selling over put buying because the expiration and deterioration of time value are not factors. This overlooks the time problem for short selling, however, which comes from regular interest payments the short seller needs to make. The risks of the short position can be reduced through buying calls, as explained in Chapter 3. The risk that the stock's market price could rise is insured against because a call will rise dollar for dollar, offsetting losses in the stock. However, the viability of selling short in this condition has to be questioned, considering the overall cost—interest on the borrowed stock, tied up collateral, and call premium. Collectively, a substantial profit has to be earned to justify this strategy. In comparison, alternative strategies of buying puts or selling calls begin to seem more reasonable.

Strategy 3: Hedging a Long Position

married put

the status of a put used to hedge a long position. (Each put owned protects 100 shares of the underlying stock held in the portfolio. If the stock declines in value, the put's value will increase and offset the loss.)

Put buying is not always merely speculative. A very conservative strategy involves buying one put for every 100 shares of the underlying stock owned, to protect yourself against the risk of falling prices. Just as calls can be used to insure against the risk of rising prices in a short sale position, puts can serve the same purpose, protecting against price declines when you are long in shares of stock. When a put is used in this manner, it is called a *married put*, since it is tied directly to the underlying stock.

The risk of declining market value is a constant concern for every investor. If you buy stock and its value falls, a common reaction is to sell in the fear that the decline will continue. In spite of advice to the contrary, many investors sell low and buy high. It is human nature. It requires a cooler head to calmly wait out a decline and rebound, which could takes months, even years. For protection against declines in value, some investors buy puts for insurance, which is known as a *hedge* strategy. In the event of a decline in the stock's value, the put can be exercised and the stock sold at the striking price; or the put can be sold at a profit to offset the lowered value in the stock, a good idea if you believe the stock's price will rebound. When you exercise a put, that action is referred to as *put to seller*.

hedge

a strategy involving the use of one position to protect another. (For example, stock is purchased in the belief it will rise in value, and a put is purchased on the same stock to protect against the risk that market value will decline.)

Example: You own 100 shares of stock that you purchased for $57 per share. This stock tends to be volatile, meaning its potential price range is broad. The potential for gain or loss is significant. To protect yourself against possible losses, you buy a put on the underlying stock. It costs 1 and has a striking price of 50. Two months later, the stock's market value falls to $36 per share and the put is near expiration. The put has a premium value of 14.

In this situation, you have two choices:

1. Sell the put and take the $1,300 profit. Your adjusted cost was $58 per share (purchase price of $5,700 plus $100 for the put). Your net cost per share is $44 ($5,700 less $1,300 profit on the put). Your basis now is eight points above current market value. By selling the put, you have the advantage of continuing to own the stock. If its market value rebounds to a level above $44 per share, you will realize a profit. Without the put, your basis would be 21 points above current market value. Selling the put mitigates a large portion of the loss.

2. Exercise the put and sell the stock for $50 per share. In this alternative, you sell at eight points below your basis. You lose $100 paid for the put, plus seven points in the stock.

Regardless of the choice taken in these circumstances, you end up with less loss by owning the married put, than you would have just owning the stock. The put provides a degree of protection. It either cuts the loss by offsetting the stock's market value decline, or enables you to get rid of the depreciated stock at higher than market value. You have a loss either way, but not as much of a loss as you would have had without buying the put.

This example demonstrates how puts can be used to protect a long position. It is also worth noting that puts are not available on all stocks; so this strategy is useful only if you happen to own shares of stock on which puts can be bought.

The put is used in this application to provide *downside protection*, which reduces potential profits because you have to pay a premium to buy the insurance. If you intend to own shares of stock for the long term, puts will have to be replaced upon expiration, so that the cost is

put to seller action of exercising a put and requiring the seller to purchase 100 shares of stock at the fixed striking price.

downside protection a strategy involving the purchase of one put for every 100 shares of the underlying stock that you own. (This insures you against losses to some degree. For every in-the-money point the stock falls, the put will increase in value by one point. Before exercise, you may sell the put and take a profit offsetting stock losses, or exercise the put and sell the shares at the striking price.)

repetitive. However, long-term investors are not normally concerned with short-term price change, so the strategy might be employed only when you believe your shares currently are overpriced, given the rate of price change and current market conditions.

In the event the stock's market price rises, your potential losses are frozen at the level of the put's premium and no more. This occurs because as intrinsic value in the put declines, it is offset by a rise in the stock's market value. Whether you end up selling the put or exercising, downside protection establishes an acceptable level of loss in the form of paying for insurance; and fixes that loss at the striking price of the put, at least for the duration of the put's life. This strategy is appropriate even for long-term investors who expect instability in the market in the short term.

Example: You recently bought 100 shares of stock at $60 per share. At the same time, you bought a put with a striking price of 60, paying 3. Your total investment is $6,300. Before making your purchase, you analyzed the potential profit and loss and concluded that your losses would probably not exceed 4.8 percent ($300 paid for the put, divided by $6,300, the total invested). You also concluded that an increase in the stock's market value of three points or less would not represent a profit at all, due to the investment in the put. So profits will not begin to accumulate until the stock's market value exceeds $63 per share.

This strategy is especially appropriate when your stock's price movement is volatile. A decline in market value is protected by the put, and an increase is still profitable once the premium cost has been exceeded.

A summary of this strategy is shown in Figure 4.4. Note that regardless of the severity of decline in the stock's market value, the loss can never exceed 4.8 percent of the total amount invested (the cost of the put). That is because for every point of decline in the stock's market value, the put increases one point in intrinsic value. This status would continue until the put expired.

PRICE MOVEMENT, UNDERLYING STOCK	PROFIT OR LOSS		NET PROFIT OR LOSS (3)	
	STOCK (1)	PUT (2)	AMOUNT	RATE
down 20 points	-$2,000	$1,700	-$ 300	- 4.8%
down 5 points	-$ 500	$ 200	-$ 300	- 4.8%
down 3 points	-$ 300	0	-$ 300	- 4.8%
no change	0	-$ 300	-$ 300	- 4.8%
up 3 points	$ 300	-$ 300	0	0
up 5 points	$ 500	-$ 300	$ 200	3.2%
up 20 points	$2,000	-$ 300	$1,700	27.0%

(1) stock purchased at $60 per share
(2) put striking price 60, premium 3
(3) return based on total cost of $6,300

FIGURE 4.4 Downside protection: buying shares and buying puts.

DEFINING PROFIT ZONES

To decide whether buying puts is a reasonable strategy for you, always be aware of potential profits *and* losses, rather than concentrating on profits alone. Pay special attention to the gap between current market value and striking price, especially if you are buying out-of-the-money puts. Remember that the wider this gap, the more difficult it will be to earn a profit. Also remember that the shorter the time to expiration, the lower the time value (which is good) but the more pressure there is to achieve adequate price movement (which is bad). The selection of a put requires balance.

Comparing limited losses to potential profits when using puts for downside protection is one type of analysis that helps you pick value when comparing puts. And when looking for a well priced speculative move, time to expiration coupled with the gap between current market value and striking price—which dictates the amount of time value premium—will help you to find real bargains in puts. Premium level is not a reasonable criterion for your selection.

The profit and loss zones for puts are the reverse of the zones for call buyers, because put owners anticipate a downward movement in the stock, whereas call buyers expect upward price movement. See Figure 4.5 for a summary of loss and profit zones and breakeven point using the following example.

Example: You buy a put with a striking price of 50, paying 3. Your breakeven price is $47 per share. If the underlying stock falls to that level, the option will have intrinsic value of three points, equal to the price you paid for the put. If the price of stock goes below $47 per share, the put will be profitable point for point with downward price movement in the stock. Your put can be sold when the underlying stock's market value is between $47 and $50 per share, for a limited loss. And if the price of the stock rises above $50 per share, the put will be worthless at expiration.

Before buying any put, determine the profit and loss zones and breakeven price (including the cost of trading on both sides of the transaction). For the amount of money you will be putting at risk, how much price movement will be required to produce a profit?

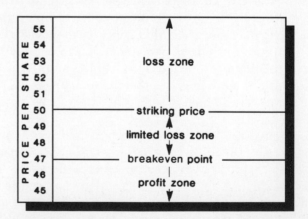

FIGURE 4.5 A put's profit and loss zones.

How much time remains until expiration? Is the risk a reasonable one?

Another example of a put purchase with defined profit and loss zones is shown in Figure 4.6. In this example, the put was bought at 3 and has a May 40 expiration. The outcome of this transaction would be exactly opposite for the purchase of a call, given the same premium, expiration, and price of the underlying stock. You will gain a profit if the stock falls below the striking price of 40. However, the point decline must be greater than the premium level of the put.

Remember this guideline: As a buyer, don't depend on time value to produce profits between purchase date and expiration, because that is highly unlikely to occur. If you do not experience a price decline in the stock's price adequate to exceed the price you paid for the put, then you will have a loss. Like call purchasing, time works against you when you buy puts. The greater the gap between market price of the stock and striking price, the more time problem you will have to overcome.

The mistake made by many investors is failing to recognize what is required to produce a profit, and failing to analyze a situation to determine whether it makes sense. Such investors, having not gone through these basic steps, have not set investment standards for themselves. They might pick up options for very little premium

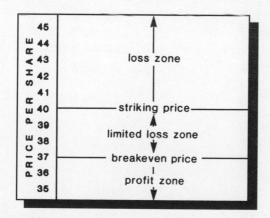

FIGURE 4.6 Example of put purchase with profit and loss zones.

cost, but in most instances, it is still a waste of money. Remember these points in evaluating put buying:

- ✔ Your motive (leverage, reduction of risk, or downside protection).
- ✔ The premium level and amount of time value premium.
- ✔ Time remaining until expiration.
- ✔ Gap between the stock's current market value and the put's striking price.
- ✔ The number of points of movement in the underlying stock required before you can begin earning a profit.
- ✔ The characteristics of the underlying stock (see Chapter 6 for guidelines for selecting stocks appropriate for your option strategy).

Collectively, these guidelines define an investment strategy, and work for you as tools for the evaluation of risks as well as for identification of profit potential. Options buyers have the opportunity to earn substantial short-term profits; they also face a corresponding high risk level represented by time, the buyer's enemy.

On the opposite side of the option transaction is the seller. Unlike buyers, sellers have an *advantage* with pending expiration. Time is the seller's friend, and higher time value represents an opportunity rather than a risk. Because time value declines as expiration approaches, the seller benefits in the same degree as the buyer is penalized. The next chapter examines strategies and risks involved with selling calls.

Selling Calls

Wisdom consists of the anticipation of consequences.
—Norman Cousins, *Saturday Review*, April 15, 1978

In this chapter, you will see how to sell an option first, and then buy it later. Most of us think about investing in a precise sequence. First, you buy a security; then, at a later date, you sell. If the sale price is higher than the purchase price, you earn a profit; if it is lower, you suffer a loss. However, when you are a call seller, this sequence is reversed.

If you buy a call and later sell it (see Chapter 3), the transaction conforms to the familiar pattern, known as the long position. The outcome to taking a short position in calls is the same as for the more familiar long position: you close by entering the opposite order (in the case of selling as a first step, a closing transaction requires that you buy). If the purchase price is lower than the original sale, then you earn a profit; if it is higher, you suffer a loss.

By starting out with an opening sale transaction, you are paid the premium at the time the order is placed. You will pay a purchase later when you close the position or, if the option expires worthless, you never pay at all. In that case, the entire sale premium is yours to keep as profit. If this all sounds like a pretty good deal, you also need to remember that taking a short position is accompanied by inevitable risks as well. These risks are explained in this chapter and examined through examples. You will discover that some types of call selling are extremely high risk and others are very low risk and conservative.

> **Smart Investor Tip**   Sellers receive payment when they initiate the opening transaction. That is compensation for accepting exposure to the risks.

Call sellers enjoy some significant and important advantages over call buyers. In the previous two chapters, many examples demonstrated how time value works against the buyer; in fact, the time value premium makes it very difficult to earn a profit consistently as a buyer. Time value represents the majority of risk involved with call buying. Even when the underlying stock's market value moves in the desired direction, it might not happen soon enough or with enough point value to offset the time value premium. This buyer's disadvantage is the seller's advantage.

Because time value evaporates, buyers see time as the enemy. For sellers, though, time is a great ally. The more time value involved, the higher the potential profit and the more that time value falls, the better. When you enter the order for an opening sale transaction, you are better off if you have the maximum time value possible. With this in mind, longer-term options tend to be better bargains for sellers, although that also represents a longer risk exposure period. While buyers seek options with the lowest possible time value and with market value within reasonable proximity to striking price, sellers do the opposite. They seek calls with the highest possible time value, preferably as far out of the money as possible. You earn a profit as a call seller due to the decline in time value. That enables you to close out the position by buying the call for a lower premium than you received at the opening sale.

> **Smart Investor Tip**   Time is the buyer's enemy, but the opposite is true for the seller. You make your profit as time value evaporates.

When you sell a call, you grant the buyer the right to buy 100 shares of the underlying stock at the striking price, at any time prior to expiration. That means that you assume the risk of being required to sell the buyer 100 shares, potentially at a striking price far below current market value. The decision to exercise is the buyer's, and that decision can be made at any time. Of course, as long as the call is out of the money, it will not be exercised. That risk becomes real only if and when the call goes in the money (when the stock's market value is higher than the call's striking price). The majority of exercise decisions take place at or near closing.

Most investment strategies contain specific risk characteristics. These are identified clearly and should be fully understood by anyone undertaking that strategy. The risks tend to have unchanging attributes. For example, the risks of buying stocks are consistent from one moment to another. The experienced stock market investor understands this and accepts the risk. However, call selling has a unique distinction. It can be extremely risky or extremely conservative, depending upon whether or not you also own 100 shares of the stock at the time you sell the call.

SELLING UNCOVERED CALLS

When call selling is reviewed in isolation, it is indeed a high-risk strategy. If you sell a call but you do not own 100 shares of the underlying stock, the option is classified as a *naked option* or *uncovered option*. You are exposing yourself to an unlimited risk. In fact, call selling in this situation could be one of the most risky strategies you could take, containing high potential for losses.

Remember that when you take a short position, the decision to exercise belongs to the buyer. You need to be able and willing to deliver 100 shares in the event that the call is exercised—no matter how high current market value has gone. If you do not already own 100 shares, you will be required upon exercise to buy 100 shares at current market value and deliver them at the striking price of the call. The difference in these prices could be significant.

 naked option
an option sold in an opening sale transaction when the seller (writer) does not own 100 shares of the underlying stock.

 uncovered option
the same as a naked option—the sale of an option not covered, or protected, by the ownership of 100 shares of the underlying stock.

Example: You sell a call for 5 with a striking price of 45 and expiration month of April. At the time, the underlying stock has a market value of $44 per share. You do not own 100 shares of the underlying stock. The day after your order is placed, your brokerage firm deposits $500 into your account (less fees). However, before expiration, the underlying stock's market price soars to $71 per share and your call is exercised. You will lose $2,100—the current market value of 100 shares, $7,100, less the striking price value, $4,500, less the $500 premium you received at the time you sold the call:

Current market value, 100 shares	$7,100
Less: striking price	−4,500
Less: call premium	− 500
Net loss	$2,100

When a call is exercised and you do not own 100 shares of the underlying stock, you are required to deliver those 100 shares *at the striking price*. This means you have to buy the shares at current market value, no matter how high that price. Because upward price movement, in theory at least, is unlimited, your risk in selling the call is unlimited as well.

Smart Investor Tip   Selling uncovered calls is a high-risk idea, because in theory, a stock's price could rise indefinitely. Every point rise in the stock above striking price is $100 more out of the call seller's pocket.

The risks of selling calls in this manner are extreme. With that in mind, a brokerage firm should allow you to sell calls only if you meet specific requirements. These include having enough equity in your portfolio to provide protection in the event of an unusually high loss. The brokerage firm will want to be able to sell other securities in your account to pay for losses if you cannot come up with the cash. You will need permission in advance from your brokerage firm before you will be allowed to sell calls. Each firm is required to ensure that you understand the risks involved; that you fully understand the options market; and that you have adequate equity and income to undertake those risks.

You will not be allowed to write an unlimited number of calls without also owning 100 shares of the underlying stock. The potential losses, both to you and to the brokerage firm, place natural limits on this activity. Everyone who wants to sell calls is required to sign a document acknowledging the risks and stating that they understand those risks. In part, this statement includes the following:

Special Statement for Uncovered Option Writers[1]

There are special risks associated with uncovered option writing which expose the investor to potentially significant loss. Therefore, this type of strategy may not be suitable for all customers approved for options transactions.

1. The potential loss of uncovered call writing is unlimited. The writer of an uncovered call is in an extremely risky position, and may incur large losses if the value of the underlying instrument increases above the exercise price.

2. As with writing uncovered calls, the risk of writing uncovered put options is substantial. The writer of an uncovered put option bears a risk of loss if the value of the underlying instrument declines below the exercise price. Such loss could be substantial if there is a significant decline in the value of the underlying instrument.

3. Uncovered option writing is thus suitable only for the knowledgeable investor who understands the risks, has the financial capacity and willingness to incur potentially substantial

[1]From the Options Clearing Corporation, "Risk Disclosure Statement and Acknowledgments"

losses, and has sufficient liquid assets to meet applicable margin requirements. In this regard, if the value of the underlying instrument moves against an uncovered writer's options position, the investor's broker may request significant additional margin payments. If an investor does not make such margin payments, the broker may liquidate stock or options positions in the investor's account, with little or no prior notice in accordance with the investor's margin agreement.

margin
an account with a brokerage firm containing a minimum level of cash and securities to provide collateral for short positions or for purchases for which payment has not yet been made.

You will be required to limit the scope of call writing when you do not also own associated shares of the underlying security. The requirement that your portfolio include stocks, cash, and other securities in order to sell calls is one form of *margin* requirement imposed by your broker. Such requirements apply not only to option transactions, but also to short selling of stock or, more commonly, to the purchase of securities using funds borrowed from the brokerage firm.

When you enter into an opening sale transaction, you are referred to as a *writer*. Call writers (sellers) hope that the value of the underlying stock will remain at or below the striking price of the call. If that occurs, then the call will expire worthless and the writer's profits will be made from declining time value (as well as any decline in intrinsic value resulting from the stock's price moving from above the striking price, down to, or below the striking price). For the writer, the breakeven price is the striking price plus the number of points received for selling the call.

writer
the individual who sells (writes) a call (or a put).

Example: You sell a call for 5 with a striking price of 40. Your breakeven is $45 per share (before considering trading costs). Upon exercise, you would be required to deliver 100 shares at the striking price of 40; as long as the stock's current market value is at $45 per share or below, you will not have a loss, even upon exercise, since you received $500 in premium when you sold the call.

It is conceivable that you could write a call and make a profit even upon exercise. Given the preceding example, if the call were exercised when the stock's market price was $42, you gain $300 before trading costs:

Current market value, 100 shares	$4,200
Less: striking price	–4,000
Loss on the stock	$ 200
Premium received	$ 500
Profit before trading costs	$ 300

Smart Investor Tip Exercise does not always mean a loss. The call premium discounts a minimal loss because it is yours to keep, even after exercise.

As a writer, you do not have to wait out expiration; you have another choice. You can close out your short position at any time by purchasing the call. Remember, as a writer, you initiate the position with a sale and close it with a purchase. There are four events that could cause you to close out a short position in your call:

1. The stock's value falls. As a result, time value and intrinsic value, if any, fall as well. The call's premium value is lower, so it is possible to close the position at a profit.

2. The stock's value remains unchanged, but the option's premium value falls due to loss of time value. The call's premium value falls and the position can be closed through purchase, at a profit.

3. The option's premium value remains unchanged because the underlying stock's market value rises. Declining time value is replaced with intrinsic value. The position can be closed at no profit or loss, to avoid exercise.

4. The underlying stock's market value rises enough so that exercise is likely. The position can be closed at a loss to avoid exercise, potentially at greater levels of loss.

Example: You sold a call two months ago for 3. The underlying stock's market value has remained below the striking price without much price movement. Time value has fallen and the option is now worth 1. You have a choice: You can buy the call and close the position, taking a profit of $200; or you can wait for expiration, hoping to keep the entire premium as a profit. This choice exposes you to risk between the decision point and expiration. In the event the stock's market price moves above striking price, intrinsic value could wipe out the profit and lead to exercise. Purchasing when the profit is available ensures the profit and avoids further exposure to risk. If the stock does rise, your breakeven price is three points higher than striking price, since you were paid 3 for selling the call.

 naked position
status for investors when they assume short positions in calls without also owning 100 shares of the underlying stock for each call written.

Whenever you sell a call and you do not also own 100 shares of stock, your risk is described as a *naked position*, which refers to the continuous exposure to risk from the moment of sale through to expiration. Remember, the buyer can exercise at any time, and that can happen whenever your naked call is in the money. Even though exercise is most likely at the time just before expiration, there is no guarantee that it will not happen before that time.

Example: You sold a naked call last week that had four months to go until expiration. You were not worried about exercise. However, as of today, the stock has risen above the striking price and your call is in the money. Your brokerage firm has advised that your call was exercised. You are required to deliver 100 shares of the underlying stock at the striking price. Your call no longer exists.

In this example, you experienced a loss on the stock because you are required to purchase 100 shares at current market value and deliver them at the striking price. However, you may have an overall profit as long as the gap between current market value and striking price is less than the amount you received when you sold the call.

You can never predict early exercise, since buyer and seller are not matched one-to-one. The selection is random. The Options Clearing Corporation (OCC) acts as buyer to every seller, and as seller to every buyer. This ensures an efficient market even when one side of the transaction is much larger than the other. When a buyer decides to exercise a call, the order is assigned at random to a seller. You will not know that this has happened to you until your broker gets in touch to inform you of the exercise.

Smart Investor Tip Because exercise can happen at any time your call is in the money, you need to be aware of your exposure; even early exercise is a possibility. If you sell an in-the-money call, exercise could happen the same day.

In order for you to profit from selling calls, the underlying stock needs to act in one of two ways:

1. Its market value must remain at or below the striking price of the call, so that time value will evaporate over time. The option will expire worthless, or it can be closed with a purchase that is lower than the initial sales price.

2. The market value must remain at a stable enough price level so that the option can be purchased below initial sales price, even if it is in the money. The decline in time value still occurs, even when accompanied by intrinsic value.

The profit and loss zones for uncovered calls are summarized in Figure 5.1. Because you receive cash for selling a call, the breakeven price is higher than the striking price. In this illustration, a call was sold for 5; hence, breakeven is five points higher than striking price. (This example does not take into account the transaction fees.)

Your brokerage firm will require that you deposit a percentage of the total potential liability at the time you write naked calls. The amount required could consist of cash or securities and will vary by broker. Because large losses can result in the event of a major change in market

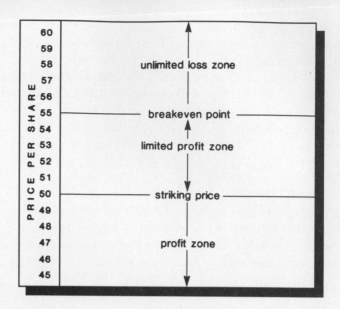

FIGURE 5.1   An uncovered call's profit and loss zones.

value, many brokerage firms restrict or even forbid naked call writing in options; or require exceptionally large deposits of cash or securities. When investors are unable to cover losses in their accounts, the brokerage firm has to make up the difference, and in sudden and large changes in market value, that can be a large sum of money.

Example: You have advised your broker that you intend to write uncovered calls. Your portfolio currently is valued at $20,000 in securities and cash. Your broker restricts your uncovered call writing activity to a level that, in their estimation, would not potentially exceed $20,000. However, as market conditions change, your portfolio value could fall, in which case your broker could restrict your uncovered call activity or require the deposit of additional funds.

Example: You want to write puts in your portfolio as part of your investment strategy (see Chapter 7). Your portfolio value is $20,000. Again, your brokerage firm will place restrictions on uncovered put writing activity based on an estimation of potential losses. However, when you write puts, your liability is not as great; stocks can fall only so far, whereas they can rise indefinitely.

Writing uncovered puts involves limited losses, since the very worst outcome possible is a stock's decline to zero. (In reality, the maximum decline should be considered the decline to tangible book value per share; book value often is overlooked in the market, but that level does provide a reasonable level for assessing liability. It is possible for market value to fall below book value, but that is not likely.) So uncovered puts are associated with a finite loss potential, whereas uncovered calls can lead to unknown levels of loss, especially if you write many uncovered calls at the same time.

> **Smart Investor Tip** While a stock's market price could fall below book value, it is rare. Using book value as a likely low point to evaluate selling puts is a good plan.

Assessing Uncovered Call Writing Risks

All investors need to practice risk assessment, as a primary means for determining what is an appropriate investment or strategy. The examples in the preceding section demonstrate that risks are substantial for uncovered call writing. In future chapters and later in this chapter, some alternatives are presented that demonstrate how writing calls is not always a high-risk venture.

For now, consider the risks involved with writing uncovered calls, especially in light of limitations that are placed on your activity by brokerage firms. These limitations are appropriate and necessary, due to the risks of potential losses. A limited value in your portfolio at large will limit the amount of uncovered call writing you will be allowed to activate. So the restrictions that are placed on this form of trading naturally limit your ability to participate in the high-risk end of this market.

The risks of uncovered call writing include the following:

✔ The stock might rise in value; you will be required to buy the call to close your position and avoid further loss and exercise.

✔ The stock might rise in value, leading to exercise, perhaps early exercise.

✔ Although the stock might remain at or below striking price for a period of time, it could rise unexpectedly and suddenly, leading to exercise; you are at risk from the moment you sell the call all the way to expiration.

✔ You lose opportunities to move your capital around in the market because your brokerage firm wants to limit your risk or loss as well as theirs; so your equity is committed as collateral for your open uncovered call positions.

✔ If you do suffer unexpected large losses, your brokerage firm may sell other securities in your portfolio to pay for those losses. This may include securities whose sale is ill-timed, thus you lose long-term value in your portfolio.

✔ Although you set standards for yourself, you might fail to take action when you should, so that today's profit disappears and you end up losing money upon exercise or having to buy the call at a loss to avoid exercise.

Smart Investor Tip It is smart to know all of the risks involved with uncovered call selling. Not knowing can lead to some very expensive surprises.

SELLING COVERED CALLS

When you sell uncovered calls, potentially large losses result if you are required to deliver shares upon exercise, or to close out positions at a loss to avoid exercise. Imagine being able to sell calls without that risk—meaning that you would never be required to suffer large losses due to an unexpected rise in the stock's market value.

There is a way. By selling a call when you also own 100 shares of the underlying stock, you *cover* your position. If the option is called away by the buyer, you can meet the obligation simply by delivering shares that you already own.

You enjoy several advantages through the *covered call*:

✔ You are paid a premium for each call that you sell, and the cash is placed in your account at the time you sell. While this is also true of uncovered call writing, the same risks do not apply. You can afford exercise because you own 100 shares of stock. Upon exercise, you would not be required to buy shares at market price.

✔ The true net price of your 100 shares of stock is reduced by the value of the option premium. It discounts your basis because you receive cash when you sell the call. This gives you flexibility and downside protection, and more versatility for selling calls with high time value.

✔ Selling covered calls provides you with the freedom to accept moderate interim price declines, because the premium you receive reduces your basis in the stock. Simply owning the stock without the discount means that declines in the stock's market value represent paper losses.

✔ By selling calls against appreciated stock, you are able to augment profits and, in the case of exercise, build in a capital gain as well.

The disadvantage to covered call selling is found in lost opportunity risk that may or may not materialize. If the stock's market value rises dramatically, your call will be exercised at the specified striking price. If you had not sold the call, you would benefit from higher market value in shares of stock. So covered call sellers trade the certainty for premiums received today, for the potential lost profits in the event of exercise.

cover
to protect oneself by owning 100 shares of the underlying stock for each call sold. (The risk in the short position in the call is covered by the ownership of 100 shares.)

covered call
a call sold to create an open short position, when the seller also owns 100 shares of stock for each call sold.

> **Smart Investor Tip** The major risk associated with uncovered call writing is the possibility of lost income from rising stock prices. But that might not happen at all; when you sell a call, you accept the possibility of lost income in exchange for certainty.

Example: You own 100 shares of stock, which you bought last year at $50 per share. Current market value is $54 per share. You are willing to sell this stock at a profit. You write a November 55 call and receive a premium of 5. Now your real basis in the stock is $45 per share (original price of $50 per share, discounted five points by the option premium). If the stock's market value remains between the range of $45 and $55 between the date you sell the call and expiration, your call will expire worthless. It would not be exercised within that price range, since striking price is 55. You can wait out expiration or buy the call, closing it out at a profit. However, if the stock were to rise far above $55 per share and the call were exercised, you would not receive any gain above $55 per share. While exercise would still produce a profit of $1,000 ($500 stock profit plus $500 option premium), you would lose any profits above the striking price level.

One of three events can take place when you sell a covered call: An increase in the stock's price, a decrease in the stock's price, or no significant change. As long as you own 100 shares of the underlying stock, you continue to receive dividends even when you have sold the call. The value of writing calls should be compared to the value of buying and holding stock, as shown in Table 5.1.

Before you undertake any strategy, you need to assess the benefits or consequences in the event of all possible changes, including the potential for lost future profits that might or might not occur in the stock. To ensure a profit in the outcome of writing covered calls, it is wise to select those calls with striking prices above your original basis; or above original basis when discounted by the call premium you receive.

TABLE 5.1 Comparing Strategies

Event	Outcomes	
	Owning Stock and Writing Calls	Owning Stock Only
Stock goes up in value.	Call is exercised; profits are limited to striking price and call premium.	Stock can be sold at a profit.
Stock remains at or below the striking price.	Time value declines; the call can be closed out at a profit or allowed to expire worthless.	No profit or loss until sold.
Stock declines in value.	Stock price is discounted by call premium; the call is closed or allowed to expire worthless.	Loss on the stock.
Dividends.	Earned while stock is held.	Earned while stock is held.

Example: You bought stock last year at $48 per share. If you sell a covered call with a striking price of 50 and receive a premium of 3, you have discounted your basis to $45 per share. Given the same original basis, you may be able to sell a call with a striking price of 45 and receive a premium of 8. That discounts your basis to $40 per share; in both instances, exercise would net a profit of $500. (Exercise at $50, discounted basis of $45 per share; or exercise at $45, discounted basis of $40 per share.) In the latter case, chances of exercise are greater because the call is five points deeper in the money.

In comparing potential profits from various strategies, you might conclude that writing in-the-money calls makes sense in some circumstances. A decline in price reduces call premium dollar for dollar, with the added advantage of declining time value. If this occurs, you can close out the position at a profit, or simply wait for exercise. As a call seller, you are willing to *lock in* the price of the underlying stock in the event of exercise; this makes sense only if exercise will produce a profit to you, given original purchase price of the shares, discounted by the call premium.

lock in to freeze the price of the underlying stock when the investor has sold a corresponding short call. (As long as the call position is open, the writer is locked into a striking price, regardless of current market value of the stock. In the event of exercise, the stock is delivered at that locked-in price.)

Assessing Covered Call Writing Risks

The seller of uncovered calls faces potentially large losses. As a covered call writer, your risks are reduced significantly. That risk is limited on the upside to lost future profits that do not always take place. On the downside, the risk is the same for simply owning shares; a decline in price represents a paper loss. The call writer discounts the basis, providing a degree of downside protection. When you write calls against stock using striking prices above your original basis, you virtually eliminate the upside market risk because upon exercise, you have a built-in profit factor.

> **Smart Investor Tip** The covered call seller has fewer risks than others because it is a safe strategy. Even if the stock falls in value, writing calls provides some downside protection.

Many investors are concerned with the lost opportunity risk associated with potential future profits in the stock. Once you sell a call, you commit yourself to selling 100 shares at the striking price, even if the stock's market value rises far above that price. Owning 100 shares covers the short position in the call; it also limits potential profit overall.

By properly structuring a covered call writing strategy, you can learn to manage the risk of losing potential future gains, in exchange of predictability and the certainty of current profits. The covered call writing strategy is going to produce profits consistently when applied correctly. So a very good return on your investment is possible through writing covered calls. You might lose the occasional spectacular profit when a stock's price rises suddenly; but for the most part, your rate of return will exceed what you could expect in your portfolio without writing covered calls. Some pitfalls to avoid in your covered call writing strategy:

✔ *Setting up the call write so that, if exercised, you end up losing money in the underlying stock.* This is possible if you sell calls with striking prices below your original basis in the stock. This is an especially serious problem if the discounted basis (considering the option premium) is not adequate to cover the loss. For example, you buy stock at $34 per share and later sell a 30 call, receiving a premium of 3. In this example, exercise produces an overall net loss of $100—$400 lost on the stock, minus $300 received for selling the call.

✔ *Getting locked into positions that you cannot afford to close out.* If you become involved in a high level of covered call writing, you will eventually find yourself in a position when you want to close out the call, but you do not have the cash available to take advantage of the situation. You need to set up an adequate cash reserve so that you can act when the opportunity is there. For example, you sold a call for 6 and since then the stock has been in the money; you think it will be exercised. However, the price dips and the call's premium value falls to 4. You would like to close the position at once, but you do not have $100 in your account; the opportunity is lost.

✔ *Writing calls on the wrong stock.* When you begin comparing premium values, you might spot an unusually rich time value in a particular option. You might be tempted to buy 100 shares of the stock and sell a call at the same time, since the option premium will discount your basis in the stock. However, the stock is likely to be volatile, which accounts for the exceptionally high premium in the call; this means that the risks associated with owning that stock are greater than for more stable issues. You might profit on the option, but trade that for losses in the stock. A moderate market correction could wipe out your profits.

CALCULATING RATE OF RETURN

If your purpose in owning stock is to hold it for many years, writing calls may not be an appropriate strategy—although, in some instances this strategy can be used to enhance returns with only a moderate risk of exercise. The call writer's objective often is quite different from that of the long-term investor and, while the two objectives can coexist, it is more likely that you will use the covered call writing strategy on a portion of your portfolio, while avoiding even moderate risks of exercise on another portion. You have three potential sources of income as a covered call writer:

1. Call premium.
2. Capital gain on stock.
3. Dividends.

Example: You bought 100 shares of stock and paid $32 per share. Several months later, the stock's market value had risen to $38 per share. You wrote a March 35 call and received 8. Your reasoning: Your original basis in the stock was $32, and selling the call discounts that basis to $24. If the call were exercised, you would be required to deliver the shares at $35, regardless of current market value of those shares. Your profit would be $1,100 if that occurred, a return of 34.4 percent. The option premium at the time you sold contained three points of intrinsic value and five points of time value. If the stock's market value remained at the same level without exercise, that five points eventually would evaporate and the call could be closed through purchase at a lower premium. If the stock's market value rises far above the striking price, you would still be required to deliver shares at the striking price upon exercise; the potential future gain would be lost. By undertaking this strategy, you exchange the certainty of a 34.4 percent gain for the uncertainty of greater profits later, if they occur.

This example shows how a potential profit may be lost, a fact that covered call writers need to accept. Simply owning stock and not writing calls against it could produce profits in the event of a large run-up in price; but it also produces losses in the event of price decline, and selling calls provides downside protection in addition to the certainty of profit. Covered call writing does limit the potential profit you can earn, so that your profits are limited but certain.

What are the chances of a stock's price soaring? It

does happen, but you cannot afford to depend on it. If you sell a call and limit your profits, have you really lost? Investors will have varying points of view about this question. Some will see potential future profits as being lost if and when they occur when the investors have also written a covered call; others will recognize that the risk is worth the certainty of current profits.

A reasonable position may be to look at profits only if they are taken. In other words, potential future profits do not exist at the time to sell an option, and by the same argument, profits in open option positions are not profits unless you close the position. Covered call writers can earn consistent returns on their strategy, but they also have to accept the occasional lost profit from a stock's unexpected price change. As a covered call writer, you seek consistent returns and, in exchange, you willingly sacrifice the occasional unexpected profit in the stock.

> **Smart Investor Tip**   Take profits when they can be taken. You cannot count paper profits because they could evaporate and never return.

By accepting this limitation associated with writing covered calls, you trade off the potential gain for the *discount* in the price of the stock. This downside protection is especially desirable when you remember that you also continue to receive dividends even though you have sold calls. You can earn better than average returns through covered call writing; it is possible for this strategy to produce greater overall profits than those to be realized from owning stock without writing calls.

A covered call writer needs to be aware of profit and loss zones that apply, as shown in Figure 5.2. A covered call's profit and loss zones are determined by the combination of two factors: option premium value and the underlying stock's current market value. If the stock falls below the breakeven price (price paid for the stock, minus the premium received for selling the call) there will be a loss. Of course, as a stock owner, you decide when and if to

discount
to reduce the true price of the stock by the amount of premium received. (A benefit in selling covered calls, the discount provides downside protection and protects long positions.)

buy stock $50 per share,
sell 1 call for 5:

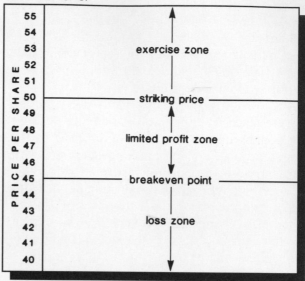

FIGURE 5.2 A covered call's profit and loss zones.

 **total
return**
the combined
return including
income from
selling a call,
capital gain from
selling the stock,
and dividends
earned and re-
ceived. (Total
return may be
calculated in two
ways: return if
the option is
exercised, and
return if the op-
tion expires
worthless.)

sell, so the loss is not realized. You have the luxury of being able to let the option expire worthless, and then wait
for a rebound in the stock's price. The option premium
discounts your basis, so by having sold the option, you
lower the required rebound level.

The writer should also calculate the rate of return
that will be realized given different outcomes. You need to
apply one critical rule for yourself: Never sell a covered
call unless you would be satisfied with the outcome in the
event of exercise. Figure the *total return* before selling the
call, and enter into the transaction only when you are
confident that the numbers work for you.

Total return in the case of exercise includes stock appreciation, call premium, and dividend income. If the option expires worthless, one rate of return results; if you
close the option by buying it before expiration, a different
return results. Because the second outcome does not include selling the stock, the rate of return can vary considerably. The return is calculated based on the original
purchase of the stock.

Example: You own 100 shares of stock that you bought at $41 per share. Current market value is $44 per share, and you have sold a July 45 call for 5. Between now and expiration, you will receive a total of $40 in dividend income.

Given the preceding information, return upon exercise would consist of all three elements:

Stock appreciation	$ 500
Call premium	500
Dividends	40
Total return	$1,040
Yield	26.0%

If the call is not exercised but expires worthless, total return does not include appreciation from the underlying stock, since it would not be called away. (Current value compared to purchase price is a paper profit only and is not included in the rate of return.) In this case, return will be:

Call premium	$500
Dividend income	40
Total return	$540
Yield	13.5%

Although the yield in the second instance is lower, you still own the stock. After expiration of the option, you can sell another call, sell the stock, or continue to hold it for long-term appreciation.

TIMING THE DECISION

A first-time call writer might be surprised to experience immediate exercise. That can occur at any time that your call is in the money. It is more likely to occur close to the expiration date, but you need to be prepared to give up 100 shares of stock at any time your option remains open. This is the contractual agreement you enter when you sell the call.

> **Smart Investor Tip** Whenever you sell a covered call, be prepared for exercise at any time when the call is in the money. The strategy makes sense only if you are willing to have your 100 shares called away.

As shown in Figure 5.3, during the life of a call, the underlying stock might swing several points above or below striking price. If you own 100 shares and are thinking of selling a covered call, keep these points in mind:

✔ When the striking price of the call is higher than the original price you paid for the stock, exercise is not a negative; it automatically triggers a triple profit—from appreciation of the stock, call premium, and dividend income.

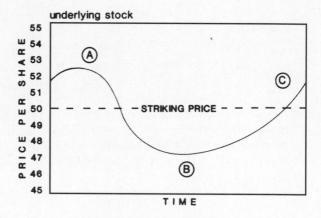

A in the money—best time
   to sell a call

B out of the money—best
   time to buy a call

C in the money at expiration
   —calls will be exercised

FIGURE 5.3 Timing of call transactions relative to price movement of underlying stock.

Example: You bought stock at $38 per share and later sold a call with a striking price of 40, receiving 3. You are not concerned about exercise because it would mean a profit of $500—$200 in stock appreciation plus $300 from option premium.

✔ If you sell a call for a striking price below your original cost of stock, be sure the premium you receive is greater than the loss you will experience in the stock in the event of exercise.

Example: You bought 100 shares of stock at $43 per share and sold a call with a striking price of 40. If exercised, your loss on the stock will be $300. Thus, if you receive an option premium of 3 or less, you lose money. This transaction makes sense only if the premium is high enough to offset losses on the stock.

> **Smart Investor Tip** Be sure that the potential loss in the stock upon exercise is less than the call premium you receive. It makes no sense to program in a loss when you sell calls against stock.

✔ In calculating potential yields, be sure to allow for trading costs on both stock and option, and both for entering and leaving the positions.

Example: You bought 100 shares of stock at $53 and later sold a call with a striking price of 50, receiving a premium of 3. In the event of exercise, losses in the stock will be offset by the option premium. However, you will actually experience a loss in this example, because you have to allow for the cost of buying and selling the stock, as well as for buying and selling the call.

✔ For the benefit of producing a consistent profit from writing calls, remember that you give up the potential for greater gains if and when the stock's current market value rises.

Example: You bought 100 shares of stock at $22 and later sold a call with a striking price of 25, receiving a premium of 4. In the event of exercise, profit will be $700—$300 in gain on the stock plus $400 for the option. However, the stock's market value recently rose to $34 and the call was exercised. You realize a 31.8 percent return—$700 on an investment of $2,200 (without counting dividends). But if you had not sold the call, your total profit would be $1,200, or 54.5 percent based on your original purchase of $2,200. This assumes, of course, that you sell the 100 shares when their value reaches $34 per share.

You cannot depend on sudden increases in a stock's market value. As a call writer, you acknowledge that this can occur, but you accept the certainty and consistency of gains from writing calls, and are willing give up the occasional bigger profit. The way you view such circumstances dictates whether or not you should write covered calls. If you would be overly concerned about the potential for big gains in the stock, then writing covered calls would not be appropriate for you. If, in the event of a big run-up in the stock's value, you find that the lost opportunity is unacceptable, then writing covered calls is also not an appropriate strategy for you.

Selection of the right covered call depends upon your original purchase price; the value of the stock today; and the available calls and their premiums. Option premium depends on the characteristics of the underlying stock and on the degree of price difference between current market value of the stock and striking price of the option. In addition, time value premium depends upon the time remaining until expiration. The more time, the higher the time value premium.

Example: You buy 100 shares of stock at $51 per share, and it then rises to $53. Rather than selling the stock, you choose to sell a call with a striking price of 50, and you are paid a premium of 7.

In this example, the premium is higher than average, with only three points of intrinsic value. The four points indicates the probability of a long time to go to expiration. Selling a call in this case provides several advantages to you:

- ✔ If the stock's current market value falls below your purchase price, you can buy the option and close the position at a profit, or wait for it to expire worthless.
- ✔ By selling the call, you discount your basis in the stock from $51 to $44 per share, providing yourself with seven points of downside protection. In the event of a price decline in the stock's market value, this is a substantial degree of protection.
- ✔ You continue to receive dividends as long as the option is not exercised.

You can also choose to sell a covered call that is deep in the money.

Example: You bought stock at $51 per share and it is now worth $53. You will receive a premium of at least 8 if you sell a call with a striking price of 45 (because there would be eight points of intrinsic value). That also increases the chances of exercise substantially. For the eight points in option premium, you would lose six points in the stock upon exercise. These outcomes would change if time value were also available. For example, a 45 call might have current premium of 11, with three points representing time value. Upon exercise, the additional three points would represent additional profit: $1,100 for selling the call, minus a loss of $600 on the stock, for a net profit of $500 upon exercise.

Smart Investor Tip Selling deep in-the-money calls can produce high profits for call sellers, especially if they want to sell their stock anyway.

Such an outcome is not an unreasonable method for producing profits. Such an outcome occurs only if the call is exercised; in the event the stock's market value falls, the call premium is reduced one dollar for each dollar lost in the stock's market value. You can buy the call to close the position, with the profit discounting your basis in the stock. Once the position has been closed at a profit, you can repeat the strategy, further reducing your basis in the stock.

Example: You bought shares of stock at $51 per share, and it is worth $53 at the time that you sell a 45 call. You received a premium of 11. The market value of the stock later falls three points, to $50 per share. The call is worth 7, representing a drop of three points of intrinsic value and one point of time value. You can close the position and buy the call for 7, realizing a $400 profit. You still own the stock and are free to sell covered calls again. For the moment, your $400 option profit reduces your basis in the stock from $51 per share down to $47 per share.

Always select options and time short sales with these considerations in mind:

- ✔ Your original price per share of the stock.
- ✔ The premium you will be paid for selling the call.
- ✔ The mix between intrinsic value and time value.
- ✔ The gap between current market value of the stock and striking price of the call.
- ✔ The time until expiration.
- ✔ Total return if the call is exercised, compared to total return if the option expires worthless.
- ✔ Your objective in owning the stock (long-term growth, for example), compared to your objective in selling the call (immediate income and downside protection, for example).

AVOIDING EXERCISE

Assuming that you sell a call on stock originally purchased as a long-term investment, you might want to take steps to avoid exercise. First, though, remember the overall guideline: Never sell a covered call unless you are willing to go through exercise and give up 100 shares of stock at the striking price. However, even with that in mind, you might be able to increase your profits from selling calls by avoiding exercise.

Call sellers—even after picking strategies well—may experience a rise in the stock and later wish to avoid exercise, if only to (1) achieve higher potential capital gains, (2) augment call premium income, and (3) simply put off selling a stock that is on the rise.

You can avoid exercise in several ways. The following examples are all based on a situation in which unexpected upward price movement occurs in the underlying stock, placing you in the position where exercise is likely.

Example: You sold a May 35 call on stock when the stock's market value was $34 per share. The stock's current market value is $41, and you would like to avoid exercise to take advantage of the higher market value of the stock.

The first method you can use to avoid exercise is to simply cancel the option by purchasing it. Although this creates a loss in the option, it is offset by a corresponding increase in the value of the stock. If time value has declined, this strategy makes sense—especially if the increased value of stock exceeds the loss in the option. A word of caution, however: The increased value in stock is a paper profit only, so to realize the profit in this case, you would need to sell the shares.

Example: You bought 100 shares of stock at $21 per share and later sold a June 25 call for 4. The stock's current market value is now at $30 per share and the call's premium is at 6. If you buy the call, you will lose $200; however, by avoiding exercise, you avoid having to sell the stock at $25 per share. You now own 100 shares at $30, and are free to sell an option with a higher striking price, if you want.

In this example, the outcome can be summarized in two ways. First, remember that by closing the call position at a loss, you still own the 100 shares of stock. That frees you to sell another call with a striking price of 30 or higher, which would create more option premium. (If you could sell a new option for 2 or more, that offsets your loss in the June 25 call.)

You can also analyze the transaction by comparing the exercise price of the option to the outcome of closing the option and selling shares at current market value. The flaw in this method is that it assumes a sale of stock, which is not necessarily going to occur; however, the comparison is valuable to determine whether avoiding exercise makes sense. A summary:

	Exercise	*Sale*
Basis in 100 shares of stock	–$2,100	–$2,100
Call premium received	400	400
Call premium paid		–600
100 shares delivered at $25	2,500	
100 shares sold at $30		3,000
Net profit	$ 800	$ 700

This comparison shows that it would be more desirable by $100 to allow exercise of the call. That is a fair conclusion only if you would be willing to give up the 100 shares after avoiding exercise. It also excludes the advantages of keeping the stock and being able to sell another call after closing the original call position. In most cases, the purpose in avoiding exercise is to be able to continue trading options on that stock, preferably at a higher market value for the underlying stock.

> **Smart Investor Tip**   A careful comparison between choices is the only way to tell whether to accept exercise or to close out the whole position.

A second technique to avoid exercise involves exchanging one option for another, while making a profit or avoiding a loss in the exchange. Since the premium value for a new option will be greater if more time value is involved until expiration, you can trade on that time value. Such a strategy is likely to defer exercise even when the call is in the money, when you remember that the majority of exercise actions take place close to expiration date. This technique is called a *roll forward*.

roll forward
the replacement of one written call with another with the same striking price, but a later expiration date.

Example: The May 40 call you wrote against 100 shares of stock is near expiration and is in the money. To avoid or delay exercise, you close the May 40 option by buying it; and you immediately sell an August 40 call—this has the same striking price but a later expiration.

You still face the risk of exercise at any time; however, it is less likely with a call three months further out. In addition, if you believe that expiration is inevitable, this strategy provides you with additional income. Because the August 40 call has more time until expiration, it also has more time value premium. The roll forward can be used whether you own a single call or several. The more lots of 100 shares you own of the underlying stock, the greater your flexibility in rolling forward and adding to your option premium profits. Canceling a single call and rolling forward produces a marginal gain; however, if you cancel one call and replace it with two or more later-expiring calls, your gain will be greater. This strategy is called *incremental return*. Profits increase as you increase the number of calls sold against stock.

Incremental return
a technique for avoiding exercise while increasing profits with written calls. (When the value of the underlying stock rises, a single call is closed at a loss and replaced with two or more call writes with later expiration dates, producing cash and a profit in the exchange.)

Example: You own 300 shares of stock that you bought for $31 per share. You sold one call with a striking price of 35, and received a premium of 4. Now the stock is worth $39 per share and you would like to avoid exercise. You buy the original call and pay 8, accepting a loss of $400 and replace it by selling three calls with a later expiration for 4 each, receiving a total premium of 12. The net transaction yields you an extra $400 in cash: $1,200 for the three calls, minus $800 paid to close the original position.

In this example, you trade one exposure on 100 shares of stock for exposure on all 300 shares; but you avoid exercise as well. At the same time, you net out additional cash profits, which reduces your overall basis in the stock. This could make exercise more acceptable later on. Of course, you can continue to use rolling techniques to avoid exercise. Another point worth mentioning is the potential tax advantage. Options are taxed in the year that positions are closed; so when you roll forward, you recognize a loss in the original call transaction, which can be deducted on your current year's federal income tax return. At the same time, by rolling forward you receive a net payment while deferring profits, perhaps to the following year.

The roll forward maintains the same striking price and buys you time, which makes sense when the stock's value has gone up. However, the plan does not always suit the circumstances. Another rolling method is called the *roll down*.

roll down
the replacement of one written call with another that has a lower striking price.

Example: You originally bought 100 shares of stock at $31 per share, and later sold a call with a striking price of 35, for a premium of 3. The stock has fallen in value and your call now is worth 1. You cancel (buy) the call and realize a profit of $200, and immediately sell a call with a striking price of 30, receiving a premium of 4.

In this case, the first call was sold four points above your original basis. The profit of $200 lowers that basis to $29 per share. The second call further reduces the basis by four more points, to $25. If the option is exercised (striking price is 30), the net profit will be $500.

The roll down is an effective way to offset losses in stock positions in a declining market, as long as the price decline is not severe. Profits in the call premium offset losses, reducing your basis in the stock. You face a different problem in a rising market. In that situation, you may use the *roll up*.

roll up
the replacement of one written call with another that has a higher striking price.

Example: You originally paid $31 per share for 100 shares of stock, and later sold a call with a striking price of 35. The stock's current market value has risen to $39 per share. You cancel (buy) the call and accept a loss, offsetting that loss by selling another call with a striking price of 40 and more time to go until expiration.

With this technique, the loss in the original call can be offset by replacement of the new call. This is true when there is more time to go until expiration. This technique depends on time value to make it profitable. Considering you will be picking up an extra five points in the striking price by avoiding exercise, you can afford a loss in the roll up as long as it does not exceed that five-point difference.

Smart Investor Tip Rolling techniques can help you to maximize option returns without going through exercise, most of the time. But the wise seller is always prepared to give up shares. That is the nature of seller options.

It is conceivable that the various rolling techniques can be used indefinitely to avoid exercise, while still producing profits. Figure 5.4 provides one example of how this could occur.

Example: You own 800 shares of stock that you bought at $30 per share; your basis is $24,000. You expect the value of the stock to rise, but you also want to write covered calls and increase profits while providing yourself with downside protection. So on March 15, you sell two June 30 contracts for 5 apiece, and receive payment of $1,000.

On June 11, the stock's market value is at $38 per share and you expect your calls to be exercised. To avoid exercise, you close the two calls by buying them, paying a premium of 8 (total paid, $1,600). You replace these calls with five September 35 calls and receive 6 for each, getting a total of $3,000.

On September 8, the stock's market value has risen again, and now is valued at $44 per share. You want to avoid exercise again, so you cancel your open positions and pay a premium of 9 each, or $4,500 total. You sell eight December 40 calls in replacement at 6, for a total of $4,800.

By December 22, the day of expiration, the stock has fallen to $39 per share. Your eight outstanding calls expire worthless. Your total profit on this series of transactions is

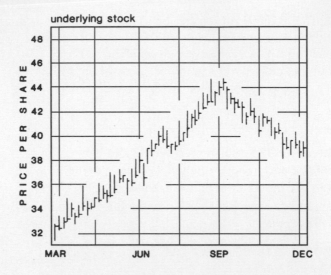

DATE	DESCRIPTION	RECEIVED	PAID
Mar 15	sell 2 Jun 30 calls at 5	$1,000	
Jun 11	buy 2 Jun 30 calls at 8		$1,600
	sell 5 Sep 35 calls at 6	$3,000	
Sep 8	buy 5 Sep 35 calls at 9		$4,500
	sell 8 Dec 40 calls at 6	$4,800	
Dec 22	Dec 40 calls expire worthless	–	–
	totals	$8,800	$6,100
	profit	$2,700	

FIGURE 5.4 Using the rolling technique to avoid exercise.

$2,700 for net call premium. In addition, you still own 800 shares of stock, now worth $39 per share, which is $7,200 above your original basis.

For the volume of transactions, you might wonder if the exposure to exercise was worth the $2,700 in profit, or 11.25 percent. It certainly was, considering that the strategy here was dictated by rising stock prices. While you received a profit, you avoided exercise while prices rose. Upon expiration of the calls, you are free to repeat the process. The incremental return combining roll up and roll forward demonstrates how you can avoid exercise while still generating a profit. You cannot depend on this pattern to continue or to repeat, but strategies are to be devised based on the situation. It helped, too, that the example involves multiple lots of stock, providing flexibility in writing calls.

This example is based on the premise that you would have been happy to accept exercise at any point along the way. Certainly, exercise would always have been profitable, as striking prices were all above original basis. If you were to sell the 800 shares at the ending market value of $39 per share, total profit would have been substantial using covered calls:

Stock

Sell 800 shares at $39	$31,200
Less: original cost	−24,000
Profit on stock	$ 7,200

Options

Sell 2 June contracts	$ 1,000
Buy 2 June contracts	−1,600
Sell 5 September contracts	3,000
Buy 5 September contracts	−4,500
Sell 8 December contracts	4,800
Profit on options	$ 2,700
Total profit	$ 9,900
Yield	41.25%

Whenever you roll forward, higher time value is a benefit. Greater premium value is found in calls with the same striking price but more time before expiration. The longer that time period, the higher your income and potential future income from selling the call. In exchange for the higher income, you agree to remain exposed to the risk of exercise for a longer period of time. You are locked into the striking price until you close the position, go through exercise, or wait out expiration.

> **Smart Investor Tip**   The key to profiting from rolling forward is in remembering that the longer the time until expiration, the more time value there will be in the call.

Your strategies to defer or avoid exercise combine two dissimilar goals: increasing your income while also holding onto the stock with value above striking price. This can be done with higher time value, in recognition of the probability that options will not be exercised until closer to expiration date. Most exercise occurs at or near expiration.

Example: You own 200 shares of stock originally purchased at $40 per share. You are open on a short June 40 call, which you sold for 3. The stock currently is worth $45 per share, and you want to avoid being exercised at $40. Table 5.2 shows current values of calls that are available on this stock. A review of this table provides you three alternatives for using rolling techniques.

  1. *Strategy 1: Rolling up and forward.* Sell one December 45 call at 5 while buying the June 40 call at 6. This produces a net profit of $200 ($500 for the December call less a $300 loss on the June call).
  2. *Strategy 2: Rolling with incremental return.* Sell two September 45 calls while closing the June 40 call at 6, producing $100 net income ($400 for the two September 45 calls, less the loss of $300 on the June 40 call).

TABLE 5.2 Current Call Option Values			
Striking Price	Expiration Month		
	June	Sept.	Dec.
35	11	13	15
40	6	8	10
45	1	2	5

3. *Strategy 3: Rolling forward only.* Sell one September 40 call at 8 while closing the June 40 call at 6, resulting in net income of $500 ($800 for the September 40 call, less the $300 loss on the June call).

Note in these strategies that we refer to the *loss* on the June call. Because that call currently is valued at 6, it requires a cash outlay of $600 to close the position. You received $300 when you sold, so your net loss is $300.

The loss of $300 is acceptable in all of these strategies because the striking price of 40 is either replaced with one of 45, which is five points higher; or additional income is produced to offset that loss by replacing the call with others that will expire later.

If the underlying stock is reasonably stable—for example, if its market value tends to stay within a five-point range during a typical three-month period—it is possible to employ rolling techniques and avoid exercise indefinitely—as long as no early exercise occurs. As stated before, however, you have to remember that when your short positions are in the money, exercise can occur at any time. Rolling techniques are especially useful when stocks break out of their short-term trading ranges and you want to take advantage of increased market value while also profiting from selling calls—all the while avoiding exercise.

To demonstrate how such a strategy can work, refer to Table 5.3. This shows a series of trades over a period of $2\frac{1}{2}$ years, and is a summary of a series of trades taken from actual confirmation receipts. The investor owned 400 shares of stock. Sale and purchase price show actual amounts of cash transacted including brokerage fees, rounded to the nearest dollar. The total net profit of $2,628 involved $722 in brokerage charges, so that profits before those charges were $3,350.

The information in Table 5.3 shows each type of rolling trade and summarizes how an effective use of incremental return helps avoid exercise as the underlying stock's market value increases. This investor was willing to increase the number of short calls as long as all were covered by shares of stock, to avoid exercise. When the stock's market value fell, the investor rolled down but did not write calls below the original striking price of 35.

		Sold		Bought			
TABLE 5.3 Selling Calls with Rolling Techniques							
Calls Traded	Type	Date	Amount	Date	Amount	Profit	Notes
1	Jul 35	3/20	$ 328	4/30	$ 221	$ 107	
1	Oct 35	6/27	235	10/8	78	157	
1	Apr 35	1/15	247	4/14	434	−187	
1	Oct 35	4/14	604	6/24	228	376	1
1	Oct 35	7/31	353	9/12	971	−618	
2	Jan 45	9/12	915	12/16	172	743	2
2	Apr 45	12/16	379	2/24	184	195	
4	Jul 40	3/9	1,357	5/26	385	972	3
4	Oct 40	6/5	1,553	7/22	1,036	517	
4	Jan 40	8/5	1,504	9/15	138	366	
		Totals	$7,475		$4,847	$2,628	

[1]A roll forward: The loss on the April 35 call was acceptable to avoid exercise, since the October 35 was profitable.

[2]A combination roll forward and roll up: The loss on the October 35 call was acceptable to avoid exercise at a low striking price. The number of calls was incrementally increased from one to two.

[3]A roll down combined with an incremental return: The number of calls changed from two to four, and the striking price of 45 was replaced with one for 40.

Any form of covered call writing should be planned well ahead. Besides checking on the attributes of the call (proximity of striking price to current market value, amount of time and intrinsic value, time until expiration, and premium), it is equally important to also analyze the underlying stock. There is no point in creating short-term profits through option writing if you do so on low-quality stock that does not have the potential for growth. If you purchase shares primarily to write options—a common practice—chances are that you will pick issues more volatile than average, since these tend to be associated with higher-premium options. The strategy makes sense in one regard: You will have ample opportunity to take advantage of momentary price swings and their corrections by timing options trades. This works as long as you call the price movement correctly, which is easy in theory but much more difficult in practice. Volatile issues are attractive to options sellers because of their tendency to have higher time value; however, that also is a symptom of the stock's greater market volatility, thus lower safety as an investment.

> **Smart Investor Tip** Stocks whose options offer greater time value do so for a reason. As a general rule, those stocks are higher-risk investments.

Whether you intend to write uncovered or covered calls, you will be less likely to succeed if you buy overpriced stocks that later fall below your basis. No call seller wants to be exercised at a level below their basis in the stock. Check Figure 5.5. This shows the profit and loss zones for an uncovered call write. In this case, a single May 40 call was sold for 2. This strategy exposes the investor to unlimited risk. If the stock rises above the striking price and then exceeds the two points equal to the amount received in premium, losses rise point for point with the stock. Upon exercise, this investor will have to deliver 100 shares of stock at $40 per share, regardless of the current market value at that time.

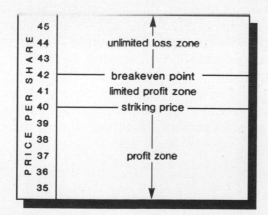

FIGURE 5.5 Example of uncovered call write with profit and loss zones.

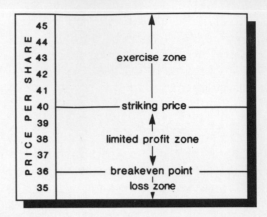

FIGURE 5.6 Example of covered call write with profit and loss zones.

The example of a covered call write shown in Figure 5.6 demonstrates that the loss zone exists only on the downside, so the strategy has a much different profile from the uncovered alternative. In this example, the investor owned 100 shares of stock that originally were purchased at $38 per share. The investor then sold a May 40 call for 2. This discounts the basis in stock by $2 per share, down to $36. As long as the stock's market value is at or below the striking price of 40, exercise will not occur. If the stock's market value rises above $40 per share, the call will be exercised and the 100 shares called away at $40 per share. In the event of exercise, profit would be $400—$200 in profit on the stock plus $200 for call premium. However, selling covered calls also locks in the striking price. In the event of a substantial price increase, profits are limited in accordance with the terms of the option contract.

As a call writer, remember that stock selection is of critical importance. The next chapter examines methods for picking stocks with a call-writing strategy in mind.

Chapter

Choosing the Right Stock

*Very few people are ambitious in the sense of having a specific image of
what they want to achieve. Most people's sights are only toward the next
run, the next increment of money.*
> —Judith Bardwick, *The Plateauing Trap*, 1988

areful, well-researched selection is the key to solid,
consistent investing success. This is true for all
forms of investing and applies to all strategies. Investors whose stock portfolios are not performing as expected might be tempted to augment lackluster profits by
becoming involved in options. Short-term income could
close a gap by offsetting small losses, improve overall
yields, and even bail out a paper loss position. However,
short-term income is not ensured, and such investors
have to face the fact that poorly selected stocks cannot be
converted through options. Your best chances for success
in the options market comes from first selecting stocks
wisely; and from establishing rules for selection and strategy that suit your individual risk tolerance. A suitable options strategy has to be a sensible match for an individual
stock, based on its volatility, your purpose in owning it,
and its original basis versus current market value.

A CHANGED INVESTING ENVIRONMENT

The challenge of selecting stocks has always been at the
crux of investment decisions. The well publicized corpo-

153

rate scandals of recent years have pointed out that the market risks are, indeed, serious. However, those problems have always existed; they simply were not as visible as they became in 2002, when the news was full of one scandal after another. The problems of accounting manipulation, aggressive booking of revenues, and outright fraud did not occur all at once; they went back many years. The companies whose demise became very public had been doctoring their books throughout most of the 1990s. Investors were shaken up, of course, by the revelations; but even more disturbing was the involvement of one of the country's most prestigious public accounting firms, Arthur Andersen.

For most investors, the security of the independent audit has always served as the foundation of fundamental analysis. You certainly want to believe, as a starting point, that the numbers are reliable. Otherwise, any analysis you perform would be flawed. You are shocked at the discovery that many of the best-known cases involved complicity or, at the very least, knowledge of the problems on the part of the independent auditing firm. In 2002, many regulatory and legal changes fixed some of the problems; but every investor should realize the inherent risks involved with owning stock, and with having capital invested. In order to be exposed to the opportunity for profit, you are also going to be exposed to various forms of risk. As events in recent years have demonstrated, the problems in corporate America and on Wall Street involve many participants: corporate management, boards of directors, auditing firms, analysts and investment bankers, and even an overly passive regulatory agency, the Securities and Exchange Commission (SEC).

Changes included passage of a new law, the Sarbanes-Oxley Act of 2002, which placed restrictions on auditing firms as well as corporate officers. While that law went a long way to cleaning up some of the problems, it did not remove all of the risks of investing. Another significant change occurred at the exchange level. Companies listed with the NYSE are now required to change the composition of boards of directors to force independence in selecting an outside auditor and in setting executive compensation. These are positive changes; however, the problem of conflict of interest between analysts and investment bankers will be far tougher to solve; the Wall Street firms involved in both of these activities are likely to resist any real reforms, even in the face of multimillion dollar fines and lawsuits.

Investors have always had to deal with the uncertainties of market risk. However, the elevated status of analysts, often without any justification, has tended to distort the true picture of how companies should be valued. Too much emphasis has been placed on earnings predictions and stock price trading targets—the favorite pastime of the Wall Street insider—and not enough emphasis on identifying value in corporations. Earnings predictions and price targets are not only short-term indicators; they also are not relevant to the more important question, Does this company represent a valuable long-term investment? In fact, the current stock price and potential trading range within the next few months is not really important to those with a long-term vision. Of course, options investors are keenly interested in short-term price trends. However, does an analyst's prediction about target price really provide any useful information?

One of the revelations concerning analysts is that they often have ignored the financial picture when identifying target prices. Some have even shunned the fundamentals as being useless in their work. However, until analysts have been trained to understand accounting, their predictions will be of no value to stock investors, and of questionable value to options speculators. The two major theories about market price movement—the Dow Theory and the Random Walk Hypothesis—agree on one fact: Short-term price indicators are unreliable. Clearly, true trends have to be developed and followed on a scientific basis, studied as part of a moving average over the long term. The momentary changes in trading range are insignificant in comparison to the identification of a value investment.

That is a company whose stock not only represents a fair value today, but who also shows the greatest promise for future price appreciation. The study of value investments has to be undertaken as part of a long-term strategy, because short-term trends involving price and even current quarter earnings have no value other than how they affect an investment in the immediate, short-term future.

The same arguments have to be taken seriously by options investors and speculators. As long as analysts' predictions are unreliable, their short-term conclusions will be misleading. If their analysis is not based on some logical and scientific study of the company, it is not a reliable source for making decisions. As an alternative, options investors should look for opportunities in underpriced or overpriced option contracts. That involves a study of current time value premium and indicates where you can make short-term profits in options, whether acting as buyer or seller. A model for time value premium is highly predictable. The tendency is for longer-term contracts to hold greater time value, and for that time value to fall out rapidly during the final weeks of the option's life. However, aberrations do occur. Unusually high time value are likely to be found in more volatile stock issues, for example. While that situation would be attractive to covered call writers, it comes with a danger as well. If you pick stocks on the basis of rich time value premium, you are likely to end up with a portfolio of high-risk stocks. Thus, if and when the market suffers a downturn—even a temporary one—those stocks are likely to react more strongly than average, and to lose market value quickly.

> **Smart Investor Tip** Option opportunities can be found in exceptional departures from the norm of time value. However, the selection of stocks and options should involve more detailed fundamental analysis in order to avoid or minimize volatility risk.

This comes down to a question of setting an investment *policy* for yourself. That includes a clear definition of acceptable risk levels, a complete understanding of the differences between short-term price or earnings targets and longer-term value, and a clear idea of how options will be used in your portfolio. They may be a separate, speculative tool, a means for enhancing income, or hedging of equity positions. This is where options can be most valuable. To the extent that you have capital at risk in the market, you are exposed to specific risks. For example, simply owning shares of stock comes with the risk that market value will fall. Anyone who invested in the fad of dot.com companies during their spectacular run-up knows that there is another side to that: Stocks that climb rapidly tend to fall with equal or greater speed. Options can be used to protect a long position; for example, if you want to continue owning shares of stock because values are rising, but you also fear as sudden decline, you can take steps to hedge your position using options.

One of the more serious dangers of stock market investment is the tendency for investors to follow fads. Thus, it is likely that new, inexperienced investors will go into the market at its top. Again, the dot.com fad demonstrated how this occurs. It is invariably a mistake to begin buying shares of stock *after* prices have risen significantly. This brings up a number of problems, however, all dealing with timing. How do you know when a price run-up is about to begin in a particular stock or sector, and once invested, how do you know when to get out?

Both of these questions involve timing and risk. When you put capital at risk, and when you decide whether to sell, you are making risk-oriented decisions. The difficulty in these core questions can be mitigated, and risks reduced, with the use of options. In that respect, options would not be purely speculative; they would be useful in reducing risk or loss as well as risk of lost opportunity.

For example, instead of buying shares today, you might consider buying calls. Even though they will expire, they require far less capital and risk exposure. On the other end—when you own stocks whose market value has risen significantly—you can buy puts to insure against unexpected losses, or sell covered calls to (1) discount your basis and (2) increase income without necessarily selling your shares. (In the event of exercise, your shares would be called away; however, as long as the striking price is higher than your adjusted basis, this outcome would be profitable for you.)

The investment policy should be the leading motivator in your investment decisions. It would be a mistake to buy shares of stock only for their current option opportunities.

The policy you set today will dictate the types of stocks that end up in your portfolio, even when the dust clears from any options trading you undertake involving those stocks. So even the most profitable covered call strategy is worthless if, as a result of picking very high time value issues, you end up with depreciated market value in your portfolio. Only after setting an investment policy for yourself should you consider also using options. Even with the best-defined policy, however, you need to also understand how options fit with the larger picture. One of the more troubling problems in selling covered calls, for example, comes up when you really do not want to sell shares of stock that you own. If you sell calls and the stock rises, you will be required to give up shares upon exercise. When your purpose in buying those shares was for appreciation, it makes no sense to have to sell when, in fact, the stock begins to appreciate. The relatively small profit from selling a call might not justify losing those shares. That is short-term thinking, and if you think of yourself as a long-term investor, a covered call strategy has to be designed and developed carefully with your long-term equity policies in mind.

A portfolio of well-chosen stocks should be considered as a long-term investment. It is true that such a portfolio can be used to produce short-term profits through options. As a general rule, stocks will hold their value over the long term whether or not you write options.

Smart Investor Tip   Value in your portfolio of stocks exists whether or not you sell options. You cannot expect to bail out poorly selected stocks by offsetting stock losses with option profits.

Every investor should ensure that their personal risk standards are given the highest priority in stock selection, and that those standards are used as a guiding force, and not just as a checklist for selection of stock. While some option strategies can be highly profitable when a stock's price changes drastically, you also need to think about your investment in shares. For example, a significant price drop represents a loss, even when you do well in selling options. It does no good to trade short-term profits for a portfolio of poor-quality stocks—especially if your basis in those stocks was higher than current market value.

One of the great advantages in selling covered calls is that a minimum profit level is ensured as long as you also remember that the first step always should be proper selection of the stock.

Example: You bought 100 shares of stock at $38 per share. At the time, you analyzed the stock and believed it would be a safe investment with prospects for long-term price appreciation. You now are thinking of selling a covered call. One call expires in three months and has a striking price of 40 and a premium of 4. During the time between now and expiration, you also will earn $60 in dividends. Your calculations ensure an annualized profit of 48.4 percent (if the call expires worthless) or 69.6 percent (if the call is exercised at the point of expiration). These returns are reported on an annualized basis in order to ensure that they are comparable.

If the Call Expires

Call premium	$ 400
Dividend	60
Total profit	$ 460
Basis in stock	$3,800
Yield if the call expires	$460 ÷ $3,800 = 12.1%
Annualized return earned in three months	(12.1% ÷ 3) × 12 = 48.4%

If the Call Is Exercised

Call premium	$ 400
Dividend	60
Capital gain ($4,000 − $3,800)	200
Total profit	$ 660

Basis in stock	$3,800
Yield if the option is exercised	$660 ÷ $3,800 = 17.4%
Annualized return earned in three months	(17.4% ÷ 3) × 12 = 69.6%

DEVELOPING A PRACTICAL APPROACH

Earning a consistently high yield from writing calls is not always possible, even for covered call writers. In addition to picking the right options at the right time, a covered strategy has to be structured around well selected stocks. In addition, even with the right stocks in your portfolio, you might need to wait out the market. Timing refers not only to the richness of option premiums, but also to the tendencies in the stock and in the market as a whole. You could be able to sell a call today rich in time value, and profit from the combination of capital gains, dividends, and call premium. But the opportunity is not always going to be available, depending on a combination of factors:

✔ The price of the underlying stock has to be at the right level in two respects. First, the relationship between current market value and your basis in the stock has to justify the exposure to exercise, to ensure that in the event of exercise, you will have a profit and not a loss. If this is not possible, then there is no justification in writing the call. Second, the current market value of the underlying stock also has to be correct in relation to the striking price of the call. Otherwise, the time value will not be high enough to justify the transaction.

Example: You bought 100 shares of stock at $43 per share and you want to write a call with a striking price of 45. If the call is exercised, you would earn a $200 profit on the stock in addition to the call premium, plus any dividends earned. In the same circumstances, it would not make sense to sell a 40 call, because that ensures a $300 loss on stock in the event of exercise.

> **Smart Investor Tip** A fairly simple analysis reveals when an option strategy is likely to produce a profit or a loss. Do the math before you execute the transaction.

✔ The volume of investor interest in the stock and related options has to be high enough to provide adequate time value to build in a profit.

Example: The stock you recently bought has had exceptionally high trading volume lately, because it is rumored that the company is negotiating a merger with a competitor. Call premiums on related options are unusually high in time value, which is the best possible situation for writing calls. Note, however, that if the rumors are true, the stock could rise suddenly so that more calls would be exercised. You could lose potential profits resulting from higher market value by writing calls now.

> **Smart Investor Tip** When time value premium is higher than average, there is always a good reason. The opportunity for covered call profits is going to be accompanied by a higher than average possibility for lost opportunity.

✔ The time between the point of sale of a call, and expiration, should fit with your personal goals. As with all other investment decisions, no strategy is appropriate unless it represents an intelligent fit.

Example: You would like to sell your stock within four months and use the proceeds to pay off a loan that is coming due. You are confident that the stock's market value will hold up and you do not want to sell now because you would like to defer capital gains until next year. In the meantime, you would like to augment your short-term income by writing a call. Because you will need proceeds within four months, that goal limits the range of calls available to you to those expiring within the next four months. You should also note that your available options strategies are restricted. You cannot avoid exercise through rolling techniques because the stock has to be sold within four months.

These circumstances demonstrate that call writing is not always timely nor practical. The ideal situation for call writing involves long-term holdings that have appreciated in value well above original basis; that you would not mind selling at a profit; and that you can afford to hold indefinitely, even if primarily to use as cover for written calls. All of these observations assume as well that the stock continues to represent a worthwhile investment on its own merits. You might have to wait until price appreciation is sufficient to justify a program of call writing.

In considering various strategies you could employ as a call writer, one common mistake is to proceed as though today's conditions were permanent. Anyone who has observed the stock market will recognize the flaw in such thinking. For example, it might be possible to earn an annualized rate of 48 percent on a single transaction, but it will not necessarily be possible to repeat that result consistently. Markets change constantly, resulting in ever-changing stock price levels and option premium. The ideal call write will be undertaken when the following conditions are present:

✔ *The striking price of the option is higher than your original basis in the stock.* Thus, exercise would produce a profit both in the stock *and* in the option. If the striking price of the option is lower than your basis in the stock, the option premium should be higher than the difference, while also covering transaction fees in both stock and option. Lacking that, a covered call would result in a loss. If the stock has appreciated considerably, you are presented with a broader range of choices. For example, you could write deep in-the-money calls and receive a considerable premium. If the call were to be exercised, you would still profit from both stock and option. However, if stock prices were to decline, you would be able to close the call at a profit.

✔ *The call is in the money, but not deep in the money.* This means it will contain a degree of intrinsic value, so stock movements will be paralleled with dollar-for-dollar price changes in option premium, maximizing the opportunity to close the call at a profit with relatively minor stock price movement. While being in the money increases the chance of exercise, it also means you will receive higher option premium upon sale of the call; there is also the likelihood that the premium will contain greater time value. In-the-money options tend to hold time value better than out-of-the-money options—not always, but often. A decline in the underlying stock's value will produce immediate profits for writers due to decline in intrinsic value. The greater the time until expiration of the call, the more likely that time value will be higher. In most strategies, you would want to avoid in-the-money calls exceeding five points, because those are more likely to be exercised; however, if your basis in stock is considerably lower than the striking price, you might accept exercise as the optimal way to sell—creating a combination of profits from stock and option.

✔ *There is enough time remaining until expiration that it represents most of the premium* Remember that even with minimal or no price movement in the stock, time value evaporates by expiration. The writer is compensated by being exposed to risk for a longer period, through higher time value. And to a degree, time value will exist whether the option is in the money or out. It is entirely possible to write an in-the-money option that remains in the money due to no change in the stock's market value, and to produce a profit strictly on the basis of declining time value. The ideal situation, of course, is when the stock's market value ends up at or below the striking price; but when the call was sold with exceptionally high time value.

✔ *Expiration will occur in six months or less.* You might not want to be locked in to a striking price for too long, and the identification of six months as a cutoff is arbitrary. The point is, the longer the time until expiration, the higher the time value; and that time value tends to fall most rapidly during the last two to three months. So clearly, your covered call strategy would be most effective when the opening sale took place in advance of the time value decline. But by the same argument, the longer that time, the longer your exposure to risk. Given changing market conditions, you need to decide how long a time is reasonable. The longer the period of time you need to forecast in the market, the less reliable your estimates will be.

✔ *Premium is high enough to justify the risk.* You will be locked in until expiration unless you later close with an offsetting purchase. In that sense, you risk price increases in the underlying stock and corresponding lost opportunity. A small premium does not justify an offsetting risk, whereas the risk could be acceptable if the premium level were higher. Every options trader needs to identify this relationship between risk and premium level in addition to the other factors used to determine validity of a short position.

Example: You own 100 shares of stock that you bought at $53 per share. Current market value is $57. You write a 55 call with five months to go until expiration that has a premium of 6. All of the ideal circumstances are present. Striking price is two points higher than your basis in the stock; the call is two points in the money, so that the option's premium value will be responsible to price changes in the stock; two-thirds of current option premium is time value; expiration takes place in less than six months; and the premium is $600, a rich level considering your basis in the stock. It is 11.3 percent of your original stock investment, an exceptional return ($600 ÷ $5,300).

In this example, you would earn a substantial return whether the option is exercised or expires worthless. If the stock's market value falls, the $600 call premium provides significant downside protection, discounting your basis to $47 per share. A worst case analysis, then, would conclude that if the stock's market value fell to $47 per share and the option then expired worthless, the net result would be breakeven.

SELECTING STOCKS FOR CALL WRITING

Some investors pick stocks based primarily on the potential yield to be gained from writing calls. This is a mistake. While a larger call premium discounts the stock's basis, it is not enough of a reason to buy shares. The best-yielding call premium most often is available on the highest-risk, most volatile stocks. So if you apply the sole criterion of premium yield to stock selection, you also assume the profile of much greater risks in your stock portfolio. Since there is a tendency among short-term investors to sell when profits are available, such a strategy often results in a portfolio of stocks with paper loss positions—all capital is committed in the purchase of overvalued stocks and investors then have to wait out a reversal in market value.

Example: You decide to buy stock based on the relationship between current call premium and the price of the stock. You have only $4,000 to invest, so you limit your review to stocks selling at $40 per share or less. Your objective is to locate stocks on which call premium is at least 10 percent of current market value of the stock, with calls at the money or out of the money. You prepare a chart summarizing available stocks and options:

Current Value	Call Premium
$36	$3
28	3.50
25	1
39	4
27	1.75

You eliminate the first, third, and last choices because call premium is under 10 percent, and decide to buy the second stock on the list. It is selling at $28 per share and call premium is 3.50, a yield of 12.5 percent. This is the highest yield available from the list. On the surface, this study and conclusion appears reasonable. The selection of the call premium discounts the stock's basis by 12.5 percent. However, there are a number of problems in this approach. Most significant is the fact that no distinction is made among the stocks other than call price and yield. The selected issue was not judged on its individual fundamental nor technical merits. Also, by limiting the selection to stocks selling at $40 per share or lower, the range of potential choices is too restricted. It may be that with only $4,000 available, you would do better to select a stock on its own merits and wait until you are able to build up your portfolio.

The method in the preceding case also failed to consider time until expiration. You receive higher premiums when expiration dates are further away, in exchange for which you lock in your position for more time—meaning more change in the underlying stock's market value will be possible. Another flaw is that these calls were not judged in regard to the distance between striking price and current market value of the stock. The yield, by itself, is a misleading method for selecting options.

Smart Investor Tip   Picking options based on yield alone is a popular, but flawed method. It fails to recognize far more important considerations, such as the quality of the underlying stock.

The value of locking in 100 shares to a fixed striking price needs to be judged in relation to the number of months remaining until expiration. Otherwise, how can you fairly judge the value of that option? For example, a 10 percent yield might be attractive for calls with three to six months remaining until expiration, but far less attractive when the call will not expire for eight months. Yield is not a constant; it depends on time.

Covered call writing is a conservative strategy, assuming that you first understand how to pick high-quality stocks. First and foremost should be a stock's investment value, meaning that option potential should not be the primary factor in the selection of stocks in your portfolio. On the contrary, if you are led by the attractiveness of option premium levels, you are likely to pick highly volatile stocks. If you first analyze the stock for investment value, timeliness, and safety, the option value may then be brought into the picture as yet another means for selecting among otherwise viable investment candidates.

Benefiting from Price Appreciation

You will profit from covered call writing when the underlying stock's current market value is higher than the price you paid for the stock. In that case, you protect your position against a price decline and also lock in a profit in the event of exercise.

Example: You bought 100 shares of stock last year when the value was $27 per share. Today the stock is worth $38.

In this case, you can afford to write calls in the money without risking an overall loss; or you can write out-of-the-money calls as long as time value is high enough. Remembering that your original cost was $27 per share, you have at least four choices in methods for writing covered calls:

1. Write a call with a striking price of 25. The premium will include 13 points of intrinsic value plus time value, which will be higher for longer-out calls. If the call is exercised you lose 2 points in the stock, but gain 13 points in the call, for an overall profit of $1,100. If the stock's market value falls before exercise, or when time value disappears, you can cancel with a purchase and profit on the option trade, which frees you up to write yet another call. Any decline in stock market value is offset dollar-for-dollar by call profit in this case.

Example: You sold a call deep in the money. A few weeks later, the stock had dropped six points and intrinsic value in the call also fell by the same amount. You can buy the call and take a profit of $600, which offsets the stock's market value decline. Any reduction in time value represents additional profit.

2. Write a call with a striking price of 30. In this case, intrinsic value is eight points, and you can apply the same strategies as in number 1. However, because your position is not as deep in the money, chances for early exercise are reduced somewhat; in the event of exercise, you would keep the entire option premium, plus gaining $300 in profit on the stock.

Example: You sold a call with a striking price of 30. Two months later, three points of time value had evaporated while the stock's market price did not change. You close the call by buying it, taking your $300 profit.

3. Write a call with a striking price of 35. With only three points in the money, chances for early exercise are considerably lower than in the first two cases. Any decline in the stock's market value will be matched point for point by a decline in the call's intrinsic value, protecting your stock investment position. Because this call's striking price is close to current market value, there may be more time value than seen in the other alternatives.

Example: You sold a call with a striking price of 35. One month later, the stock had declined one point, but the call lost three points overall, representing lost time value. You are able to buy the call to close it and take a profit of $300.

4. Write a call with a striking price of 40 or 45. Since both of these are out of the money, the entire premium represents time value. The premium level will be lower since there is no intrinsic value; but the strategy provides you with two distinct advantages. First, it will be easier for you to cancel this position at a profit because time value will decline even if the stock's market value rises. Second, if the option is eventually exercised, you will gain a profit in the option *and* in the stock.

Example: You bought a 40 call when the stock's market value was $38. Your original basis was $27 per share. The call was eventually exercised, and your overall profit includes all of the call premium plus $1,300 profit on the stock.

If you are holding stock with an appreciated market value over your basis, you face a dilemma that every stockholder has to resolve. If you sell and take a profit now, that is a sure thing but you lose out in the event that further profits could also be earned by keeping those shares. You also face the risk of a decline in market value, meaning some of today's appreciated value will be lost. Long-term investors may be less concerned with short-term price changes; however, it remains valid that anyone would like to ensure a degree of safety in their paper profits.

Covered call writing could represent the best way to maximize your profits while providing downside protection. As long as your call is in the money, every point lost in the stock is matched by lost points in the call; a paper loss in the stock can be replaced with profits in the call position. The time value premium is potentially all profit, since it will disappear even if the stock's market value goes up, an important point that too many options traders overlook (especially buyers). When your basis is far below striking price of the call, you lock in a capital gain in the event of exercise.

Smart Investor Tip Time value declines over time, even when the stock's market value goes up. This is a problem for buyers, but a great advantage for sellers.

Example: You bought 100 shares of stock several years ago at $28 per share. Today it is worth $45. You sell a 45 call with four months to go until expiration. The premium was 4, all of which is time value. This discounts your original basis down to $24. If the stock were to fall four points or less, the call premium protects the paper profit based on current stock price. If the market value rises and the call is exercised, your shares would be called away at $45 per share.

In this example, two levels of downside protection are evident. First, the original basis is protected to the extent of the call premium; second, paper profits in the current market value have the same degree of downside protection. When stock has appreciated beyond its original cost, it makes sense to protect current value levels, and call writing is a sensible alternative to selling shares you would not otherwise want to give up. Most investors would see a decline in market value as a loss off the stock's high, even when the corrected stock price remains above original cost. Call writing solves that dilemma.

Selection Risks

Picking the best possible option is not as simple as it appears at first glance. Remember that the real value of any option is a factor of the value in the underlying stock. This includes the fundamental value of the company—its sales and profits, dividend history, competitive strength, and other dollars and cents comparisons. It also includes the technical aspects of the stock, which encompass overall market perception of future value and directly affects option time value. Market perception also is reflected largely in the stock's current price; because perception can be a fleeting thing, the more change in perception, the greater the swing in price. For covered call writers, the best selection should always be based upon the proper selection of stock with many questions in mind, including the recognition of the relationship between rich time value and market risk. Once that is done, options should be chosen based on several factors:

✔ *The current price of the stock, versus your original basis.* This comparison certainly affects your decision about which options to write. If your stock's current market value is lower than your original cost, call writing is a problem. Premium level needs to be high enough so that, in the event of exercise, call profit offsets stock loss. If this is not possible, then there is no good reason for writing a covered call. When the price is far higher than your cost, you have a wide range of flexibility in your choice, and you can even write deep in-the-money calls hoping for expiration and high profits.

✔ *Your goals in writing calls.* If your stock has appreciated but you have no intention of selling it, writing calls might not be appropriate, even if you could use the short-term income. In this situation, you should restrict call writing to out-of-the-money calls, reducing the exposure to exercise. That means lower call premium, but less chance of having shares called away.

✔ *The comparison between intrinsic value and time value.* This is always a crucial test for option selection. The higher the time value, the greater your potential profit. However, higher time value is accompanied by more time until expiration, meaning less chance for early exercise *and* longer exposure to the locked-in position. High time value might also be a symptom that the underlying stock is a higher risk than you thought, a question worth investigating.

✔ *Time until expiration.* The longer the time, the more time value premium you will receive. Compare the number of months to the difference between available options. You might discover that for a relatively small difference in premium, you can cut three months off your exposure term. Shorter term also means that time value will decline more rapidly, a clear advantage to you as seller. You can succeed in covered call writing by dealing primarily in short-term contracts, profiting from rapidly disappearing time value.

✔ *Premium level versus lock-in risks.* You might find that for many stocks, premium levels simply are too low to justify locking in your stock to a fixed striking price. Even with all other signals in place, you need to be able to justify the short position in terms of premium dollars you will receive as compensation for exposing yourself to the risk. You might need to wait until more favorable conditions arise.

AVERAGING YOUR COST

You can increase your advantage as a call writer using a strategy known as the *average up*. When the price of stock has risen since your purchase date, this strategy allows you to sell calls in the money on stock you own, when the average basis in that stock is always lower than the average price you paid.

If you buy 100 shares and the market value increases, buying another 100 shares reduces your overall cost so that your basis is lower than current market value.

 average up
a strategy involving the purchase of stock when its market value is increasing. (The average cost of shares bought in this manner is consistently lower than current market value, enabling covered call writers to sell in the money when the basis is below the striking price.)

The effect of averaging up is summarized by examples in Table 6.1.

How does averaging up help you as a call writer? When you are writing calls on several hundred share lots of stock, you also need to be concerned about the consequences of falling stock prices. While that means you would profit from writing calls, it also means your stock loses value. The more shares you own of a single stock, the higher this risk. For example, if you are thinking about buying 600 shares of stock, you can take two approaches. First, you can buy 600 shares at today's price; second, you can buy 100 shares and wait to see how market values change, buying additional lots in the future. This means you will pay higher transaction costs, but it could also protect your stock's overall market value. By averaging your investment basis, you spread your risk. In effect, you use time as a form of diversification.

Example: You buy 600 shares of stock on January 10 at $26 per share. Market value later falls to $20, so you have a paper loss of $3,600. Later, the price rises to $32, so that you have a paper profit of $3,600.

Example: You buy 100 shares on the tenth of each month, beginning in January. The price of the stock changes over six months so that by June 10, your average basis is $29.50.

The second example, as illustrated in Table 6.1, enables you to reduce your risk. The average price is al-

TABLE 6.1 Averaging Up			
Date	Shares Purchased	Price per Share	Average Price
January 10	100	$26	$26
February 10	100	28	27
March 10	100	30	28
April 10	100	30	$28\frac{1}{2}$
May 10	100	31	29
June 10	100	32	$29\frac{1}{2}$

ways lower than current market value as long as the stock's price continues moving in an upward trend. A critic of this method will point out that buying 600 shares at the beginning would have produced greater profits. But how do you know in advance that the stock will rise?

Averaging up is a smart alternative to placing all of your capital at risk in one move. The benefits to this approach are shown in Figure 6.1.

By acquiring 600 shares over time, you can also write 6 calls. Because your average basis at the end of the period is $29.50 and current market value is $32 per share, you can sell 30 calls and win in two ways:

1. When the average price of stock is lower than the striking price of the call, you will gain a profit in the event of exercise.

2. When the call is in the money, movement in the stock's price is matched by movement in the call's intrinsic value.

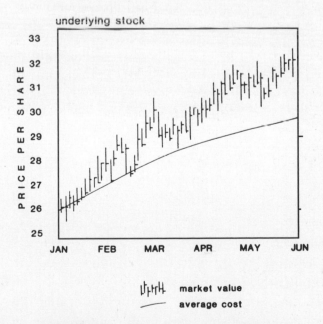

FIGURE 6.1 Example of averaging up.

average down

a strategy involving the purchase of stock when its market value is decreasing. (The average cost of shares bought in this manner is consistently higher than current market value, so that a portion of the paper loss on declining stock value is absorbed, enabling covered call writers to sell calls and profit even when the stock's market value has declined.)

What happens, though, if the stock's market value falls? You also reduce your risks in writing calls if you *average down* over time. An example of this strategy is summarized in Table 6.2.

One risk in buying stocks is that if market value falls, you cannot afford to sell calls later. Striking prices with any worthwhile premium value will be below your basis in the stock. If basis is higher than current market value, you will lose money in the event of exercise. As a general rule, you should never sell covered calls if exercise would produce an overall loss.

 Smart Investor Tip   When the stock's market value declines, selling covered calls is unlikely to produce profits. Never write calls when exercise would produce a net loss.

If you sell calls with higher striking prices when your stock has lost value, premium will be so minimal that the strategy is not worth it. The solution may be to buy stock through averaging down.

Example: You buy 600 shares of stock on July 10 when the price is $32 per share. The price rises eight points and you have a profit of $4,800. The stock later falls to $24 per share, resulting in a paper loss of $4,800.

TABLE 6.2 Averaging Down			
Date	Shares Purchased	Price per Share	Average Price
July 10	100	$32	$32
August 10	100	31	31½
September 10	100	30	31
October 10	100	30	30¾
November 10	100	27	30
December 10	100	24	29

Example: You buy 100 shares of stock each month, beginning on July 10, when market value is $32 per share. By December, after periodic price movement, the current market value has fallen to $24 per share. Average cost per share is $29.

Your average cost is always higher than current market value in this illustration using the average down technique, but not as high as it would have been if you had bought 600 shares in the beginning. The dramatic difference made through averaging down is summarized in Figure 6.2.

By owning 600 shares, you can write up to 6 covered calls. In the first example, you are at a disadvantage. Your basis is $32 per share, and current market value is eight points lower. You would need to write deep out-of-the-money calls, for which premium will be minimal It will be nearly impossible to justify this strategy, given the circumstances. For example, to lock in all 600 shares at a striking price of 30, would not be worthwhile. Upon exercise, you would lose two

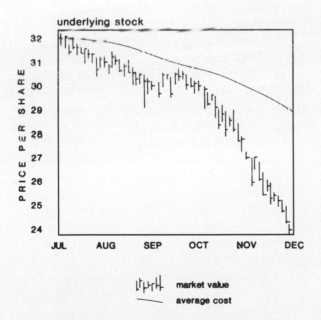

FIGURE 6.2 Example of averaging down.

points per share of stock; yet, it is unlikely that you would gain enough in call premium to justify taking the short position.

In the second example, average basis is $29 per share. By writing calls with striking price of 30, you would gain one point of capital gain on the total of 600 shares in the event of exercise. This is a significant difference in comparison to the first example. It demonstrates how averaging down can be beneficial to call writers in the unfortunate event that the stock's market value falls.

Both averaging techniques are important tools that help you to mitigate the effects of quickly changing stock prices. In a fast-moving market, price changes represent a problem to the call writer, since locked-in positions cannot be sold without exposing yourself to greater risks in the short call position. Both techniques are referred to as *dollar cost averaging*. Regardless of price movement, the strategy always results in protection of capital. (A variation of dollar cost averaging is the investment of a fixed dollar amount over time, regardless of per-share value. This is a popular method for buying mutual fund shares. However, in the stock market, direct purchase of stock makes more sense when buying in round lot increments.

Whether stock prices move up or down, averaging provides some degree of price change protection. By averaging out the cost, you reduce exposure to loss in paper value of the entire investment. For the purpose of combining stock and option strategies, owning several hundred shares is a significant advantage over owning only 100 shares. Transaction costs involving multiple options contracts are reduced; in addition, owning more shares enables you to use many more strategies involving options. For example, if you begin your strategy by selling one call, you can avoid exercise by rolling up and increasing the number of calls sold. This provides you with more premium income as well as avoiding exercise, even when the stock's market value is rising. By increasing the number of options sold with each subsequent roll up, you can increase profits over time. The technique is difficult if not impossible when you only own 100 shares of stock.

dollar cost averaging
a strategy for investing over time, either buying a fixed number of shares or investing a fixed dollar amount, in regular intervals. (The result is an averaging of overall price. If market value increases, average cost is always lower than current market value; if market value decreases, average cost is always higher than current market value.)

ANALYZING STOCKS

Stock selection is the starting point for covered call writing. Remember that options themselves are valued based upon market value of the stock in comparison to striking price and expiration date of the option. As such, options do not contain any fundamental or technical features of their own. Valuation is a direct result of fundamental and technical conditions in the underlying stock.

Smart Investor Tip   Don't look for fundamental or technical indicators in options when you should be studying the attributes of the underlying stock.

Many novice investors buy stocks on recommendations from others, without understanding the source of the recommendation. They make a second mistake in failing to question whether the particular stock is a good match for them, given their own individual risk tolerance level, long-term investing goals, and available capital. It is easier to make mistakes when buying on the word of someone else and without doing their own research; but that is a lazy approach and, unfortunately for the inexperienced investor, it may lead to losses that they cannot afford. Options traders are especially vulnerable to the temptation to buy stocks for the wrong reason—namely to take advantage of high-priced option opportunities. The failure to investigate the reasons for exceptionally high premiums leads, again, to selection of stocks that might be too risky for their own situation, given their goals, risk tolerance, and available capital.

The disturbing revelations of corporate misdeeds on the part of Enron and many other companies point out the importance of performing tests to select stocks. The lessons of the corporate scandals include:

✔ *If the information provided by the company is too complicated to understand, you should not invest.* In the past, some of the explanations provided by management or disclosed in footnotes were so obscure that they could not be understood, even by expert analysts. This is a danger sign. The explanations provided in annual reports and quarterly filings with the SEC should be easily understood. If something is especially complex, it is management's job to explain it so that shareholders do not have problems understanding what is going on.

✔ *If a stock continues to rise beyond reasonable expectations, this could be a sign of trouble.* It is rarely a good idea to buy shares in a company just because the stock's price has risen to impressive levels. Are those levels justified by earnings? In the past, we have seen many examples of stock prices continuing to climb even when there was no fundamental justification. In fact, some companies have seen this occur even though they have never reported a profit! The numbers should dictate the realistic level of stock price; market perception is worth only so much and, of course, is going to be reflected in the price of the stock. The P/E ratio is an expression of the market's anticipation of future earnings potential. But when a stock's P/E rises over 100, investors should question what is driving that run-up. The higher the P/E and the faster the run-up, the greater the danger of an equally fast fall in price.

✔ *You need to apply tests that look beyond recommendations, rosy estimates of future earnings, and other suspicious indicators.* Too many investors have placed faith in so-called "experts" on the market. The analyst often has worked in an atmosphere of glaring conflict of interest. For example, when an analyst recommends that you buy a stock but that analyst's firm is also the investment banker for the same company, you are not necessarily getting sound advice. Recommendations coming from analysts, stockbrokers, friends and relatives, and anyone else, should be reviewed with great suspicion. You are better off investigating companies on your own, remembering that free advice may be more expensive than the kind you pay for.

✔ *Methods for valuing companies have to go beyond the traditional—and overly optimistic—tests so common in the market.* The common methods for determining whether or not a company represents a sound investment need to be reviewed. In fact, it is wise to question the traditional assumptions and methods for picking companies to begin with. All too often, stocks are highly rated merely because sales and profits continue to rise year after year. That alone does not define "good" because a steady increase in sales and profits can also result from manipulation of the numbers. You need to relate changes in sales and profits, to changes in balance sheet accounts. Study ratios and trends in accounts receivable, bad debt reserves, inventory levels, current and long-term liabilities, and capital assets. If you spot a departure from the trend in these areas, it could mean that the company is applying creative accounting to artificially create the outcome of the numbers. This was the primary method employed by many of those companies investigated after the discovery of irregularities among some of the larger publicly traded corporations. While a lot of reform in law and regulation may curtail such practices in the future, you need to continue to look for signs of trouble on your own. Never depend on law and regulation to protect you completely. Too much of the regulatory environment is responsive, moving in to investigate after problems have occurred and investors have lost money.

✔ *Intelligent analysis has to depend on valuing companies rather than identifying target price and earnings levels.* The corporate scandals proved that some of the basic methods of operation on Wall Street are flawed. As a rule, investors have become addicted to short-term forecasting, at the expense of longer-term analysis. Even those investors who think of themselves as investing for the long term often react to today's news about earnings, for example. An analyst predicts the earnings per share, often merely repeating what corporate management reports; and then the company is judged based on how close its reported earnings are to the forecast. Analysts also pick target trading ranges or prices for stocks, again based on anything but fundamental information. Recent history demonstrates that these short-term methods of investing are dangerous and flawed. Instead of predicting price-related value in the next three months, analysts should be studying and reporting on the value of companies over the next 5 to 10 years.

core earnings
as defined by Standard & Poors, the after-tax earnings generated from a corporation's principal business.

Standard & Poors has changed its method for valuing companies, and their revised definition of "*core earnings*" is helpful in getting around many of the creative methods used in the past to inflate earnings and mislead investors. The S&P definition of core earnings are "the after-tax earnings generated from a corporation's principal business."

Under this definition, many items are excluded, including gain or loss from the sale of capital assets, gains on pension investments, and fees related to mergers and acquisitions. In the past, the inclusion of these items caused a lot of distortion in reported profits and corporate value, so that investors had unrealistic and inaccurate ideas of a company's investment value.

The definition includes many expenses and costs that have been excluded or capitalized in the past, such as restructuring charges, write-down of amortizable operating assets, pension costs, and purchased R&D costs. Again, in the past companies excluded or capitalized these items, leading to a deceptive picture of a company's real value.

Smart Investor Tip Refer to the S&P website for more information about the newly defined core earnings and its application, at http://www.standardandpoors.com/PressRoom/Equity/Articles/051302_CoreEarningsPR.html.

EBITDA
a popular measurement of cash flow, which stands for earnings before interest, taxes, depreciation, and amortization.

The move by S&P to arrive at a standardized definition is a positive trend. It enables like-kind comparisons between many different corporations, without the very real concern for inconsistent treatment and interpretation of the numbers. The S&P definition makes more sense than the more widely used *EBITDA*, which is "earnings before interest, taxes, depreciation, and amortization." To some, EBITDA is a measurement of cash flow or cash-based earnings for a company; however, this measurement is also flawed.

Under EBITDA, no provision is included to account for purchasing of capital assets or paying down debts. Rather than a clarifying calculation, EBITDA has been used more as a way to make things look better. For example, when accounts receivable are rising, EBITDA does not include a distinction between cash sales and credit sales—an area where abuse has occurred in the past and where it is all too easy to alter the true numbers.

As a starting point in the analysis of corporate reports, the core earnings help you to study many different companies on the same basis. Going beyond that, you also need to identify what analysts call *quality of earnings*. While this term has many definitions, it is supposed to mean the earnings that are reliable and true, as opposed to those that are overly optimistic. For example, if a company reports income based on accounts receivable that might never be collected, that is not a good quality of earnings. The higher definition would include revenues that are likely to be collected and not created out of accruals, acquisitions, or accounting tricks.

In addition to the importance of selectively identifying companies based on quality of earnings, it remains important to apply specific fundamental tests. Fundamental analysis—the study of financial information, management, competitive position within a sector, dividend history, volatility, volume, and more—is a common and popular method for analyzing stocks. The fundamentals provide you with comparative analysis of value, safety, stability, and the potential for growth and increase in the stock's long-term value. Collectively, the fundamentals are referred to as the "strength" of a corporation. Financial and economic information, corporate management, sector and competitive position, and other indicators involving profit and loss, all are part of fundamental analysis. The fundamentalist studies a corporation's balance sheet and income statement to judge a stock's long-term prospects as an investment. Other economic indicators may influence a person's decision to invest or not, such as pending lawsuits, product-related problems, labor troubles, and competition—in other words, anything that could affect profitability.

The essential problem all investors face with the fundamentals is reliability of information. Perhaps the most

quality of earnings
the real value of earnings as reported, which should include nonrecurring earnings, revenues from acquisitions, earnings resulting in changes in accounting methods, pro forma estimated earnings that depend on future performance, and other nonpermanent items; and including recurring earnings from primary lines of business, adjusted for bad debts.

disturbing aspect of the corporate scandals that came to light in 2002 was that we cannot necessarily rely on what is being reported. Corporate executives and boards of directors, accounting firms, Wall Street analysts, and regulators, all failed to do their jobs. Investors suffered because of the widespread abuse and conflict of interest on many levels. This is why a study of the fundamentals has to involve study on two levels. The traditional level is a study of trends, to identify changes in financial strength and competitive position. Second is an equally important study of balance sheet ratios, with the purpose of ensuring that a company is not artificially inflating earnings in order to deceive investors.

The fundamental analyst believes in the numbers. However, part of a scientific analysis has to include verification of the core data as a starting point. The fundamental analyst has to not only be able to interpret the information, but also to use some basic forensic accounting skills to make sure the numbers are real. Those skills include a study of the basic ratios in a search for suspicious or questionable changes. If those changes are discovered and not adequately explained, the discovery should serve as a warning that something could be wrong.

The technician will be less interested in the forensic aspects of current or past information. Technical analysis involves a forward-looking study relating almost exclusively to price of the stock, market forces affecting that price, and anticipation of changes based on supply and demand, market perception, and trading ranges. The technician uses financial data only to the extent that they affect a current trend, believing that trends provide the key to anticipating the future price movement of stock. The primary concern for technicians is price movement and patterns of price change. Many market analysts believe that price change is random, especially short-term price movement; but some technicians, notably the *chartist*, prefer to believe that patterns of price movement can be used to predict the direction of change in the stock's price.

The relative value of either fundamental or technical analysis is debated continuously. The fundamental approach is based on the assumption that short-term price movement is entirely random and that long-term value is best identified through a thorough study of a corpora-

chartist
an analyst who studies charts of a stock's price movement in the belief that recent patterns can be used to predict upcoming price changes and directions.

tion's financial status and strength. The technical approach relies on patterns in price of the stock and other price-related indicators that are associated more with the market's perception of value and less with financial information. Obviously, a current report on the corporation's net income will affect price, at least temporarily, and technicians acknowledge this. However, their primary interest is in studying pricing trends.

Many successful investors recognize that both schools have value, so they apply parts of both fundamental and technical analysis in their own monitoring program. The purpose of monitoring the market is in order to make the four important decisions that every investor needs to be able to make: buy, hold, sell, or stay away. The wise investor knows that analysis in all of its forms is a tool for decision making, and that no analysis provides insights that dictate decisions on their own. Common sense and discriminating personal judgment based on experience are the extra edge that successful investors bring to their investments. Even so, there remains a large contingent of people in the market who cling to the belief that some particular analytical tool does, indeed, point the way to beating the market every time. The reality is that everyone is wrong at times. Smart investors know that successful investing results when they are able to use analysis so that their estimates are right more often than they are wrong.

Smart Investor Tip There are no formulas that will make you right all of the time. Investing success comes from applying good judgment, from increasing your chances of being right about market decisions.

Call writers should never overlook the need to continuously track their stocks. They tend at times to ignore changing attributes of the stock over time because their interest is in watching the options. So call writers may be inclined to ignore signals relating to the stock when, if they were not involved with writing options, they might be more inclined to watch their portfolios. Call writers are preoccupied with other matters: movement in the stock's price (but only insofar as it affects their option positions); chances of exercise and how to avoid or defer it; opportunities to roll forward; and other matters relating to immediate strategies. As important as all of these matters are for call writers, they do not address the important questions that every stockholder needs to ask continuously: Should I keep the stock or sell it? Should I buy more shares? What changes have occurred that could also change my opinion of this stock?

The time will come when, as a call writer, you will want to close an open call position and sell the stock. For example, if you own 100 shares of stock on which you have written several calls over many months or years, when should you sell the stock? For a variety of reasons, you might conclude that the stock is not going to hold its value into the future as you once believed. Even investors buying stock for the long term need to rethink their positions through constant monitoring. It would be a mistake to continue holding stock because it represents a good candidate for covering call sales, when in fact that stock no longer makes the grade based on analytical tests that you use.

Fundamental Tests

The success call writer tracks ever-changing call status of the call—time and intrinsic value, risk of exercise, timing of decisions—*and* the stocks on which those calls are written. A number of fundamental indicators are useful in deciding when to buy or sell stock; and these tests should always override the considerations that attract you to call writing. Remember, options are always related to stock valuation, and trying to make profit through options on stocks that are not worthwhile investments, is a losing strategy.

The current market value of the stock reflects the buying public's current perception of its current and future value. This perception is affected by virtually all information available in the market at any time, including financial as well as nonfinancial, fact and rumor, and industry or sector news not directly related to the company itself.

One indicator that enjoys widespread popularity is the *price/earnings ratio* (P/E ratio). This is a measurement of current value that utilizes both fundamental and technical information. The technical side (price, of a share of stock) is divided by the fundamental side (*earnings per share* of common stock) to arrive at a numerical value.

Example: A company's stock recently sold at $35 per share. Its latest annual income statement showed $220 million in profit; the company had 35 million shares outstanding. That works out to a net profit of $6.29 per share: $220 ÷ $35. The P/E ratio is: $35 ÷ $6.29 = 5.6.

Example: A company earned $95 million and has 40 million shares outstanding, so its earnings per share is $2.38. The stock sells at $28 per share. The P/E is calculated as: $28 ÷ $2.38 = 11.8.

The P/E ratio can be described as a relative indicator of what the market believes about the particular stock. It reflects the current point of view about the company's prospects for future earnings. As a general observation, lower P/E ratio means lower risk for investors. Any ratio is useful only when it is studied in comparative form. This means not only that a company's P/E ratio may be tracked and observed over time; but also that comparisons between different companies can be instructive, especially if they are otherwise similar (in the same sector, same product profile, etc.). In the preceding examples, the first company's 5.6 P/E would be considered a less risky investment than the second, whose P/E is 11.8. However, P/E ratio is not always a fair indicator of a stock's risk level, nor of its potential for future profits, for six reasons. These include:

1. *Financial statements may themselves be distorted.* A company's financial statement may be far more complex than it first appears, in terms of what it includes and what it leaves out. For example, the income statement might include adjustments, called "extraordinary items." And as everyone now realizes, even an audited financial statement is not necessarily a reliable report on the company's

price/ earnings ratio a popular indicator used by stock market investors to rate and compare stocks. The current market value of the stock is divided by the most recent earnings per share to arrive at the P/E ratio.

earnings per share a commonly used method for reporting profits. Net profits for a year or other period are divided by the number of shares of common stock outstanding as of the ending date of the financial report. (The result is expressed as a dollar value.)

real numbers. Even when extraordinary items and other nonrecurring charges are fair and accurate, they will not be part of recurring operations. They may result from large gains or losses in currency exchange, payments resulting from lawsuits, changes in inventory valuation methods, and accounting adjustments for previous years.

2. *The financial statement might be unreliable for comparative purposes.* The financial reports of companies whose stock is listed must be audited by an independent auditing firm every year. While many investors take assurance from this and trust the accuracy of financial reports, it is less widely acknowledged that companies have considerable leeway in the way that they report income, costs and expenses, and profits, even within the rules. In fact, differences of opinion between auditors and company accountants may even be negotiated to a degree so that an accepted final version can be arrived at. Anyone who has studied the profit reports of some of the largest corporations may be impressed at the consistency of profits as reported from year to year. The perception among many corporate managers is that investors want reliability and consistency, so some transactions may be deferred to the following period. This is not necessarily deceptive as defined within the auditing rules. The leeway enables corporate management to make some adjustments in their current reports. The auditor's job is to ensure that no outright fraud is taking place. As a general rule, corporate financial reporting is a reliable science with rules that have to be followed, even in light of past problems involving auditing conflicts of interest. Still, the adjustments do raise the question of how reliable the P/E ratio is as a result. In addition, even when audited statements are fair and consistent, P/E has to be expected to vary from one industry to another. To keep a comparison realistic, it is not accurate to compare companies in dissimilar industries and draw a conclusion from differences in the P/E ratio.

3. *The number of shares outstanding might have changed.* Because shares outstanding is part of the P/E ratio equation, its comparative value can be altered when the number of shares changes from one year to another. A corporation may issue additional shares or split shares, for example, so that any comparison from one year to the next is distorted. Some companies buy their own shares on the market when they consider current price to be low. Shares purchased in that way are called "treasury stock," and they are retired, which means that the number of outstanding shares is lowered as well.

4. *The ratio becomes inaccurate as earnings reports go out of date.* If the latest earnings report of the company was issued last week, then the P/E ratio is based on relatively updated information. However, if that report was published three months ago, then the P/E is also outdated. The status of the company's earnings might be vastly different today from what it was as of the last published report. The greater the time lag between the latest report and today, the less reliable the P/E ratio. However, most market watchers accept and compare P/E ratios on all issues without considering the problem of outdated earnings reports.

5. *The comparison is between dissimilar forms of information.* The P/E ratio compares a stock's price—a technical value based on perceptions about current and future value—with earnings, which is historical and fundamental in nature. In one regard, this is the advantage of the P/E ratio; it bridges technical and fundamental in a logical manner to report on perceptions. However, it can also be problematical in the sense that these forms of information are entirely separate from one another. It raises the question about whether a purely technical matter such as market price can even be compared to a purely historically and fundamental matter such as earnings.

6. *Perceptions about P/E ratio are inconsistent.* This indicator is widely used and accepted as a means for evaluating and comparing stocks. However, not everyone agrees about how to interpret P/E to select stocks. A higher P/E generally means that, in the market's overall perception, the company has better than average prospects for high future stock price appreciation. So to some people, a high P/E translates to an investment more likely to do well in the future. Conversely, a lower than average P/E would indicate that the stock is less likely to appreciate in the future. Historically, however, lower P/E stocks have outperformed the market, and higher than average P/E stocks have been poor performers. This may reflect the market's tendency to overrate the potential of popular issues, and to underrate the earnings potential of less interesting ones. A company that reports a net loss cannot even have as P/E ratio so, by definition, it is impossible to compare a company reporting a net loss, with another reporting a profit, at least on the basis of the P/E ratio. There is no such thing as a negative P/E, which would imply a market expectation of future loss multiples. So P/E can be used only to compare companies reporting net profits. Given the opportunity for losses due to nonrecurring charges, P/E has limited value as a consistent (or singular) analytical tool.

How, then, should you use the P/E ratio? This remains a valuable indicator for measuring market perception about value of a stock, especially if you are tracking the P/E ratio for a single stock and watching how it changes over time. Comparing P/E between two different stocks may be more of a problem in terms of reliability. Companies in different industries, for example, may have widely different norms for judging profits. In one industry, a 3 percent or 4 percent return on sales might be considered average, and in another an 8 percent return is expected. So comparing P/E ratios between companies with dissimilar profit expectations, is inaccurate.

P/E ratio is a useful method for tracking changes in perception about a stock, and to a degree for comparing a stock to a broader standard. For example, you might decide to narrow down a selection of likely stock candidates by setting rules based on P/E ratio. You might exclude stocks whose P/E exceeds a mid-range P/E, for example. This tends to eliminate stocks on which market perception may be too high. The test may serve as one of several methods you use to reduce the range of stock purchase candidates. So P/E may serve more as a tool for eliminating stocks more than an indicator of which stocks to follow. If a company reports a net loss and thus has no P/E, or if the P/E is unreasonably high, you may eliminate those issues from a field of stocks you want to study further.

An additional fundamental test that every investor will want to consider is the *dividend yield*. This shows the current yield from dividends, expressed as a percentage of the share price. Of course, as the stock's market price changes, so does the dividend yield. Compare:

dividend yield
dividends paid per share of common stock, computed by dividing dividends paid by the current market value of the stock.

$3.50 ÷ $65 per share = 5.4%

$3.50 ÷ $55 per share = 6.4%

$3.50 ÷ $45 per share = 6.8%

As the price per share falls, the dividend yield rises. When you are considering buying stock, the dividend yield is a useful method for calculating your return from dividends—*based on the price per share that you pay*. However, once you own stock, your return from dividends is fixed as it represents a return on the price you paid (as long as the dividend per share paid by the corporation does not change). For purposes of ongoing analysis, the comparison between dividend per share and price per share has no value. In fact, continuing to study it based on current share price is distorting. Dividend yield is a valid form of analysis only when dividend payments are reflected based on the price per share that you paid.

When you consider which stock to buy from among several, dividend yield should be seen as potentially a large portion of your total return. More generous dividend yield could reflect a buying opportunity at the moment. That yield, added to capital gains as well as returns from selling covered calls, could add up to a very healthy overall return. Like comparisons between P/E ratio, the dividend yield is a useful indicator you can use for narrowing the field when you are picking stocks for investment.

A corporation's profitability is another important test. After all, long-term price appreciation occurs as the result of the corporation's ability to generate profits year after year. Short-term stock price changes are less significant when you are thinking about long-term growth potential of the stock, and for that, you want to compare *profit margin* from one company to another. This is the most popular system for judging a company's performance. It is computed by dividing the dollar amount of net profit by the dollar amount of gross sales. The result is expressed as a percentage.

The profit margin, as useful as it is for comparative purposes between companies, and for year-to-year analysis, often is not fully understood by investors. As a consequence, many market analysts and investors develop unrealistic expectations about profit margin. A couple of points worth remembering:

 profit margin
the most commonly used measurement of corporate operations, computed by dividing net profits by gross sales.

✔ *An "acceptable" level of profit varies among industries.* One industry may experience lower or higher average profit margin than another. For example, attributes of the insurance industry are vastly different from attributes of companies in computer technology. They cannot be realistically expected to generate the same profit margin, given the operational differences and structures of their companies. One sells a service, the other sells a product. One depends on investment returns, while the other competes in a retail marketplace. This and many more differences make it impractical to arrive at a singular standard for measuring profitability; the unique aspects of each sector should be used to differentiate between corporations. Comparisons should be restricted to those between corporations in the same sector.

✔ *It is not realistic to expect that one year's profit margin should always exceed that gained in the previous year.* Once a corporation reaches what is considered a respectable profit margin, it is unrealistic to expect it to continuously grow it terms of higher percentage returns. The financial elements and nature of costs and expenses naturally restrict the degree of profitability that is possible. So if a corporation's earnings match only the previous year or even come up short, that is not a negative indicator. Even so, analysts and investors often react by selling stock when earnings reports fail to meet their expectations, even the unrealistic ones.

A less frequently used method for evaluating your investments measures return to you as an investor. While this makes perfect sense, it often is overlooked. It is ironic that the market is preoccupied with stock prices, but its analysis is restricted in many instances to measurements of sales and profits. In practical terms, it is equally significant to judge how well a corporation performs in terms of what it returns to its investors, *that is*, stockholders. Divide net profits by outstanding capital to arrive at the percentage of *profit on invested capital*.

This indicator demonstrates how well a corporation is able to maintain consistent returns to its investors. It is related to a study of sources of capitalization. Corporations capitalize their operations through equity (stock) and debt (bonds and notes), and both forms of capitaliza-

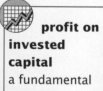

profit on invested capital

a fundamental test showing the yield to equity investors, computed by dividing net profits by the dollar value of outstanding capital.

tion require compensation. Stockholders are paid through dividends and capital gains, whereas bondholders are paid interest. An important point for stockholders to remember is that as debt capitalization increases, an increasing portion of operating profit is paid out in interest. That means that, in turn, there remains less operating profit available for dividends. If debt capitalization increases steadily over time, stockholders lose out as their dividend income is eroded. A secondary consequence is the erosion of market price resulting from ever-growing reliance on debt capitalization, which translates to lower long-term capital gains. The study of sources of capital is more complex than a simple ratio, but profit on invested capital does provide you with the means for tracking a company's management of its capitalization over several years.

Closely related to this should be a continuing analysis of your own return on invested capital. Whenever you buy stock, you may be compensated through capital gains and dividends, as well as covered call premium. Collectively, these represent your overall profit on invested capital. It is the means by which you judge your own investment performance, not only for one stock against another, but for your portfolio at large as well.

All of these fundamental tests are best reviewed in comparison with past statistics, and always computed in the same manner. Only then will you have a valid and useful analysis. Financial information is worthwhile only when tracked over time, and when they reveal the direction of a trend.

No single indicator should ever be used as the sole means for deciding what actions to take in the market. Fundamental analysis should be comprehensive. You can employ combinations of information, including a thorough study of all of the tests that reveal trends to you. They may confirm a previous opinion; or they may lead you to change your mind. Either way, the purpose in using the fundamentals is to gather information and then to act upon it.

Technical Tests

A well-rounded method for judging the value of a stock does not have to be arrived at with only one method. The combination of both fundamental and technical tests helps you to review the question of viability of a stock from several different points of view. While the fundamentals help you to gain insights into a company's overall financial and capital strength, technical indicators help you to judge market perception about future potential. In this regard, the fundamentals look back at a company's history to estimate the future; and technical indicators are used to make estimates based on current market information.

Most investors are aware of the importance of tracking a stock's price over time. In fact, price is the most popular indicator used by technicians. Even those describing themselves as acting based on the fundamentals often are, in fact, more interested in the market value of stock from day to day. It is an easy value to find; it is widely reported in the financial press and online. And while the short-term price movement of a stock is not valuable as a long-term indicator, it is interesting in technical terms. It is also of utmost importance to every options trader. Remember, there is an inconsistency between long-term value of stocks and short-term value of options. You need to be concerned with both.

Smart Investor Tip Long-term value of stocks is inconsistent with valuation methods for options, which are by nature short term. You need to track and monitor both.

Often overlooked in this analysis is the study of volume in a stock. You may apply volume tests to the market as a whole and several popular technical tests review trading volume on a daily basis. Volume can also be applied to individual stocks. When it increases, it indicates increased market interest in the stock. Of course, if that interest is led by buyer interest, then it means the price probably will rise. If the interest is generated by sellers, then the price will be driven downward. The direction of movement of the stock indicates which of these applies.

Obviously, all trades will have both buyer and seller. The point is that high volume can have two opposite conclusions, and that will be manifested in the direction that the stock's price is moving on a particular day. You often see a mix of buying and selling, high volume with little change in price. This is important information as well. It indicates that while shares of stock are changing hands, the current price range is considered reasonable by the market as a whole.

You can watch the movement in volume as well as in price in the financial press or on the Internet. Charting is widely available and free on numerous sites. Look for those offering easy directions and combination price and volume charts. The analysis of price and volume together reveals trading patterns in stocks that will improve your insight into the way that a stock acts in the market. There are no universal formulas. Each stock will develop its own trading pattern and the price will vary with changing volume, often in ways unique to the stock itself. This may be affected by the mix of ownership. If a stock is heavily invested through mutual funds, for example, then trading would tend to occur in large blocks. Thus, changes in volume may appear more drastic than volume in stocks owned more by individual investors, where a large volume of relatively small lots of stock would be expected. The point is, you need to assess each stock based on the mix of ownership, historical price and volume patterns, and overall volatility in the stock's market price.

Smart Investor Tip   Free charts of stock price and volume are available on dozens of sites, free of charge. Check these websites for a sampling:

Investor Guide	http://investorguide.com/
Stockmaster	http://www.stockmaster.com/
Financial Times	http://news.ft.com

A chartist, one who tracks patterns and trends in a stock's price, believes that by identifying patterns, it is possible to predict how a stock's price will act in coming days, weeks, or months. While most people believe that short-term price movement, in fact, is random and unreliable as an indicator, chartists do present some valuable observations concerning trading ranges of a stock.

For example, the chartist is especially interested in watching a stock's *support level*, which is a range of price identified as the lowest likely price level, given current conditions. On the other side of the chart is the *resistance level*, the highest price or price range a stock is trading under current conditions. The concepts of support and resistance are not only keys to the chartist's approach to studying stock price movement; they also are revealing because they indicate a stock's relative volatility. The wider the range between support and resistance, the more volatile a stock; and of course, the thinner that trading range, the more stable the stock. In this respect, the visualization of a stock's trading pattern can help every investor to identify a stock in terms of volatility over time.

As long as the price remains within the trading range between support and resistance, the chartist is satisfied that the stock's price is stable. However, eventually the stock's price will test either support or resistance by threatening to break through on the downside or on the upside. When the price does move beyond the trading range, it is described as going through a *breakout* pattern. The essence of charting is to try to identify in advance of the breakout when it is going to occur. The chartist believes that by studying the trading patterns, it is possible to predict price movement.

The support and resistance levels as well as breakout patterns are shown in Figure 6.3. In the illustration, an initial trading range is shown at the left, with a breakout on the upside; this establishes a new trading range and is then followed with a breakout on the downside. The breakout patterns are indicated by the arrows.

Predictions concerning future price movement are based upon detailed analysis of the patterns in the trading range. Chartists point to past patterns as confirming evidence that in fact, the movement in a stock's price is predictable. However, looking ahead to future price changes, chartists probably do not perform much better than anyone else in trying to predict what is likely to occur next. It will be difficult to convince a serious market

support level
the price for a stock identifying the lowest likely trading price under present conditions, below which the price of the stock is not likely to fall.

resistance level
the price for a stock identifying the highest likely trading price under present conditions, above which the price of the stock is not likely to rise.

breakout
the movement of a stock's price below support level or above resistance level.

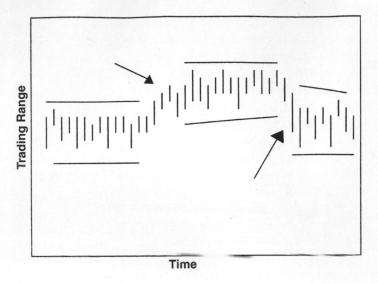

Trading Range

Time

FIGURE 6.3 Chart patterns.

watcher that charting has any predictive value. Its value is found, however, in the definition of the trading range. The Idea of support and resistance is a valuable tool for judging volatility.

Options traders can make good use of the support and resistance concepts. By observing the pattern of recent trading ranges, you may better judge a stock's price stability. The problem with a purely mathematical analysis of volatility is that it presents a year's summary in a single number. That volatility could be the result of a single change in price, or part of a pattern of widely varying prices. You cannot differentiate the two with the traditional volatility formula.

The chart reveals more for options traders. By studying the chart's pattern over time, you can judge whether the trading range is broad or thin; whether it is changing and, if so, to what degree; and how often previously established trading ranges have been changed by breakouts. The length of time a trading range remains unchanged is also revealing, as it helps options traders to determine a stock's tendency to react to market changes in general, or goes along on its own timing and trading pattern. Remembering that all of these observations may change at any time, charting is nonetheless valuable for comparing stocks to one another; and for arriving at conclusions about volatility that cannot be revealed through the price range formula that looks at an entire year.

Accompanying an in-depth review of volatility, a sound analysis of a stock may include a study of the high and low price ranges over time. This demonstrates several things. For example, the more volatile stocks—those with broader high and low ranges—may, in fact, be volatile at the beginning of the period but not at the end, or vice versa. A simple one-year summary is not reliable in terms of today's tendency. In addition, the study of high and low price ranges reveals where that stock's price stands today in relation to the longer-term trading range. Is it at the high end, low end, or somewhere in the middle?

The stock reports in the financial press present only the 52-week high and low price ranges. Given the many possible varieties of trading patterns that can result in the same high and low summary, this information is highly unreliable. A more detailed study is required.

Example: Three different stocks have what appear to be highly volatile status today. They all have 52-week trading ranges with a spread of 40 points. However, upon more detailed examination, you discover three different scenarios, making the simple 52-week summary unreliable for your comparative analysis:

Stock A began the year at $22 per share and has risen consistently throughout the past 52 weeks. Today, the stock is valued at $62 per share.

Stock B has been trading between $55 and $58 for most of the year. Eight months ago, it was rumored to be a takeover candidate and the stock soared to $96 per share, at which point trading was halted. The rumor proved to be untrue and when trading was reopened, the stock resumed trading at $64, quickly falling back to its previous three-point range.

Stock C began the year at $107 per share. This stock is in a highly competitive market sector and is one of the less strongly capitalized corporation in the field. It began losing share value early in the 52-week range, slipped over the first three months to the 90s and has been falling more since then. It currently is trading at $67, its lowest point in the past year.

In each of the three scenarios, the summarized 52-week high and low analysis means completely different things. In fact, stock A is trading at the high point in its 52-week range but few people would describe it as trading too high today, given its trading pattern. Stock B appears volatile, but in fact it is a very stable stock with an exceptionally small trading range. And stock C might look like a well-timed buying opportunity because it currently is at its 52-week low. However, a closer look at the stock's history points to some competitive problems that are perceived by the market as making it a high-risk alternative.

Some investors pick stocks by religiously studying the 52-week high and low ranges. The use of this information cannot be restricted to the conclusions as shown in the financial press, however. It is essential that the character of the high and low range be more fully explored so that its exact nature can be identified.

No single fundamental or technical test can be used reliably to identify good purchase candidates. The high and low ranges, for example, might represent a fair starting point for stock selection, but the analysis should explore further into the timing and attributes of the stock and its trading range. The more information available, the more accurate your analysis. You can evaluate stocks by tracking key indicators over time, looking not only for patterns, but also for the emergence of *new* pricing trends. For example, you might decide to track a stock you are thinking of buying, combining dividend rate, P/E ratio, high and low range, and current price (close each day) of a stock. The worksheet in Figure 6.4 can be used for this purpose. You might use the close each Friday to track a particular stock. After entering information on each line, you can begin to see how each piece of information changes or interacts with the others.

The problem with analysis is that it takes time. And the more time you spend on analysis, the more quickly it goes out of date. Having online charting services available without charge makes your task much easier. As an options trader, you may also be able to limit your analysis to the relatively small number of stocks on which options are traded.

stock name _____

DATE	DIVIDEND RATE	P/E RATIO	HIGH	LOW	CLOSE

FIGURE 6.4   Stock evaluation worksheet.

Deciding Which Tests to Apply

Entire books have been written about the hundreds of
possible fundamental and technical tests you may use for
picking stocks, tracking them, and deciding when to sell.
How do you determine which of these tests is most useful
to you? This is no easy question, since the answer depends on your own opinion. Before deciding upon how to

pick one form of analysis over another, be aware of these important points:

✔ *Many analysts love complex formulas.* A difficult to understand theory that requires a lot of mathematical ability is probably entirely useless in the real world. An academic approach to the market might be interesting in an academic setting, where professors and students take a theoretical approach to studying stocks, but are likely to have no actual investing experience. Avoid the complex, recognizing that useful information also tends to be straightforward and easily comprehended.

✔ *You can perform your own tests. You do not need to pay for analysis.* Even though some of the accounting-related ratios can be complex and difficult to follow, the actual tests leading to decisions to buy, hold, or sell are going to be very basic and straightforward. Keep your focus on verifying the reliability of financial information, tracking trends in moving averages while looking out for red flags, and seeking indicators that the basic value of a company has changed. It does not have to be any more complicated than that.

✔ *Price has nothing to do with the fundamentals.* This is one of the often overlooked realities in the market. The price of any stock (or option) reflects the market's perception about future potential value, whereas the financial condition of that company is historical. A study of fundamentals certainly indicates good long-term investment prospects, but it has nothing to do with today's price or the way that the price is likely to change tomorrow or next week.

✔ *The actual net worth of a company has nothing to do with price.* Some investors fall into the mistaken belief that the price of stock represents the value of the company. That is not true; the two have nothing to do with each other. Current market value is determined through auction between buyers and sellers, and not by accountants at the company's headquarters. The actual value of the stockholders' equity in a corporation is found in the *book value* of shares of stock. This is the net worth of a company, divided by the number of outstanding shares. However, book value per share has little to do with current market value per share; it often is considerably lower and

 book value
the actual value of a company, more accurately called "book value per share"; the value of a company's capital (assets less liabilities), divided by the number of outstanding shares of stock.

in some instances, might even be higher. Most investors and analysts completely ignore book value.

✔ *The past is not an infallible indicator.* You may attempt to predict patterns of price, profits, or competitive posture within an industry; but in fact, the past is unreliable. In corporate offices, accountants continuously try to estimate future sales, costs, expenses and profit through the budgeting process. This itself is more art than science. When investors attempt to predict price movement through studying the fundamentals, they face an even more elusive task, since the fundamentals do not affect short-term price movement as much as other factors, such as perception of the market as a whole. As much as investors would like to be able to predict the future, it simply cannot be done. Every investor is well-advised to remember the wisdom that the stock market has no past.

✔ *Predictions abound, but reliable predictions do not exist.* Anyone can get lucky and make an accurate prediction once in a while. Doing so with any consistency is far more difficult. You can study any number of factors, either fundamental or technical, but none will enable you to accurately predict future price movement of stocks. Technicians spend a lot of time trying to prove that there is a correlation between market prices and other events; some have even attempted to tie market trends with social, political, or even sporting events. Some have been even more farfetched, including studies trying to show that market prices are affected by weather patterns or the thickness of tree rings! None of these unrelated factors are related to pricing of stocks and the elements that make them change. The truth is, no one really knows what causes price changes overall. Numerous theories address part of the cause, and it is certain that all market, economic, financial, and technical indicators play a part. An entire predictive industry convinces subscribers that a particular formula will provide insight, and the desire to beat the averages results in many dollars going into the pockets of newsletter and newspaper subscriptions. The truth, though, is that no one can predict price movements of the market as a whole, or of individual stocks. However, you can gain informed insight that will help you to make an intelligent decision.

✔ *Common sense is your best tool.* Investing is more likely to be a successful experience if you employ common sense, backed up with study, analysis, and comparison. If you seek fast riches through easy formulas, you are more likely to lose money than to make money in the stock market. Getting rich without hard work is no easier in the stock market than anywhere else. All too often, promoters of schemes or tricks appeal to many inexperienced people; and now that the Internet is accessible to so many investors, new schemes like day trading are being promoted as the way to get rich—promotions often fail to mention that opportunities are accompanied with exceptionally high risks as well.

✔ *Stock prices, especially in the short term, are random.* Most predictive theories acknowledge that, while long-term analysis can accurately narrow down the guesswork, short-term price movement is completely random. In the stock market, where opinion and speculation are so widespread, no one can control the way that stock prices change from one day to the next. Long-term investment prospects can be identified through a study of the fundamentals; but trying to guess where a stock's price will be within the next few months is virtually impossible, and any system that attempts to provide a means for such predictions should be viewed with great skepticism.

The two major theories directing opinions about stock prices are the *random walk* theory and the *Dow Theory*. Both of these deserve consideration, because while they differ in their approach, both agree on one important issue: Short-term prices cannot be used as reliable indicators, because they cannot be predicted. For the options investor, this is an interesting observation. If short-term price movement is unpredictable, that means that stock selection has to be done on a long-term basis. However, at the same time options investors have an exceptional opportunity. You *know* in advance how time value premium is going to change. That change occurs only due to time, and is not affected by changes in the stock's market price. So while you should select long position stocks with the long term in mind, whichever theory you accept about how price is determined, the methods used for selling short position calls are going to involve two elements not affected by stock valuation: option premium richness

 random walk
a theory about market pricing, stating that prices of stocks cannot be predicted because price movement is entirely random.

 Dow Theory
a theory that market trends are predictable based on changes in market averages.

(meaning time value) and the amount of time remaining until expiration.

Even though you know in advance how time value is going to change over time, the degree of time value is affected by the stock's volatility. More volatile stocks (higher-risk stocks) will tend to have higher time value when the time until expiration is greater. So you will have greater profit potential and less chance of exercise due to higher time value in those cases, offset by higher market risk associated with owning the stock.

Options traders should be especially aware of the theories underlying both the random walk and the Dow Theory, since both agree on one key point: Short-term prices cannot be accurately predicted. This idea has ramifications for options traders and, if both theories agree on that point, it probably has considerable merit.

efficient market hypothesis
a theory stating that current stock prices reflect all information publicly known about a company.

A third idea about market pricing only supports the theory about pricing as expressed in the two broad theories. This idea is called the *efficient market hypothesis*. An efficient market is one is which current prices reflect all information known to the public. Thus, prices are reasonable based upon perceptions about markets and the companies whose stock is listed publicly. If the efficient market hypothesis is correct, then all current prices are fair and reasonable. Again, this idea has ramifications for all options traders.

All three of these theories deserve some further study, at least regarding short-term price movement. Options traders deal exclusively in the short-term, so the theories about market pricing should be observed carefully. Of course, no theory is absolutely right. A theory is intended only to offer observations about price behavior. Understanding how and why a theory is developed can help you to understand markets and stock prices, but no theory can ever be used as a guiding force for making decisions about when (or if) to buy or sell.

The Random Walk In one regard, the random walk contradicts the other theories. If, in fact, prices are entirely random, then there is no explanation for price behavior. There is a 50-50 chance that price will rise, and a 50-50 chance that prices will fall. Thus, if the theory were absolute, then there would be no need for market analysis. Fundamental and technical indicators would provide no useful information.

However, in another sense, the random walk makes a point about short-term price movement that conforms to the principles of the Dow Theory and the efficient market hypothesis. There is no way to know how short-term prices will change. Virtually everyone agrees that short-term price changes are highly unreliable, and that they do not act or react with any consistent logic whatsoever. The random walk emphasizes the absolute importance of selecting stocks with strong fundamental and technical characteristics. For options traders, the strength of the underlying stock is a long-term attribute; the value of stock selection is the most important consideration for options sellers. It is the proper selection of stock for long-term value that determines whether or not your portfolio has intrinsic strength. Only after selecting stocks through careful research, should you ever consider writing calls.

Remembering the random walk, an option seller cannot know how short-term price changes will occur. So the need to look at all possible outcomes is always essential to succeeding in an option writing plan. Only when you will be satisfied will all possible outcomes does it make sense to sell options against stock. It is one of the few strategies that can be designed so that you will profit no matter what happens to the underlying stock. Some outcomes are going to be more desirable than others, but it is possible to create situations where profits are virtually guaranteed (the one exception being an unexpected significant drop in the stock's market value, in which case the writer can only wait for a rebound).

The Dow Theory   While the Dow Theory has been around for more than 100 years, its origins go back to Charles Dow, who developed the system as a means for tracking business trends. He did not originally intend for this analysis to be used in the stock market. However, he and his partner Edward Jones founded the Dow Jones Company and began publishing a newsletter that grew into the *Wall Street Journal*. Dow's editorial comments and ideas were expanded upon by his successors.

What was originally a rather straightforward idea has developed into an overall market theory based largely on the premise that the averages concocted by the Dow Jones Company can be used to predict market price changes. Among the tenets of the Dow Theory are the identification of three movements in the stock market: primary, secondary, and daily. The primary movement is an overall trend in the market, most often described as bull or bear. The secondary movement is a reaction to the first, characterized by opposite movements—a rally in a bear market or a decline during a bull market. The daily movements are variously described as unimportant or meaningless.

If you select stocks based on the Dow Theory, you face a difficult task. Used primarily to predict overall price movement, the Dow Theory is less reliable for selection of individual stocks, whose price changes may more accurately be traced to the company's fundamentals. The Dow Theory utilizes a number of precepts concerning the identification of changing trends, but it is of little use in picking out one stock from among thousands. However you select stocks, the significant point to remember as an options trader is that daily movement is considered as mere ripples among the tide (primary movement) or the wave (secondary movement). The Dow Theory is applied to the broad market; even so, the theory itself can be used in the analysis of individual stocks. It is puzzling that even the most faithful Dow Theory proponents rarely apply the theory to individual stock analysis, where it would be more useful.

The Efficient Market   The theory of the efficient market, in some people's view, is the most cynical. It is particularly resisted by market professionals whose livelihood depends upon convincing customers that their analyses are valuable. The efficient market theory essentially debunks all analysis that might be used to time market decisions. If it is correct, then both fundamental and technical analysis are useless.

Anyone who has observed how the market works understands that the efficient market is a pure theory, but it is not always applicable. For example, Value Line divides the stocks it studies into five groups, from the highest-rated for safety and timeliness, down to the lowest. The first two tiers beat market averages with consistency, proving that there is value in going through the analysis of prices, price movement, and the range of fundamentals. A reasonable approach is to believe that the market is efficient, but only to a degree. Market observers will acknowledge that the investing public tends to overreact to news in the market. Prices rise beyond a reasonable level on good news, and decline beyond a reasonable degree on bad news. So in short-term trading, prices cannot be called efficient by any means. In fact, all of the various market theories would agree that, for whatever cause, short-term market price movement is highly chaotic and unpredictable. The often unrealistic pricing swings present momentary opportunities for speculators—including options investors.

In intermediate timing—meaning weeks or months rather than the short term, hours or days—the efficient market theory might hold a degree of validity. In other words, news, whether true or not, has an effect on prices. However, it takes some time for the overreaction to simmer down, often resulting in what appears more efficient. If a rumor proves untrue, the intermediate-term effect is that the stock price is not effected at all. If it is true, then the effect is more reasonable than the initial price reaction.

Like the other two theories, the efficient market points out the danger and opportunity for options traders. Short-term price changes cannot be predicted with any reliability whatsoever, even in the efficient market; so options traders really have no reliable *options-related* method for selecting which ones to trade. However, the characteristics of the underlying stock can be used reliably to select a profitable portfolio. It is fair to surmise that a stock with strong fundamental and technical characteristics is not only a good long-term investment, but also a viable candidate for writing covered calls. The options buyer, on the other hand, undertakes considerable risks, remembering that none of the theories place any reliability on short-term price changes.

Smart Investor Tip All theories agree that short-term price changes provide no useful information. This presents problems for options buyers; for options sellers, the volatility of short-term prices can have a positive effect on time value, meaning opportunities for profits.

APPLYING ANALYSIS TO CALLS

To select stocks for writing calls, the essential requirement is that you pick issues with strong long-term growth potential. Keep the major market theories in mind when you study stocks, and emphasize the characteristics that should be used for picking them. These characteristics do not include exceptionally rich option premium. The volatility test is appropriate for picking stocks, given that you are able to distinguish between different causes of volatility. So is it a general tendency, a momentary spike in an otherwise stable price range, or an upward or downward pricing trend? Volatility needs to be studied in more detail than is normally provided in the financial press. A study of a year-long stock price chart yields more useful information.

Many investors believe that moderate volatility is a positive sign, as it demonstrates investor interest. A stock that has little or no volatility is, indeed, not a hot stock and such conditions will invariably be accompanied by very low volume as well, and a consistently low P/E ratio. So some short-term volatility might demonstrate not only that investor interest is high, but also that option activity and pricing will be more interesting as well. As a technical test of a stock's price stability, volatility should be analyzed in terms of both short-term and long-term levels. Ideally, your stocks will contain long-term stability, but relatively volatile price movement in the short term. The volatility test will not be a constant, and stocks that are popular in the market will change in terms of volatility as markets change and as their price moves from one moment to another.

With the distinctions in mind between different causes and patterns of volatility, the selection of stock may be based on a comparative study of the past 12 months. First, ensure that the stocks you are considering as prospects for purchase contain approximately the same causes for their volatility. Then apply volatility as a test for identifying relative degrees of safety.

Example: You are considering buying several stocks. Their volatility patterns are similar, with price ranges tending to be consistent over the past 12 months. (You have eliminated stocks whose volatility resulted from price spikes.) One stock's price range over the past 12 months was between $28 and $49 per share. To compute volatility, divide the difference between high and low, by the low. Multiply the result by 100 to arrive at a percentage representing volatility:

$$\frac{\$49 - \$28}{\$28} \times 100 = 75.0\%$$

Example: A second stock in your comparison had a 12-month price range between $67 and $72 per share. Volatility is computed as:

$$\frac{\$72 - \$67}{\$67} \times 100 = 75.0\%$$

The stock in the second example is considerable less volatile than the one in the first example. The trading ranges of each might contain similar pattern characteristics, but it is the degree of change, or the width of that gap, that defines volatility. For call writers, the degree of volatility is an indication of risk as well as potential richness in call premiums. Obviously, you will want to seek stocks with long-term price appreciation potential but high short-term volatility. This attribute is easy to spot in hindsight, but difficult to predict—especially since short-term volatility also means difficulty in predicting any price movement over the next few months. So a lower volatility, as in the second example, indicates more predictability in stock price movement, but lower likelihood of call premium richness. The obvious choice for call writers is to select stocks with a history of short-term volatility, and the best possible long-term growth potential.

Fundamental and technical tests are complemented with the use of another feature in a stock's price used to define volatility—that is the stock's *beta*. This is a test of "relative" volatility; in other words, the degree to which a stock tends to move with an entire market or index of

beta
a measurement of relative volatility of a stock, made by comparing the degree of price movement in comparison to a larger index of stock prices.

stocks. A beta of 1 tells you that a particular stock tends to rise or fall in the same degree as the market as a whole. A beta of 0 implies that price changes of the stock are independent of price changes in the broader market; and a beta of 2 indicates that a stock's price tends to overreact to market trends, often by moving to a greater degree than the market as a whole.

Example: Over the past year, the composite index—the overall value of the stock market—rose by approximately 7 percent. Your stock also rose 7 percent, so its beta is 1. If your stock rose 14 percent, its beta would be 2.

As a general rule, the more volatile stocks will also tend to have greater time value premiums associated with their options. That is because the stocks represent greater risks, and option premium reflects that risk. It is an advantage for sellers, and a problem for buyers, because high-beta stocks will also experience more rapid decline in their options' time value than the rate of decline for low-beta stocks. So if your portfolio contains high-beta stocks, you will receive higher premiums for selling calls, but your stock will be more volatile as well.

Because time value tends to be higher than average for high-beta stocks, premium value, like the stock's market value, is less predictable. From the call writer's point of view, exceptionally high time value that declines rapidly is a clear advantage, but it would be shortsighted to trade only in such stocks, especially if you also want stability in your stock portfolio.

Example: You own 100 shares of stock that you bought at $62 per share. You recently sold a May 65 call at 5. Last week, the stock fell six points and the call's value fell to 1. You buy, realizing a profit of $500 on the call. However, you lost $600 in the underlying stock.

In this example, the fast turnaround in the option reflected high volatility and was offset by a paper loss in the stock. Investors often choose volatile stocks in full awareness of the risk, planning to move in and out of short option positions several times—trading on volatility, in other words. In the preceding example, you walked away with a profit of $400 and you still own the stock. If it were to jump in value above your basis, you could sell another call and wait for yet another decline in value. You cannot control the frequency or the direction of price changes in the stock, but when its price moves in the desired direction, you can profit by selling calls with high time value.

A more elusive but interesting indicator that helps select options is called the *delta*. When the price of the underlying stock and the premium value of the option change exactly the same number of points, the delta is 1.00. As delta increases or decreases for an option, you are able to judge the responsiveness (volatility) of the option to the stock. This takes into consideration the distance between current market value of the stock and striking price of the call; fluctuations of time value; and changes in delta as expiration approaches. The delta provides you with the means to compare interaction between stock and option pricing for a particular stock.

Delta measures aberrations in time value because, if all delta levels were the same, then overall option price movement would be formulated strictly on time and stock price changes. Because this is not the case, it is obvious that we also need to use some means for comparative option volatility, apart from the volatility of the underlying stock. The inclination of a typical option is to behave predictably, tending to approach a delta of 1.00 as it goes in the money and as expiration approaches. So for every point of price movement in the underlying stock, you would expect a change in option premium very close to one point when in the money. Time value tends to not be a factor when options are deep in the money. Time value is more likely to change predictably based on time until expiration. For further-out options, notably those close to the striking price, delta is going to be a more important feature. In fact, the comparison of delta between options that are otherwise the same in all of their features, will indicate the option-specific risks and volatility not visible in a pure study of the stock itself. Many beginning options traders overlook this important fact, forgetting that time value does not rise in most situations; it tends to fall as expiration approaches. However, time value can and does change for longer-term options close to the money. The delta can work as a useful device for studying such options.

 delta
the degree of change in option premium, in relation to changes in the underlying stock. (If the call option's degree of change exceeds the change in the underlying stock, it is called an "up delta"; when the change is less than the underlying stock, it is called a "down delta." The reverse terminology is applied to puts.)

When the option is at the money, you can best judge option tendency by observing delta. For example, if the option's delta is 0.80 when at the money, you would expect a change of eight-tenths of one point for every change out of the money in the stock's market price. In addition, however, the direction of the stock's movement may also affect response in the option's premium. This is true because movement in one direction puts the option in the money; and movement in the other direction moves the option out of the money. So as the stock moves in the money, you would expect the delta to approach 1.00. If it were higher when movement occurred in the money, that would be an aberration worth watching. For the call seller, the aberration is invariably an advantage.

Example: You are tracking an in-the-money call. Its striking price is 35 and the underlying stock's market value is $47 per share. You notice that each point of movement in the stock's market price is paralleled by a corresponding change in the option's premium value. The only variance is evaporating time value.

Example: An option is at the money. You observe that as the underlying stock's price changes, it affects premium value by about 80 percent. This option's delta is 0.80.

Example: A call is out of the money. The striking price is 65 but current market value of the stock is $52 per share. Minor changes in the stock's market value have little or no effect in the call's premium value, all of which is time value. As the gap widens between striking price of the call and current market value of the stock, you observe that there is even less effect on the call's premium value. In this case, delta is almost inapplicable, since the call is so far out of the money. Time value premium declines as expiration approaches; the only factor that could increase the time value would be the sudden closing of that gap, presenting a prospect that the call could move into the money.

Being aware of delta enables you to take advantage of conditions and improve your timing, whether you are operating as a buyer or as a seller.

Accompanying these indicators of relative volatility, you may also follow *open interest*. This is the number of open option contracts on a particular underlying stock. For example, one stock's July 40 calls had open interest last month of 22,000 contracts; today, only 500 contracts remain open. The number changes for several reasons. As the status of the call moves higher into the money, the number of open contracts tends to change as the result of closing sale transactions, rolling forward, or exercise. Sellers tend to buy out their positions as time value falls, and buyers tend to close out positions as intrinsic value rises. And as expiration approaches, fewer new contracts open. In addition to these factors, open interest changes when perceptions among buyers and sellers change for the stock. Unfortunately, the number of contracts does not tell you the reasons for the change, nor whether the change is being driven by buyers or by sellers.

open interest
the number of open contracts of a particular option at any given time, which can be used to measure market interest.

Applying the Delta

The delta of a call should be 1.00 whenever it is deep in the money. As a general rule, expect the call to parallel the price movement of the stock on a point-for-point basis, an observation that is more the case when the call is closer to expiration. In some instances, a call's delta may change unexpectedly. For example, if an in-the-money call increases by three points but the stock's price rose by only two points (a delta of 1.50), the aberration represents an *increase* in time value, which rarely occurs. It may be a sign that investors perceive the option to be worth more than its previous price, relative to movement in the stock. This can be caused by any number of changes in market perception. For example, buyers might drive delta by way of increased time value when an in-the-money call is viewed as having profit potential based on rumors about the company. Figure 6.5 summarizes movement in an option's premium relative to the underlying stock, with corresponding delta.

Time value is reasonably predictable in the pattern of change, given looming expiration. It does not move in a *completely* predictable manner, since perceptions about the option are changing constantly. However, it is fair to say that increases in time value are rare. Of

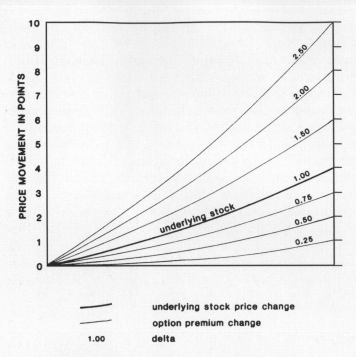

FIGURE 6.5 Changes in an option's delta.

course, perceptions about both the stock and the option
will affect time value to a degree, and increases in time
value premium can occur, especially if the option has
several months to go until expiration. You can track a
call's delta in order to better time a covered call write.
The most likely aberration in time value would be
greater than expected decline too early, followed by a
period of catch-up, in which time value changes more
slowly to equalize the rate of decline.

Example: You bought 100 shares of stock at $48 per
share. During yesterday's market, the stock rose from $51
to $53, based largely on rumors of higher quarterly profits
than predicted by analysts. The 60 call rose from 4 to 8,
an increase of four points (and a delta of 2.00).

In the preceding example, it is apparent that the
market overreaction to current news presents a call selling
opportunity. Increases in time value are invariably corrected in the near future. Once the news hits and is absorbed, the time value in the example is likely to correct

itself as quickly as it appeared. Distortions in value often are momentary and require fast action. The covered call writer needs to be able to move quickly when opportunities are presented.

The same strategy can be applied when you already have an open covered call position and you are thinking of closing it. For example, your call is in the money and the stock falls two points. At the same time, option premium falls by three points, for a delta of 1.50. This could be a temporary distortion, so profits can be taken immediately on the theory that the distortion will be corrected within a short time.

FOLLOWING YOUR OWN PERSPECTIVE

All market analysts depend on their best estimates in making decisions. You cannot time your decisions perfectly nor consistently; so you have to depend on a combination of fundamental and technical indicators to provide yourself with an edge. That means you improve your percentages, and not that you will be right every time. As a call writer, it is crucial that you base your entire strategy on the thorough analysis and well-thought-out selection of stocks. You should always pick a stock on its merits as a long term investment and not merely to provide coverage for short option positions.

Also recognize that covered call writing is one way you create downside protection and to improve overall return from your stock portfolio. In exchange for much-improved returns, you might lose the occasional sudden rise in market value of a stock. The fixed striking price ensures a limited but consistent profit. If writing covered calls is contrary to your overall long-term objectives, you should not participate in this market. For example, if you buy a stock because you believe it is grossly underpriced, then you expect its market value to rise in the future. In that case, it would not make sense to sell calls and fix the striking price.

Example: You bought 300 shares of stock last year as a long-term investment. You have no plans to sell and, as you hoped, the market price has been inching upward consistently. Your broker is encouraging you to write calls against your shares, pointing to the potential for additional profits as well as downside protection. Your broker also observes that if exercised, your calls will still earn a profit. However, remembering your reasons for buying the stock, you reject the advice. Call writing is contrary to your goal in buying the stock.

You usually can avoid exercise by rolling up and forward, as long as the price increase in the stock is not too severe. Exercise could be unavoidable when a stock's market price takes off. Call writers should understand such risks before entering into short positions; the loss of potential market value in the stock might not be worth a relatively small call premium. Exercise is always possible when a call is in the money, so you need to be completely satisfied with the return from call premium and the capital gain if the option is exercised.

As an options trader, never overlook the need for continued monitoring of the stock. By preparing a price performance chart like the one shown in Figure 6.6, you can track movement by week. A completed chart helps you to time decisions, notably on writing covered calls. If you have access to the Internet, you can also use free sites to produce price and volume charts. Three out of the many sites that provide this free benefit are listed earlier in this chapter.

Successful call writers have learned that it is important to track both the option and the underlying stock. If profits in one are offset by losses in the other, there is no point to a strategy. By observing changes in the option and the stock, you will be able to spot opportunities and dangers as they emerge.

Example: You bought 100 shares in each of four companies last year. Within the following months, you wrote covered calls in all four. Today, three of the four have market values below your basis, even though the overall market is higher. You add up the total of call premium, dividends, and paper capital gains and losses, and realize that if you were to close out all of your positions today, you would lose money.

This example indicates that stocks were poorly

stock _____ dates: _____ to _____

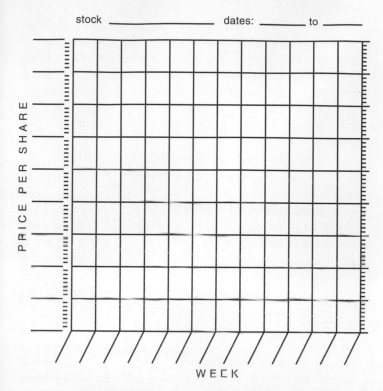

FIGURE 6.6 Stock performance chart.

chosen or poorly timed. While paper losses might have been greater had you not written calls, they also raise questions about why a particular mix of stocks was chosen. A critical review of your selection criteria might reveal that you are picking stocks based on option premium value rather than on the stock's fundamental and technical indicators. Relatively safe stocks tend to have little options appeal, because time value is minimal in stocks that do not change much. So more volatile stocks are far more likely candidates for premium action. That does not mean they are worthwhile investments; it could mean that option profits will be offset by capital losses in your portfolio.

Perhaps the greatest risk in call writing is the tendency to buy stocks that are overly volatile because they also have higher time value premium in their options. You will do better if you look for moderate volatility as a secondary strategy.

1. Select stocks with good growth potential and hold them for a while without writing options. Give the stocks a chance to appreciate. This gives you much more flexibility in picking options and ensuring profits regardless of the outcome. The combination of premium, dividends, and capital gains can be built into your strategy with ease, assuming that current market value is higher than your original cost per share.

2. Time your decision to sell calls on stock you already own, to maximize your potential for gains from the options.

3. Remember the importance of patience. You might need to wait out a market that seems to be moving too slowly. Your patience will be rewarded if you select stocks properly. Opportunity does come around eventually, but too many novice call writers give in to their impatience, anxious to write calls as soon as possible. This is a mistake.

Putting Your Rules Down on Paper

Setting goals helps you to succeed in the options market. This is equally true if you buy stocks and do not write options. By defining your personal rules, you will have a better chance for success. Define several aspects of your investment plan, including:

✔ Long-term goals for your entire portfolio.

✔ Strategies you believe will help you reach those goals.

✔ Percentages of your portfolio that are to be placed in each type of investment.

✔ Definitions of "risk" in its many forms, and the degree of risk you are willing to assume.

✔ Purchase and sales levels you are willing and able to commit.

✔ Guidelines for review and possible modification of your goals.

Those investors who write down their rules tend to succeed more than those who do not have clearly defined rules of practice. If guidelines are overly vague or generalized, it is easy to modify them as you go, not giving in to temptation that you cannot afford in the market. In a sense, hard and fast rules provide you with a programmed response to evolving situations, and improve your performance and profits. This does not mean you have to be inflexible; only that you know the limits of risk you are willing to take.

The next chapter explains how you need to adjust your approach in volatile markets.

Strategies in Volatile Markets

Change is inevitable in a progressive society. Change is constant.
                    —Benjamin Disraeli, speech, October 20, 1867

Profiting in the market is easy, as long as it is rising. Many first-time investors begin their investment program during these bull markets; unfortunately, they are cyclical and those uptrends can and do turn suddenly.

First-time investors, as a general rule, have never experienced losses. So when they do occur, it takes investors by surprise. Experienced investors understand that success has to be defined differently from the absolute of winning or losing. They know that being right more often than being wrong defines investing success. Experienced investors also know how to diversify and limit risk even in a rising market, and they understand the old wisdom that stocks climb a wall of worry.

Smart Investor Tip Success in the market should be defined as being right more often than being wrong. Expecting loss is realistic; if a loss takes you by surprise, then you need to take a second look at your expectations.

Hindsight always clarifies the periods of upward and downward trends. However, it is far more difficult to identify the type of market we are experiencing at this moment, and what is going to happen next. At any given time, some observers think the market is rising, others think it is falling, and a third group adopts a wait-and-see approach. Each of these groups can cite plenty of market data to support their points of view, but they cannot all be right. The dilemma for investors in this constant environment of uncertainty is finding a way to build a portfolio of stocks while also minimizing the risk of catastrophic losses. Of course, you want to take advantage of emerging rises in the price of stocks and at the same time, limit your risk exposure. Many investors flee the market in times of uncertainty such as the period of corporate scandals revealed in 2002. However, it's all a matter of timing. How do these investors decide when (or if) to go back into the market? Or do they simply conclude that there are just too many risks and that they are better off putting their money into a mutual fund, just hoping that they pick one that will perform well?

These problems are severe for anyone who has been in the market before. It used to be an automatic assumption that audited statements could be trusted to be reliable, that boards of directors would prevent executives from raiding a corporation's assets, and that Wall Street analysts would give their clients good advice. Now that we have discovered the flaws in all of these traditional assumptions, the very idea of investing has to be reevaluated.

Fortunately, reform has occurred on a broad front and will continue. The Sarbanes-Oxley Act of 2002 drastically changed the way that corporations report their operations and imposed severe liability and penalties for deception. Reforms in requirements to list stock on the exchanges affected the composition of boards of directors, including a majority of independent board members and control over independent auditors by the boards' audit committees. Changes in the SEC enforcement and investigation divisions were helped by a significant budget increase, and new leadership at the SEC may also lead to more aggressive preventive measures. Reforms in the Wall Street brokerage firms that aimed at separating research and investment banking operations will eventually remove that conflict of interest as well.

While all of these changes are significant, they will not completely remove the problems of conflict of interest, corruption, or outright fraud. However, it is collectively a start. More reform will be needed, but investors will eventually return to the markets, and however investing is viewed today, it will be different tomorrow.

For those who want to be invested in sound long-term stocks, options can play an important role in mitigating risks, diversifying your portfolio, and preventing or reducing unexpected losses in a volatile investing market.

VARYING STRATEGIES BY MARKETS

As a starting point in defining a market strategy, each investor will benefit from examining the basic assumptions that go into how and why particular decisions are made. How do you pick a particular company? Do you study their fundamentals, follow price chart patterns, or buy stocks on the basis of name recognition?

Some common errors characterize the way that some investment decisions are made. These include the following 10 mistakes:

1. *Failing to follow your own rules.* Many people define themselves as believers in the fundamentals, and then defy their own standards. They don't follow the fundamentals at all. Instead of monitoring trends in the important areas of statements, they find themselves tracking stock charts or making decisions based on index movements. If you are comfortable making decisions based on technical indicators, you will be in good company; many investors believe that is a valid method to use. However, they need to define their approach to investing, and to understand themselves, if only to know how much weight to give to varying types of information. Options investors will do well to select stocks for long-term investing based on a thorough examination of the fundamentals, and then use technical indicators to time short-term option positions.

2. *Forgetting your risk tolerance limits.* More than anything else, investors need to continually examine and reexamine their own limitations. *Risk tolerance* means just that: the amount of risk you can afford to take and are willing to take. If you cannot afford to lose, then you should not expose yourself to a high risk of loss. Options investors should avoid placing an entire portfolio at risk by buying options, hoping for quick profits. For the majority of investors, this would be a foolish decision. As a long-term investor, you also need to remember that your risk tolerance level is going to change over time. As your income increases, family status changes, and investment knowledge expands, your risk tolerance will grow as well. A more valuable portfolio requires greater diversification and protection against a single form of loss. And just as a growing family needs life, health, and homeowners insurance, an expanded portfolio can also be protected through the thoughtful use of options and other forms of diversification.

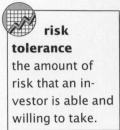

risk tolerance
the amount of risk that an investor is able and willing to take.

3. *Trying to make up for past losses with aggressive market decisions.* No one is happy about losing capital. Losses can happen very suddenly, or they can accumulate over time, eroding your portfolio value. In either case, losses are troubling not only because of the monetary loss, but also because they represent ill-timed decisions. Some investors try to make up for big losses by taking unacceptable risks. This form of desperate market strategy is not a good idea. It transforms you from investor to gambler and, while you might beat the odds and recapture lost capital, it is more likely that aggressive decisions will lead only to higher losses. When you lose capital in your investment portfolio, keep a cool head, reevaluate your position, and go forward from there. Remember, options can be used not only to augment profits in your portfolio, but also to help you recover from unexpected losses. Seek smart strategies employing options to offset portfolio losses. If your original plan was sensible, stay with it, recognizing that cyclical change means well-selected stocks will eventually recover.

4. *Investing on the basis of rumor or questionable advice.* The Internet chat room is not a good place to get market information. You have no idea who is online, nor what their experience or knowledge levels are and, realistically, those with good information are *not* likely to go online to share it with strangers. By the same argument, unsolicited phone calls, pop-up advertisements, or mail solicitations for investment solutions, promising fast and easy profits, are not going to make anyone rich. Advice from friends, relatives, co-workers, or people you talk to on the bus or train, should be discarded. By the time you understand options well enough to incorporate an option strategy into your portfolio, you should also realize that rumors and advice from strangers should be discounted and largely ignored.

5. *Trusting the wrong people with your money.* Market insiders often provide valuable advice to their clients. However, it has also become clear in recent years that the majority of analysts have not performed well. As a group, analysts' advice has led to net losses for their clients. Those analysts working in firms that also provide investment banking services live with an inherent conflict of interest. This conflict cannot be removed simply by changing the titles of buy, hold, or sell recommendations, nor by separating research and investment banking functions within the company. The pressure from the investment banking side to move shares of stock to the market compromises the advice. Options investors do not need the help of an analyst to devise strategies and, for the most part, will do better making their own decisions regarding both stock and option strategies. It makes more sense to subscribe to a service such as Value Line or Standard and Poors than to trust an advisor—especially given the track record of the industry as a whole.

6. *Adopting beliefs that simply are not true about the markets.* The market thrives on beliefs that, although strongly held, are simply not true. For example, history demonstrates over and over that the majority is wrong more often than it is right; so the obvious solution is to make decisions opposite from the majority. The strategy employed by the contrarian is popular because it works. Widespread beliefs are difficult to overcome. For example, the vast majority of investors avoid any discussion of options because they believe them to be high risk. Exposure to a basic covered call strategy disproves this belief, yet it persists. The majority also faithfully follow the Dow Jones Industrial Averages, even though the method used to weight the index gives a lot of influence to a few corporations. Few question the periodic re-placement of one stock with another, and the reasons are not publicized. However, The Dow has become syn-onymous with the market to such an extent that it is ac-cepted without question.

7. *Becoming inflexible even when conditions have changed.* Some investors find a method that works for them; they stick with it, even when conditions have changed and the strategies are no longer working. The stock market is changing constantly. New regulations, new investment products and derivatives, and the Inter-net, all change the way the market works. Strategies should be reviewed continually and, when they become outdated, they should be replaced. When a particular se-ries of options become a particularly profitable source for call writing, it makes sense to go with that program. How-ever, the situation is likely to change as the underlying stock's character changes. In this situation, it would not make sense to continue a program based on the original conditions, when those conditions have changed. In-vestors need to maintain their flexibility, recognizing that markets are in a continual state of change.

8. *Taking profits at the wrong time.* The temptation to take profits when available is a strong one. However, the timing of profit taking should depend more on your over-all strategy than on a momentary opportunity. If you buy stock as a long-term investment, taking profits presents two problems. First, you then need to decide where to reinvest the funds, and it is likely that many other stocks will have run up in value if the profit-taking opportunity is market wide. Second, your overall portfolio will suffer. If you always take profits when available, you will end up with a portfolio full of stocks whose current market value is lower than their original cost. When you remove prof-itable investment and leave the losses, you program your portfolio to perform below market levels. It makes more sense to balance your decisions to sell. If you determine to remove a profitable stock, sell off a losing one as well. That frees up capital and helps offset a capital gain with a capital loss. You can also use options to protect paper profits or even to enhance the profitable position, without needing to sell off shares that continue to hold out long-term growth value.

9. *Selling low and buying high.* The old advice Buy low and sell high is easily given but harder to follow. It is all too easy to make investment decisions on the basis of panic (at the bottom) or greed (at the top). A worthwhile piece of market wisdom states that Bulls and bears often are overruled by chickens and pigs. Unfortunately, this means that many investors buy and sell at the wrong time. As prices approach a market top, more buyers enter the market; and as prices bottom out, many sell at a loss. Repeating this pattern over and over, their timing makes no sense. So long-term investors will be better off buying shares on sound research, holding those shares, and monitoring conditions. If you want to keep your long-term investments and still play market movements, options are the best way to go. Covered call strategies can maximize changing market conditions, adding to profits with little risk, and without your having to sell valuable shares.

10. *Following the trend instead of thinking independently.* Finally, it is worth remembering that crowd mentality is most likely to be wrong. This is true because crowds really don't think; they react. So mistakes are likely to occur when individuals give way to the less dependable ideas of the crowd. Admittedly, when the market is depressed, it is very difficult to commit capital and buy low-priced shares. Not knowing whether prices will continue to fall, it is far easier to agree with the crowd and stay away. By the same argument, it is difficult to resist the temptation to buy when prices have run up to all-time high levels. But the higher the run-up, the greater the risk. As an options investor, you are likely to succeed by resisting the crowd mentality, staying with your long-term program, and using options to ride out market trends—without making ill-timed decisions in your long-term portfolio.

MODIFYING YOUR RISK TOLERANCE

Your ability and willingness to be exposed to risk is a matter of degrees. Your risk tolerance is defined by capital resources and income, investing experience, family status, condition of the market, and personal attitude. It is ever-changing because as your own circumstances evolve, all of these other areas evolve as well.

> **Smart Investor Tip** Risk tolerance is an ever-
> changing matter, reflecting your attitude at the
> moment. It will be different next year and the year
> after, so you need to review risk tolerance constantly.

Capital resources and income define your ability to undertake certain risks. If you have a large amount of capital to invest, you will be more willing to consider a wider array of possible investments than if your assets are more limited. Of course, that also means that you will be likely to not be aware of the risks associated with some deci sions. Having a large amount of capital available might contain an inherent risk of its own in that regard; so if you inherit a large sum of money, sell your home, or take other actions that bring you a large nest egg to invest, you also need to still pay attention to risk. The same arguments apply to income levels. An individual with a comfortable level of income will be more inclined to diversify in terms of investment products *and* risks. As a strategy, it makes sense to vary the risk levels of your portfolio as long as it is part of a plan. The danger arises when risks come about unexpectedly.

Investing experience has a lot to do with the risks you take on and with the manner in which you evolve as an investor. As you become familiar with options, for example, you will be willing to try advanced strategies, use options in different ways within your portfolio, and diversify risks with option positions. Experience has another side; those who have lost money in the market learn about risk the expensive way. Many people walk away from the market permanently, which is a risk decision. They decide that the market is simply not a safe investing environment. In fact, it can be if investors learn how to mitigate specific risks. Anyone who invested all of their 1997 assets in Yahoo! or all of their 2001 assets in Enron or WorldCom understands the problem: lack of diversification and lack of fundamental analysis. The fate of the dot.com industry or companies whose accounting was misstated does not define the entire market. Experience teaches us that there are many ways to protect capital, and the use of options is one of those ways.

Family status has a lot to do with the types of investments you choose. If you are a young single person making good money, you will be inclined to take greater risks; if you are married, buying a home, and raising young children, you will of necessity have to think about security, college education expenses, and retirement savings. Major events, like marriage, birth of a child, divorce, losing a job or starting a new one, relocating, health problems, or the death of a loved one, will have an understandable major impact on how you invest, because such events change your risk tolerance profile. And of course, these are not absolute profiles; there are many degrees in between. This is why options present a flexible method for mitigating risks, enhancing profits, or pure speculation. All of these uses could be elements within your portfolio to one degree or another, depending on today's and tomorrow's family status.

Condition of the market will also change your risk tolerance. When the market is going through a broad-based bull period, it is relatively easy to feel confident and to make money in the market. As a result, there is a tendency for investors to lower their concern about loss. In these conditions, it makes sense to buy and hold securities as long as the good times last; but at the same time, be aware of risks. Markets can turn around quickly and you can use options to protect your portfolio. This is especially valuable in the very common situation where you own shares that have grown in value, which you would like to continue holding, but when you also are concerned about the possibility of loss. Options can be bought to provide temporary insurance, so that your paper profits will be protected. When markets are depressed, investors are naturally more fearful and aware of the risk of loss. Many who held onto shares during a downturn will be concerned about their prospects. Will value ever rise again? Would it be best to sell now and cut losses? It is normal to have a keener sense of risk at such times, but it is worth remembering that market cycles have their own timing and cannot be predicted accurately. As long as companies were selected carefully and continue to represent sound long-term investments, it is wise to hold on through the downturns. Here again, options can be used to protect against further price declines—so that you do not have to sell at the market bottom—or to maximize profits when the situation does turn around—so that you are able to take advantage of cycles without putting more capital at risk by buying low-priced shares. Purchasing calls when prices are low is an alternative strategy.

> **Smart Investor Tip** Even recognizing the fact that markets change continually, some investors make the mistake of fixing their definition of risk, and never changing. As a consequence, their profile is perpetually outdated.

Personal attitude will have more to do than anything else with the definition of risk tolerance. Some investors are ultraconservative and prefer to leave the majority of their portfolios in low-yielding insured money market accounts. Others can tolerate high risk and seek the highest possible returns and will speculate in long shot investments. Most people are somewhere in between. Diversification may call for leaving a portion of your portfolio in conservative accounts and reserving another portion for speculation; but the majority is likely to be invested in well-managed companies whose stock has been fairly stable over time, and has the potential for solid long-term growth. Attitude is affected by experience, family status, and available capital, of course; but even beyond those other factors, the attitude of each investor tends to dictate the general approach to investing and to risk.

SOME MARKET REALITIES

Risk tolerance is going to grow and change with experience; however, you also need to be sure that you have a realistic expectation about the market itself. Unfortunately, many misconceptions persist about investing and the markets. Some investors make their decisions based on these misconceptions, and as a result, they make mistakes.

The biggest misconception for investors is the belief that you can trust Wall Street brokerage firms. Between 2000 and 2001, these firms offered hundreds of buy recommendations and almost no sell recommendations. Their emphasis on companies like Priceline.com, Amazon.com, Enron, and WorldCom cost trusting investors $5.2 trillion in just over one year.[1]

Beyond the losses in individual stocks, the troubling corporate scandals that developed throughout the 1990s and came to light in 2002 reveal that accounting misstatements and manipulation were commonplace among listed companies; that independent auditing firms knew of the problems and did nothing to stop them; and that a complacent and passive regulatory environment allowed the problems to go forward without penalty. In addition to creative interpretations of reporting rules, many companies simply falsified their records, reporting nonexistent sales, capitalizing expenses, and acquiring smaller companies only to create artificial and inflated operating results. The big myth is that investors can trust those whose job is to report, audit, and report on companies. Wall Street analysts were in a position to know, and they did not do their jobs. There is no reason to expect that they will willingly fix their conflict of interest problems in the future. The truth is, investors are on their own and no one is going to help safeguard their capital. The regulatory structure is designed to provide protection; but until the SEC and other agencies start doing their jobs, you should not trust others to give you good advice. You are better off investigating companies on your own.

The widespread corporate deceptions of recent years demonstrate an important risk not previously discussed in investing literature: the risk that you might not get accurate accounting information from companies whose stock you buy. If earnings are falsified or exaggerated, then all other indicators—P/E ratio, earnings per share, and so on—are unreliable as well. For this reason, you need to

---

[1]Martin D. Weiss, *The Ultimate Safe Money Guide*, John Wiley & Sons, 2002, p. 3.

perform the standard balance sheet ratio tests and look for unexplained distortions. When you find ratios out of line with acceptable limits and recent trends, that could be a sign that you are getting a false picture.

Smart Investor Tip You need to perform your own basic tests on financial reports. One lesson we all have to learn from recent events is that corporate reports cannot be taken at face value. They have to be verified.

Equally troubling is the practice among brokers of artificially inflating stock prices. This is achieved by investment bankers getting institutional buyers to commit to buying shares of a specific issue at a fixed price. This has the effect of running the market price up far beyond its reasonable level. Then, individuals and smaller institutions get in at the top and the whole thing collapses. This is outright stock fraud, but in the past this form of "pump and dump" was common for new issues and went unpunished. Many of those companies hyped by brokers later went out of business. For example, more than 500 Internet companies have gone bankrupt since the beginning of 2000. On average, more than 35,000 companies file for bankruptcy each year.[2] Thus, even companies whose stock has little or no value can be promoted by unscrupulous brokers, with investors ultimately losing everything.

The problems we have all discovered about the flaws of corporate management, boards of directors, auditing firms, analysts, and regulatory agencies all come down to one overall problem: These groups have not done their jobs. That is disturbing and reform can go a long way toward fixing some of the problems. This process has begun already: Congress has significantly increased the SEC's investigative budget, new laws curtail conflicts among auditing firms, and new stock exchange rules limit CEO

[2]American Bankruptcy Institute, *www.abiworld.org.*

access and contact with outside auditing firms. Most significantly, CEOs and CFOs are now required to personally certify their reported financial results. The discovery of false information could lead to a loss of incentive compensation, a ban on serving in their capacity for any corporation, and even criminal fines or jail. Corporations now face the challenge of transparency in reporting. This has two primary aspects. First, their reports to stockholders must disclose everything, including alternative reporting methods and the effect those alternatives would have had on reported earnings. Second, corporations need to explain their financial results so that everyone can understand what they mean. This is not a difficult task, given the army of accountants and public relations staff big companies have on hand; it's just that in the past corporations have not always wanted to explain everything to their stockholders. So change is underway, and future reporting will disclose more than ever before.

The problems assigned to corporations and deceptive reporting practices are only half of the problem. The other half involves self-education. Far too many investors choose to believe a lot of Wall Street lies, and are too quick to accept those lies as truths. The market is a myth-laden community, and far too many people constantly seek out insider secrets to quick and easy wealth. Of course, there are no quick and easy answers and, in spite of what analysts claim, no one can foretell the future.

One of the big lies, for example, is the claim that a crash like the big one in 1929 is unlikely to ever take place again, because new laws and exchange rules would prevent those problems from recurring. However, between 1999 and 2002, an ever bigger crash did occur. There really is no protection for investors buying stocks that have been hyped up and that later crash. If you were unlucky enough to buy into tech stocks at their peak, you have probably lost most of your money already.[3]

A closely related form of deception in the market is the claim that you are better off placing your money into well-managed mutual funds. The claims of impressive

---

[3]Martin D. Weiss, *Op. Cit.*, p. 30, citing NASDAQ losses of 68.4 percent from the exchange's peak.

long-term returns on invested capital reflect compound returns from reinvested dividends and capital gains, and cloak dismal performance by a majority of funds. Only about one in four mutual funds performed better than the S&P 500 in recent years.[4] Without exception, every tech stock lost money in the big tech decline. Three-quarters of those funds lost more than the NASDAQ Composite Index.[5]

THE NATURE OF MARKET VOLATILITY

As a measurement of relative risk, volatility is a valuable indicator. It often is used to describe markets in the broad sense; however, for selection of stocks and options, it can and should be applied to individual issues. (Overall market volatility is useful to identify index option investing opportunities by the same argument.) This does not mean that overall volatility trends should be ignored; however, because options are specific to a single stock, the study of volatility can be used to measure risk, to identify market conditions, and to identify option opportunities.

Market volatility follows cyclical patterns just as prices do. However, volatility seems to be associated with degrees of price changes. When prices for specific stocks, sectors, or the overall market, rise rapidly, the tendency is that such run-ups are accompanied by increases in the interim price and shares traded volume. The violent movements associated with rapid price change define the type of rally. A short-term rally is likely to be characterized by a corresponding short-term volatility as well, meaning prices can range in both high and low directions within a single day or week. A longer-term rally—lasting several weeks, for example—will tend to be broader based. Market volatility will slow down as the rally slows, which is one way to identify the top of the market—not always, but often.

When volatility occurs on the downside, there tend to be fewer interim upward spikes. Some degree of opposite-

[4]*Ibid.*, p. 32.
[5]Weiss Ratings, Inc., www.weissratings.com.

movement volatility will be caused by those who are buying shares in the belief that the downturn is temporary.
However, as the downward trend continues, the offsetting
upticks will appear less frequently.

Of course, these are generalizations and are not to be
found in all rallies or declines. A study of past market
trading patterns reveals what has happened in the past,
but such patterns are far more difficult to detect as they
occur. This is so because while volatility tendencies are
predictable, the timing is not. So in one rally or decline,
identifiable volume markers might appear on a daily basis
and with predictable timing; in another, more erratic period, those markets could occur in spaces of several days
or weeks and without any discernible pattern. So being
aware of market volatility does not necessarily provide
you with a key to the timing of option decisions. In fact,
in the most volatile of markets, it is the uncertainty of the
timing of events that makes the market the most interesting, and the most dangerous.

Smart Investor Tip   Volatility demonstrates both
risk and opportunity. The very uncertainty associated
with big price swings provides options traders with
the best environment for profits—if properly
understood.

If we could identify clearly when markets top off or
bottom out, it would be easy to make money using stocks
and options. However, volatile markets by their nature
put out many false signals. To some who follow markets
closely, it is easy to begin to believe that the market is a
conscious entity that enjoys teasing its hapless investors,
telling them to buy when they should sell, or to sell when
they should hold. Of course, the market is not conscious
(although it often is cruel); investors who follow short-
term trends too closely tend to transfer their own trepida-
tion onto the market and assign it a consciousness. This is
misleading, and is a trap to be avoided.

Volatility is an expression of conflicting investor interests converging at the same moment. A high demand or a high supply resulting from higher than usual volume among investors has an immediate effect on prices of shares and, of course, on option premium as well. When time value is distorted during such periods, the corresponding advantage is immediate and will disappear rapidly. Distortions occur most often during highly volatile periods for a specific stock, but the offsetting reaction among options investors tends to correct the condition within the same trading day. So if you wish to take advantage of time value price distortions, you will need to track the market throughout the day. Because the change occurs quickly, you will need to close positions immediately when the reversal occurs.

> **Smart Investor Tip** Options traders who plan to take advantage of short-term price aberrations have to be prepared to track prices closely, and to act quickly. This demands a lot of time.

This strategy works as long as you are following the trend carefully. You have to be able to recognize and understand the distortion to make a proper decision. Thus, be sure that what looks like an advantage today could be a correcting adjustment from yesterday's momentary distortion. Be sure that your option-position decisions are made with an awareness of the full picture, not just a view in today's smaller window.

MARKET VOLATILITY RISK

Understanding the nature of volatility is important to options investors; but in a larger sense, it is equally important to be aware of the risks associated with market volatility. Everyone who uses options to accompany positions in stock should be aware of how volatility affects their equity position, and not just how it presents short-term profit opportunities in options.

This danger—market volatility risk—is especially important for those desiring to write covered calls. If you select stocks for long-term growth and concentrate on that as the primary means for finding investment candidates, you are taking a wise approach. However, if you pick stocks primarily based on the richness of option premium levels, it is a shortsighted decision, and one that may lead to losses. There is no sense in exchanging short-term option profits for losses in stock value. Remember, the richer option premiums are associated with more volatile stocks. The higher premium levels exist because the stock itself is higher risk.

Many covered call writers have fallen into this trap. It has been aggravated by stockbrokers and advisors as well. When you think about buying stock without considering the related options, you will tend to look at financial information, long-term competitive stance, the sector, management, dividend yield, and price history, among other indicators. However, when you are looking for covered call writing opportunities, it is tempting to buy 100 shares and sell an option at the same time—with the discounting effect (return from the option) the primary consideration. As long as you ignore other elements related to the risk of the particular stock, this is a mistake. The more volatile stock is, of course, far more likely to lose market value in a broader market decline, often to a greater degree than the market average.

Some stockbrokers market to their customers by calling with a proposal to buy shares and sell calls at the same time. They emphasize the various outcomes in terms of return, but without necessarily discussing the risks associated with the stock itself. The stockbroker will tend to identify opportunities with richer than average

Smart Investor Tip Beware the tempting rates of return available from buying stock and selling covered calls at the same time. Don't overlook the need to analyze the stock as a starting point, not as a subordinate point to the option's value.

premiums, just as investors themselves will tend to do. So the net result is making a recommendation to buy shares of an exceptionally volatile stock, discounting by a richer than average option premium.

To a degree, that discount does mitigate the market risk of placing capital into shares of stock. However, the larger question should be, Does the option discount the share price adequately to justify the higher risk? If the option profit serves only to equalize the market risk of the stock, are there more sensible alternatives? It makes more sense to purchase less volatile companies and wait out price movement; and then sell covered calls with striking prices well above your purchase price, thus ensuring higher profits even in the event of exercise. While this strategy is more conservative and may require more time to build profits, it also avoids the problems of market volatility.

The comparative analysis of market volatility emphasizes price. However, an equally important form of volatility involves the financial results of the company. A study of *fundamental volatility* is a valuable method for picking stocks wisely.

Investors like predictability. So they tend to take faith in companies whose sales increase gradually and predictably from one year to the next, and whose profits remain within an expected range. This preference has led to many problems, including pressure on companies to equalize earnings through accounting decisions. Some publicly listed companies report each year a gradual, but somewhat predictable increase in sales and profits, with dividend payments steady and regular. Investors like this a lot; they feel safe when their investments have such predictable outcomes, without a lot of disturbing and unpredictable volatility.

In the real world, however, sales and profits do not materialize consistently and steadily. Actual outcome is far more chaotic. How, then, do companies even out their results, and isn't that fraud? Unfortunately, the Generally Accepted Accounting Principles (*GAAP*) rules give corporations a lot of flexibility to interpret and report their numbers.

The GAAP guidelines exist in no one place, but are a series of published opinions, guidelines, and regulations

fundamental volatility
the tendency for a company's sales and profits to change from one period to the next, with more erratic change representing higher volatility.

GAAP
acronym for Generally Accepted Accounting Principles, the rules and standards for reporting financial results among companies and auditing firms.

developed by many groups, with the American Institute of Certified Public Accountants (AICPA) serving as a sort of clearinghouse for GAAP application. The Financial Accounting Standards Board (FASB) develops new guidelines and also serves as a clearinghouse for developing standards for the accounting profession.

Smart Investor Tip   Check the AICPA and FASB websites to learn more about these organizations and the role they play in developing GAAP standards: These are found at www.aicpa.org and www.fasb.org.

The GAAP rules are broad enough so that corporations can bank earnings one year and recognize them the next, so that the results are less volatile. This is called "cookie jar" accounting and, as long as the justification appears to make sense, it is allowed under GAAP. In fact, because earnings are being deferred, the bending of the rules is far more acceptable than the opposite, booking nonexistent revenues and hoping to absorb them in better sales periods of the future.

In the typical cookie jar entry, some of this year's earnings, along with corresponding costs, are deferred and set up in a liability account. These are not true liabilities, just credit-balance accounts. So the "deferred credit" is reversed the following year and recognized as income. This is only one of many techniques used to reduce fundamental volatility.

More troubling are entries that inflate current results to improve an otherwise dismal operating result. For example, current-year expenses may be capitalized and applied over several years, increasing the current year's profits. Depreciation can be spread out over a longer period than normal by making an election under Internal Revenue Code rules. Or reserves set up during acquisitions can be reversed to inflate current profits.

All of these types of entries *might* be allowed under GAAP; but whether accountants can justify questionable interpretations or not, the fact remains that these practices are deceptive. They give investors a distorted and inaccurate picture. As long as you make investment decisions based on inaccurate or unreliable information, you are being deceived. Even if, for the sake of argument, such practices are not illegal, it remains true that it is not right to misuse the complexities of GAAP to equalize results.

The distortions created by these practices can be found by studying balance sheet ratios, and also by comparing cash flow to earnings. Cash flow and earnings have a natural relationship and should approximate one another, given year-to-year variations like depreciation expense. However, when distortions appear, this means the company is manipulating results in some way. A comparison between Cash Flow from Operations (on a company's Statement of Cash Flows) and Net Income (on the Income Statement) may reveal quite a lot. If the company is reporting a net profit, but shows a negative cash flow, the difference has to be made up somewhere. Typically, you will see big increases in Accounts Receivable, and such discrepancies are warning signs. While cash flow and net profit will not be the same due to changes in other asset and liability accounts and noncash expenses, the differences should not be unexplained; and there should be a correlation that makes sense.

In the future, full disclosure might also mean higher fundamental volatility. While this might be unsettling, it is always better to see an accurate result than to settle for the short-term comfort you gain from low volatility, but with inaccurate reporting. For options investors, higher volatility could have a positive effect on premium levels. If you write covered calls, you will profit when time value is higher as a consequence of greater fundamental volatility.

Smart Investor Tip A new environment including more accurate, consistent reporting probably will also mean greater fundamental volatility. Ironically, the more honest financial statements could show higher than average volatility, so it may be important to change opinions about both volatility and risk.

INFORMATION RISK

In the new investing environment, options investors must deal with the problems associated with misinformation—whether coming from analysts, corporations, or auditing firms—as part of their analysis of stocks and option contracts. This is not a new risk, because the market has always had an abundance of misinformation; in fact, it appears to thrive on it. The difference, however, is that we have all discovered that misinformation and, in some cases, outright fraud, have come not from the rumor mill or the chat room, but often from the most trusted of sources. Related problems, those of passive law enforcement or lack of will to undertake any reform, have only made the situation worse.

Most experienced investors tolerate the rather silly rumors that everyone hears, ranging from rather innocent speculation about soon to be published new product announcements or earnings reports, to the downright bizarre: conspiracy theories, coming monetary collapses, and other catastrophic events. But the sources that should disturb everyone have been previously credible and trusted ones, including:

✔ *Corporate management*—America used to hold its corporate executive class in high esteem. They were handsomely paid in multimillion dollar incentive packages because they were talented, inspiring leaders who took losing concerns to all-time profits. The image of Lee Iacocca leading Chrysler from the brink of total failure to a profitable company is the model that every investor has believed in. We have discovered, however, that some corporate leaders have misled investors, employees, and boards of directors, enriching themselves by taking undeserved incentive pay while falsifying the financial results. This has happened with rubber stamp boards who often shared in the wealth. Some executives were less imaginative, and simply stole corporate funds. We have learned that corporate executives cannot always be trusted. The majority probably are honest, ethical people, but it makes sense to keep an eye on them anyhow, because it is difficult for the average investor to tell the good guys from the bad guys.

✔ *Boards of directors*—Investors also have a less than accurate image of a corporation's board of directors. In the recent past, boards did little or nothing to curb practices by CEOs and CFOs, often gaining for themselves at the expense of the investor. Boards were the ultimate good old boys club with no real enforcement action. Even when the board's audit committees tried to bring problems to the attention of boards, no action was taken in some of the worst cases. Fortunately, new exchange rules require a majority of independent board members, and audit committees now have responsibility to hire and deal with independent auditors. Executive compensation will also be determined by a board's compensation committee rather than by merely appropriating outrageous and undeserved payments without independent oversight.

✔ *Auditing firms*—The demise of Arthur Andersen took most Wall Street insiders by surprise. The extent of conflict of interest by the Houston office of the big auditing firm involving Enron accounting reports, was not anticipated by anyone. However, the scope of problems led to quick and significant reform. Under provisions of the Sarbanes-Oxley Act of 2002, auditing firms are barred from providing most types of consulting services for their audit clients, an attempt to do away with an important area of conflict of interest. Investors have always placed supreme confidence in the independence of professional audits, and in the certification of financial statements as being fair, accurate, and complete. The discovery that this assumption was not well-founded has been troubling, to say the least and has led to dozens of investor lawsuits, many of which were quickly settled by auditing firms.

✔ *Analysts*—Among the many culprits in the Wall Street community, analysts have been the worst. They have abused their influence for years, elevated themselves to esteemed positions of power among investors, and lied to their clients to enrich themselves. Even knowing that many companies were of the lowest quality, practically all recommendations were to buy shares; the only alternative seemed to be "hold" and rarely did a "sell" recommendation go out. Analysts working for big firms that also offer investment banking services have an unavoidable conflict of interest. However, even in the light of multimillion dollar penalties and widespread negative publicity, the big firms still don't get it. They believe the solution to the problem is to separate investment banking and research services, or to change the titles of recommendations that they make. Moving departments to another floor does not remove the conflict of interest; and redefining buy, hold, or sell with different names or recommendation ranges are halfhearted efforts at best. What is really needed is a change of the core attitude among analysts and their corporate leadership. It is insulting to think that investors will be placated by changed titles of recommendations alone, a sign that the insiders think investors are stupid and will accept the appearance of reform in place of real change. It may require many more millions of dollars in penalties to get the idea across that the functions of investment banking and research cannot coexist in the same organization.

✔ *The SEC*—When the scandals came to light in 2001 and 2002, the newly appointed head of the SEC was Harvey Pitt. He took the brunt of criticism for lax enforcement and a passive approach to the serious problems of accounting misrepresentation, in some degree unfairly. Pitt was certainly a Wall Street insider, whose private practice clients had included all of the big accounting firms and such notorious figures as Ivan Boesky. Pitt believed that a lot of reform should happen within industries, and was not an advocate of legal reforms. This was his downfall. However, in fairness to Pitt, it should be remembered that the accounting irregularities uncovered in 2001 and 2002 usually went back at least five years. Previous SEC enforcement had failed to turn up any problems. And even though auditing firms often found out about those problems, change was not undertaken within companies. With little or no prospect of being caught or punished, the wrongdoing accelerated without stop. The failure of the past SEC to uncover or correct those problems was made worse by an outdated and inadequate enforcement budget. Although the SEC failed to prevent the problems by finding out about them in Pitt's tenure or even in the many years before, investors may see a more aggressive stance on the part of federal regulators now that the agency's enforcement budget has been boosted.

Clearly, the problems uncovered in the corporate scandals of 2001 and 2002 were the culmination of years of passive enforcement, widespread wrongdoing, and the failure in many sectors to perform jobs, provide oversight investors believed was being provided, or put a stop to glaringly obvious abuses among executives, boards of directors, auditing firms, analysts, and regulatory agencies. Investing today and in the future may actually be safer than in recent years. Seeing previously powerful executives taken away in handcuffs must have a chilling effect on other executives. Having to pay a $500 million fine for deceiving investors may have an equally chilling effect on Wall Street brokerage firms. And seeing a prestigious auditing firm cease to exist in a few months will certainly cause the remaining Big Four—Deloitte & Touche, PricewaterhouseCoopers, KPMG, and Ernst & Young—to reexamine their own practices. Hopefully, prosecution of individual analysts will also lead to some real reforms.

None of these changes can recapture the lost capital for investors. However, reforms and a newly aware market community could lead to some intrinsic and needed changes. These changes may create a safer investing environment. Change creates fear and uncertainty, and the market is changing significantly. However, there remain many opportunities in stocks, and investors can also protect themselves by using options to avoid losses in stock positions. The uncertainty itself can lead to specific opportunities for options traders.

OPTIONS IN THE VOLATILE ENVIRONMENT

The more uncertain a trading environment, the greater the fear among investors. As corporate scandals came to light one after another in 2002, market values fell. Who would want to invest capital in that environment? It was especially disturbing to see many large, well-respected companies in the news and under suspicion. In one form or another, many well-established companies received negative publicity. Well-known names, like Xerox and General Electric, were among those firms criticized for some form of accounting irregularity, excessive executive compensation, or regulatory investigation.

One solution involving options should be considered

by anyone interested in long-term equity, but still fearful about the timing of investment decisions. The dilemma in a volatile market is well known. When prices are very low, people are fearful about placing capital at risk, especially if they have already lost money in the market. At the same time, we all know that such moments are buying opportunities.

The Long-term Equity AnticiPation Securities (*LEAPS*) is a long-term option that can be used in volatile markets to solve this problem. A LEAPS has a life up to three years, so, unlike the relatively short-lived equity option, a LEAPS can be used as a form of contingent purchase of shares of stock. The LEAPS works just like the shorter-term equity option in every respect but, because of its longer life, it can present an alternative to outright stock purchase.

The long-term option—because of its extended life—can be employed for some strategies that are not practical with shorter-expiration contracts. LEAPS can be used as an alternative to buying stock and placing large sums of capital at risk. This could change the way that you invest in volatile market conditions.

 LEAPS

Long-term Equity AnticiPation Securities, long-term option contracts that work just like standardized options, but with expiration up to three years.

Example: You have approximately $10,000 to invest. You have been following five stocks that you believe will increase in value over the next two to three years; but you cannot buy 100 shares of all of these with your limited capital. And because the market has been very volatile lately, you are not even sure that the timing is right for committing money right now. You don't want to miss an opportunity, and you remain uncertain about short-term volatility.

In the circumstances just described, there are three problems: (1) limited capital, (2) uncertainty about short-term price volatility, and (3) the desire to profit from longer-term change. Everyone faces these conditions from time to time; many face them continually. LEAPS options address all three concerns. With a $10,000 capital base as described, it might be possible to buy calls for all five of the stocks. As long as options are picked out of the money, the premium cost will be lower than it would be for an in-the-money option on the same 100 shares. This diversifies the $10,000 capital into five different 100-share lots; but because these are options and not shares, the risk of loss is limited.

> **Smart Investor Tip** The LEAPS option removes the most inhibiting factor of the options market, the short-term nature of contracts and ever-looming expiration. A three-year lifespan is an eternity in the options market.

Is it prudent to buy calls, given the risks of long positions as a general rule? It could make sense more so than buying shorter-expiring standardized calls, which will expire in a few months. Remember, a LEAPS contract has a life up to three years, and a lot can happen in that time. If you believe that stocks will rise in value during those months, then buying long-term options represents a smart strategic choice. If the market value does not rise, you lose the option premium. However, since you will be spreading a limited amount of capital among options on several different stocks, you stand a good chance of profiting overall as long as the market direction is upward during the lifetime of the LEAPS.

There are three possible outcomes in this strategy:

1. The LEAPS expires worthless. If the stock fails to rise above the LEAPS striking price, the strategy produces a loss.

2. The LEAPS increases in value and you close it at a profit. You might decide later on that you would rather take the option profit when available, and give up the opportunity to buy shares later.

3. The stock value rises and you exercise the LEAPS option, purchasing shares at the fixed striking price. This is the strategy to aim for; LEAPS are used to own the right to buy 100 shares at a fixed price, with the idea that you will want to make the purchase as long as fundamental conditions do not change.

Of course, LEAPS can be used in all of the ways that short-term options can be used. LEAPS calls can be bought to insure against losses in short stock positions; and LEAPS puts can be used to insure against losses in long stock positions. You can also sell LEAPS, either naked or covered. The covered call strategy will produce far higher premium income because of higher time value. Of course, in exchange, you also will be required to keep your stock tied up to cover the short option for a longer period of time. The typical time value pattern for LEAPS is that it remains fairly stable and then rapidly falls off during the last three months. Thus, covered call writing on very long-term periods should be analyzed and compared with shorter-term alternatives.

Smart Investor Tip The risk-reward question for LEAPS covered call writers has to be adjusted. The question of time is one aspect only, and the other aspect—exposure to exercise—is much longer term than for standard short-term options.

You also can sell LEAPS calls or standard calls against longer-term LEAPS long positions. For example, if you have bought a LEAPS call expiring in 30 months, you can sell a call against that position expiring in 3 months. This often is referred to as a "covered call" position or writing short-term calls against the LEAPS. However, because both positions are options, this is actually a spread. (For more on option spreads, see Chapter 9.)

The potential uses of LEAPS beyond expected purchase (or sale) of shares in the future, can become quite interesting. When you combine the longer expiration of LEAPS options with the features of shorter-term expirations, some of the typical trading techniques become more advantageous, especially on the short side. Remember, time works for the seller and against the buyer. As a seller of a LEAPS option, you are going to have more time value to work with, and a longer time until expiration. As a buyer of a LEAPS option, you still work against time;

but because expiration is so far out, the potential for profit—or at least the uncertainty of what will happen—makes buying options far more feasible.

The same arguments favoring buying calls in anticipation of an upward-moving market, apply just as well when you expect market values to fall. You can buy LEAPS puts when you have seen a big run-up in value and you anticipate a reversal. This strategy makes sense whether you own stock or not.

When you own shares and the market value has risen substantially, you face a dilemma. Do you take your profits now, while you can and risk missing out on even more appreciation? Or do you wait, risking losses when prices fall? You may continue to think of the company as a sound long-term investment, so you don't want to sell; but you are worried about short-term corrections to market price. If you buy a LEAPS put in this situation, the downward price movement in the stock will be matched point-for-point by increasing value in the in-the-money LEAPS put.

When you don't own shares and market value has run up, buying a put is a speculative move. You anticipate a correction; when prices fall, you will experience a corresponding increase in value of the LEAPS put. Without taking a short position or selling calls—both high-risk strategies—you can profit if you are right when stock market prices fall, by owning the put. And because expiration is further out, you have as much as three years to be proven right.

> **Smart Investor Tip** Using LEAPS to time market swings or insure other positions is more practical than with short-term options. The longer time until expiration provides better value, enabling you to protect paper profits more economically.

The advantage of longer expiration overcomes the option buyer's ongoing struggle with time, at least to a degree. You will pay more for time value but you have more

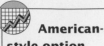 **American-style option**
an option that can be exercised at any time before expiration. All equity options and some index options are American-style.

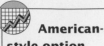 **European-style option**
an option than can be exercised only during a specified period of time immediately preceding expiration. Some index options are European-style.

time; in so many instances, options buyers are right about prospects for price movement, but time runs out for the option before that movement occurs. In a volatile market, your chances of profiting with LEAPS calls and puts are greater because expiration is not immediate.

In addition to trading in LEAPS on individual stocks, you can also buy or sell index LEAPS. These are somewhat more complex because the relationship between striking price and index value is not the same as for individual stocks. In addition, index LEAPS may be exercised in one of two ways. *American-style options* can be exercised at any time prior to expiration. All short-term options and LEAPS in stocks are exercised as American-style options. However, some index options are *European-style*, which means that exercise is allowed only during a shorter period of time immediately before expiration.

Selling Puts

A wise man turns chance into good fortune.
> —Thomas Fuller, *Gnomologia*, 1732

Options traders are well aware of the special risks involved in selling calls. The underlying stock could rise indefinitely, so that in theory, risk is un-limited when the call is not covered; even those writing covered calls face the risk of lost future profits because striking prices lock in the option seller to a fixed price in the event of exercise.

The situation is completely different when you sell puts. Recalling that a put is the opposite of a call, a put seller hopes that the value of the underlying stock will rise. As the stock rises, the value of the put falls, creating a profit for the put seller. The seller also faces the risk that the stock's market value will fall. In that case, the seller will experience a loss. However, this loss is finite. The greatest loss possible, in theory, is zero. However, for practical reasons, a stock is unlikely to fall that far. A well-selected company's stock will have a limited likely range of market price; for example, while market value could fall below a company's book value per share, it does not stand to reason that market price would decline far below that level.

Even a drastic decline in a stock's market value has limited consequences for the put seller. It could be defined as the difference between striking price and book value as the "lowest likely" price level. This is no guarantee, as the market has shown time and again that price levels are relatively oblivious to the intrinsic value of stock. In other words, the fundamentals serve as a valuable means for evaluating a company's long-term growth potential, but short-term price changes are unreliable; the fundamentals mean little in terms of pricing over the next few months. Short-term indicators are recognized as unstable for any purpose of analysis, by proponents of the Dow Theory as well as the random walk hypothesis. The market can be viewed as having reliable intermediate and long-term trends showing up through indicators; but whose short-term trends are highly chaotic and unreliable.

Tangible book value per share—book value minus all intangible assets such as goodwill—is a fundamental support level for the valuation of stock. It is today's value in terms of financial worth, without considering any prospects for future growth. A popular expression today, "value investing," means just that. Investors should buy a company's value, not a stock's price. So when analysts publish a target range for a stock, it makes sense to question (1) how the target range was arrived at, (2) whether price targeting is based on fundamentals, and (3) how price equates to the company's long-term investment value.

The primary question a value investor asks is, "What could this company be sold for today, if it were on the market?" Another might be, "If I owned this company, how much would I expect the value per share to be?" Upon analysis, you may arrive at a reasonable value for a company; by comparing this to the market value of the stock, you can gain a sense of whether it is undervalued or overvalued.

With these ideas in mind, it is easier to evaluate a stock by comparing current market price per share to the value of the company. However, while this is a valid form of analysis for long-term purchase of shares, it may not be a good indicator for selling short-term puts. A stock's value could fall below book value per share. For example, if the market perception is that a company will not be able to maintain its position in the market sector, or that current problems will spell disaster for sales and profits, or other significant defects in products and services spell problems in the future, then current price could reflect a dire outlook. The consequence could be that market price plummets well below book value per share, at least temporarily. For the put seller, a temporary drop in price could present a problem; at such a time, exercise is possible and, for puts deep in the money, automatic.

By and large, a put seller takes a reasonable position in assuming that book value per share is a fair support level, and it is unlikely that the stock's price will fall below that level. So a stock selling at $50 per share with book value of $20 per share could be assessed at having a maximum risk range of 30 points.

A put is an option to *sell* 100 shares of the underlying stock, at a fixed price by a specific date in the near future. So when you sell a put, you grant the buyer the right to "put" 100 shares of stock to you at the striking price, or to sell you 100 shares. In exchange for receiving a premium at the time of your opening sale transaction, you assume the risk of exercise. You are willing, then, to buy 100 shares of the underlying stock even though at the time of exercise, current value of the shares will be lower than the fixed striking price.

Smart Investor Tip   It makes sense to sell puts as long as you believe that the striking price is a fair value for that company's stock.

As a put seller, you reduce your exposure to risk by selecting stocks within a limited price range. For example, if you sell puts with striking prices of 50 or less, your maximum loss is 50 points, or $5,000; that, of course, would occur only if a stock were to become worthless by expiration date. If you sell puts with striking price of 25 or lower, that cuts the maximum exposure in half, to $2,500 per contract. However, the more realistic way to assess maximum risk is to identify book value per share in comparison to striking price. That gap represents a more likely range of risk.

EVALUATING STOCK VALUES

If you consider the striking price to be fair and reasonable for 100 shares of the underlying stock, selling puts has two advantages:

1. You receive cash at the point that you sell a put.
2. The premium discounts the price of the stock in the event of exercise.

If you are willing to purchase shares of stock at the striking price, then selling puts is a smart strategy. In one regard, there is no actual risk because you think the price is reasonable. Of course, in the event of exercise, you would own 100 shares whose current market value would be lower than your purchase price, and that ties up capital.

Buying shares above market value may be acceptable if you plan to keep those shares as a long-term investment. Remember, however, that if the difference between striking price and current market value at the time of exercise, is greater than the amount you received in premium, you have a paper loss at the point of exercise. You will need to wait out the time required for the stock's price to rebound before you recapture that loss. It might be true that over the long term, that company represents a profitable investment. But put sellers would prefer to not experience exercise, so they use the same techniques to avoid it—rolling forward and rolling down, for example. Once you identify the degree of risk involved with exercise, you need to compare that to the premium income in order to determine whether placing yourself in a short position is worth that risk exposure. If you embark on a heavy program of put writing, you will need to have available adequate capital to purchase the shares of stock involved, an important factor that limits the degree of put writing you are likely to undertake. If you experience a high degree of exercise, you will use up your available capital and fill your portfolio with shares of stock acquired above current market value. So you should limit put writing to those stocks you would like to own, whether or not you write puts.

Example: You sold a put with a striking price of 55 and received 6 (discounting the net price per share to $49). You considered $49 per share a reasonable price for those shares. Before expiration, the stock's market value fell to $48 and your put was exercised.

Two observations need to be made concerning this transaction:

1. The outcome is acceptable as long as you believe that $49 per share is a fair price for the stock. You would then also believe that current market value—only one point lower than your basis—represents a temporary depression in market value, and that is likely to rebound in the future. If your assumption is correct, the loss is a paper loss only and it will turn out to be a worthwhile investment.

2. If the stock's market value had risen, you would have profited from selling the put. It would not have been exercised and would have expired worthless; or time value would have evaporated, enabling you to buy to close at a profit. In those outcomes, the put sale would have produced a profit. So selling puts in a rising market can produce profits for investors unable or unwilling to tie up capital to buy 100 shares, with limited risk exposure.

Put sellers who seek only the income from premiums need to select stocks that they consider to be good prospects for price increase. Fundamental and technical tests of a company and its stock can be applied to a degree against the market in general, but it makes more sense to apply such tests to individual issues, because you cannot depend on a stock to follow market trends. Premium value is only half the test of a viable put sale; the other half is careful selection of stocks. If risks are too great, then you cannot justify the strategy.

EVALUATING RISKS

Stock selection contains specific risks for call sellers. More attractive options premiums are associated with more volatile stocks. So covered call writers may be prone to selecting higher-risk stocks in order to sell higher-than-average time value.

The same risks apply to put sellers. You will find that higher time value premiums for puts are going to be found on stocks with higher-than-average volatility. The direction of price movement you desire is different with puts than with calls, but the risks in the underlying stock are the same. Put sellers face the risk that the underlying stock's market value will fall. The more drastic the fall, the greater the risk of exercise. However, a put seller's perception of risk has to be different than that of the call seller. The key to selecting puts should not be the size of the premium, but your willingness to buy the stock at the striking price in the event of exercise.

With this in mind, the evaluation of risk is different than for call selling. The put seller needs to apply those fundamental and technical tests to a stock in the same way as call sellers. The difference, however, is that while covered call writers own shares of the stock when they sell a call, the put writer can be willing to buy the stock only if exercise does occur. Because not every put will be exercised, put sellers enjoy greater leverage than call sellers. Your risk is limited to the degree of short position risk you can assume at one time and, of course, the risk exposure your brokerage firm will allow you to carry in your portfolio. You will need to be able to demonstrate that you have equity available to pay for shares in the event of exercise. A short position always carries a degree of risk and if the market trend turns downward, several puts could be exercised within a short period of time.

Given the possible outcome that exercise results in gaining shares at or slightly below current market value, why bother to sell puts at all? In the examples in the previous section, the net result of selling a put was acquisition of stock at $49 when market value was $48. Remember, however, that exercise is only one possible result. The put seller should be happy to acquire the stock for an adjusted basis of $49, given what analysis of the company reveals. A value analysis should indicate that $49 per share is a good bargain. At the same time, put sellers will also profit if the stock rises. As this occurs, puts lose value and will expire worthless, or can be closed at a profit. So rather than simply buying shares (placing more capital at risk) the put seller has a two-part strategy. If exercised, the net cost is considered a fair value, in spite of potentially lower current market value. And if the put falls in value as a result of rising market value in the stock, then the put sale is profitable. As a form of leverage, put selling produces profits from market movement without the requirement of investing in 100 shares of the stock.

PUT STRATEGIES

There are five popular strategies you may have in mind for selling puts: to produce short-term income, to make use of idle cash deposits in a brokerage account, to buy stocks, to cover short stock positions, or to create a tax put.

Strategy 1: Producing Income

The most popular reason for selling puts is also the most apparent: the purely speculative idea of earning short-term profits from put premiums. The ideal outcome would be a decline in put value from declining time and intrinsic value, enabling the put seller to purchase and close the position at a profit. Time is on your side when you sell, so the more time value in the total premium, the better your chances for profit. A corresponding higher risk will be associated with high time value.

Example: Last January, you sold a June 45 put for 4. At that time, the underlying stock's market value was $46 per share. Because market value was higher than the striking price, the entire premium was time value. (Remember that for puts, in-the-money is opposite that for calls.) If the stock's market value remained at or above $45 per share, the put would eventually expire worthless. If by the exercise date the stock is valued between $41 and $45 per share, you would earn a limited profit or break even in the event of exercise (before trading costs). The $41 per share level is four points below striking price, and you received $400 for selling the put.

A short position can be canceled at any time. As a

seller, you can close the position by buying the put at the current premium price. However, remember that an open put can also be exercised at any time by the buyer. So whenever you sell a put, you are exposed to exercise whenever that put is in the money (when the stock's market value is lower than striking price). For the premium you receive, you willingly expose yourself to this risk.

A smart put seller is always aware of the profit and loss zones in their positions, and they decide in advance at what point to close their positions and when to keep them open. This self-imposed goal is related to premium level, of course, the status of current market value in relation to striking price, and the degree of time value premium still in the premium value. If a profit becomes unlikely or, in the seller's opinion, impossible, it might be necessary to close the position and limit the loss.

Smart Investor Tip   Options traders recognize that they cannot be right all of the time. It often is wisest to accept a small loss rather than continue to be exposed to potentially greater losses.

An example of profit and loss zones for selling a put is shown in Figure 8.1. This is based on a striking price of 50 with put premium of 6. The premium creates a six-point limited profit zone between $44 and $50 per share. Below that, the put seller will have a loss. This visual range analysis helps you to define when and where you will close a position, based on proximity between a stock's current market value and loss zone.

Example: You sold a 50 put for 6. Your profit zone is any price above the striking price of 50. If the stock's market value falls below 50, the put will be in the money. As long as the price range remains between $44 and $50 per share, the loss upon exercise is limited because the premium you received discounts your potential basis in the stock in the event of exercise. If the stock's market

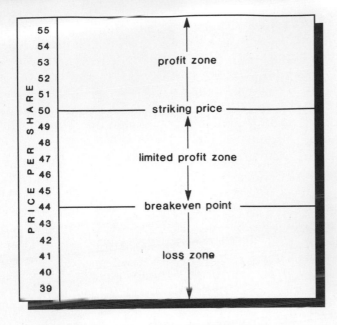

FIGURE 8.1 Put selling profit and loss zones.

value falls below $44 per share, you will experience a loss upon exercise.

It is possible for a stock's market value to fall below striking price by several points, and still enable you to close the put at a profit. This relies, of course, on time value decline. The analysis of profit and loss zones above is based on the worst-case assumption of where a stock's price will lie at the point of expiration. If the premium contains a good amount of time value, a put seller can profit merely by trading in the put, even when considerable price movement occurs. Of course, whenever it moves to an in-the-money range, you also risk exercise.

Conceivably, you could select stocks that will remain at or above the striking price and earn premium profits repeatedly, without ever experiencing exercise. However, foresight about which stocks will achieve such consistent price support is difficult. It takes only a single, temporary dip in price to be exposed to exercise, a risk that cannot be overlooked. Exercise is not necessarily a drastic step; but it does tie up your capital because it requires that you buy stock above current market value. While you wait for the stock's price to rebound, you might miss other market opportunities.

Remember the basic guideline for selling puts: You need to be willing to buy 100 shares of the underlying stock at the striking price, which you consider a fair price for that stock. If current market value is lower than the striking price, you should believe that the price is going to rebound, justifying the purchase you will be required to make upon exercise.

If you consider the price a fair one, that does not mean you would welcome exercise. It only means that you would not mind owning those shares. You might still want to avoid exercise whenever possible by rolling positions, remembering that exercise of many puts means you end up with an overpriced portfolio of stocks.

Example: You sold several puts in the past few months. This month the entire market fell several hundred points. Five of your puts were exercised at the same time, requiring you to purchase 500 shares of stock. All of your available capital now is tied up in these shares. Consequently, your portfolio's basis is higher than current market value for *all* of the shares you own. The market is recovering, but very slowly. Even considering your premium income, you are in a large paper loss position. You have no choice but to sit out the market and hope for a rebound in the future.

The net cost level for stock acquired through exercise of puts is the striking price, minus premiums you received when you sold the puts. Allowing for transaction fees paid (both when you sold the put and when you bought the shares), your basis will be higher still. You should not overlook the potential paper loss position you could experience in the event of a correction. The tendency in such times is for a broad-based drop in most stock prices, meaning you could have many exercised puts at the same time.

You reduce the risk somewhat by avoiding selling puts with the same expiration month, and spreading your put sales among different market sectors. Diversification takes many forms, for put sellers need to be aware of the strategic spreading of exposure to risk. Even if you believe that the striking price represents a reasonable price for shares, your point of view could change in the event of a large market correction.

Your brokerage firm will require cash or securities to satisfy margin requirements if you want to sell puts. Whenever you open a short position, the brokerage firm will want to ensure that it will not be stuck picking up losses because their clients do not have the resources. If you have numerous short positions open at the same time, the brokerage firm will want to be assured that in the event of exercise, you are able to honor your commitments and buy the shares assigned to you. If you are unable to honor your commitment, the brokerage firm is stuck with overpriced shares.

The brokerage firm is also aware that you cannot cover short puts as you can cover short calls. The call writer who owns 100 shares of stock faces no risk in the event of unexpected market rallies, because the shares can be delivered upon exercise. The put seller, however, cannot cover a potential exercise. So the put seller has to be able to demonstrate the financial ability to pay for shares upon exercise.

Example: You have $12,000 available to invest in the market today. Taking the traditional route, you could buy shares of stock up to $12,000 in market value. However, you may also decide to sell puts as an alternative. Your brokerage firm will decide how much your $12,000 deposit will allow you to write in puts—in other words, the brokerage firm will define how much risk you can expose yourself to for your $12,000 equity.

A brokerage firm might allow you to exceed your maximum point value (in the example above, $12,000 deposit is also called 120 points, so option premium can add up to that point value without risk to the brokerage firm). Your brokerage firm might allow you to exceed the 120-point level in written puts, in two circumstances. First, the put premium you earn upon sale may be deposited in your account and held as a reserve, increasing your maximum point level. Second, you might be allowed to exceed total point exposure on the condition that you would be required to finance exercise in excess of your reserves, through a margin account. In that outcome, you not only end up with a portfolio of overpriced stocks, but a portion of your purchase price would be accumulating interest.

The put seller needs to evaluate strategies differently from call sellers, because the risk position is entirely different. Call sellers will not always see exercise as a negative; in many circumstances, it is viewed as the most desired outcome. Profits can be built into the strategy. But when a put is exercised, stock will always be bought at a level above current market value, without exception. This outcome is advantageous only when the put premium exceeds the number of points between striking price and the stock's current market value; and this is a limited advantage only.

As a put seller, you can avoid exercise by using rolling techniques. Rolling forward buys time and might help avoid exercise, remembering that while exercise can occur at any time, it is most likely near expiration. Avoid increasing the number of puts in a rolling technique on a single issue, because that only increases your risk. Since rolling is most likely to occur in the money, it does not make sense to increase risks through rolling forward *and* picking up more short puts.

Example: You sold a put two months ago for 4. The stock's market price recently declined below striking price and you would like to avoid exercise. The put expires later this month, but you believe the stock's price will rebound. Premium level currently is 6. You close the position and replace it with two puts expiring in four months, each with a premium of 4. You receive $800 for opening the new puts, less the $600 you paid to purchase and close the original put.

A problem in this strategy is that it also increases your risk. You buy extra time and get an additional $200 in premium, but you end up with two puts instead of one. If both are exercised, you will be required to buy 200 shares above market value. An alternative is to roll forward the single put and replace it with another. In the example, you would purchase the first put at 6 and buy a later one at 4. That creates a cash outlay of $200. You originally received $400 when you sold the put; now you reduce that profit to $200 for the purchase of extra time. Another alternative to avoid exercise would be to buy the put and take a $200 loss. The decision depends on how much you want to avoid exercise; how willing you are to buy 100 shares at the striking price; how long you are willing to remain at risk; your basis in the stock discounted by premium received; and how much value you place on the current premium level.

Strategy 2: Using Idle Cash

When investors sell options, their brokerage firms require deposits of cash or securities for a portion of potential losses. With puts, the maximum risk is identified easily. It is equal to the striking price of the put.

Investors may hold their capital on the sidelines, believing that stocks they want to buy are overpriced and will be attractive buying opportunities in the future. The dilemma is that the longer cash is held in reserve, the more they miss opportunities to put that money to work. Idle cash does not earn money, and there is no way to know how long it will take for conditions to present themselves, making the desired move practical.

One way to deal with this problem is by selling puts on the targeted stock. In this way, capital is still kept in reserve, yet you earn money from put premiums *and* you discount the basis in the stock in the event of exercise. You will profit from selling the put if the stock's price rises; and you will end up buying shares at the striking price (less premium discount) if the stock's market value falls. In either event, the premium you receive will be yours to keep.

Example: You are interested in buying stock as a long-term investment. However, you believe that the current market price is too high, and that a correction is likely to occur in the near future. One possible solution: Sell one put for every 100 shares you want to buy, instead of buying the stock. Place your capital on deposit with the brokerage firm as security against your short position in the puts. If the current market value of the stock rises, your short puts will fall in value and can be closed at a profit or allowed to expire worthless. In this way, you benefit from rising market value without placing all of your capital at risk.

If market value of the stock declines, you will purchases the shares at the striking price. Your basis will be discounted by the value of premiums you received for selling the puts. As a long-term investor, you will be confident that the share price will grow over time, and the current paper loss will be partially offset by the premium.

Strategy 3: Buying Stock

The third reason for selling puts is to intentionally seek exercise. Selling a put discounts the basis in stock in the event of exercise, and using the strategy of looking for exercise, you will not be concerned with price drops in the stock.

Example: You have been tracking a stock for several months, and you have decided that you are willing to buy 100 shares at or below $40 per share. The current price is $45. You could wait for the stock to drop to your level, which might or might not happen. However, an alternative is to sell a November 45 put, which has a current premium value of 6. This is all time value. If the market value of stock rises, the put will become worthless and the $600 you received is yours to keep. You could then repeat the transaction on the same argument as before, at a higher price increment. If the stock's market value falls, the put will be exercised. Your basis would be $39—striking price of 45 less 6 points received in put premium—which is one dollar per share below your target purchase price.

In this example, the put was sold at the money and the premium—all time value—was high enough to create a net basis below your target price. Even if the stock's market value were to fall below $40 per share, your long-term plans would not be affected. You considered $40 per share a reasonable purchase level for the shares. Long-term investors are not concerned with short-term price changes. Simply waiting for the right price to come along means you expose yourself to the risk of losing the opportunity to get the stock at your price. Selling puts discounts current market value and makes it worthwhile to wait for exercise.

Example: You are interested in buying stock at $40 per share. Current market value is $45. You sell a put with a striking price of 45 and receive 6. Willing to take exercise, you reduced your potential basis to $39 per share by selling the put. However, instead of falling, the stock's market value rose 14 points.

In this scenario, the put will expire worthless and you keep the $600 as profit. But if you had bought shares instead of selling the put, you would have earned $1,400 in profit. However, once your put expires, you are free to sell another one, offsetting the lost opportunity and perhaps exceeding that potential profit. Remember, the lost $1,400 is easy to recognize after the fact; however, at the time of making the decision to sell a put, you have no way of knowing whether the price will rise or fall. If share price were too high, you could risk *losing* $1,400 just as easily as you miss the opportunity for profiting by the same degree. This is why selling puts sometimes presents an attractive alternative to buying shares outright.

You risk losing future profits in two ways as a put seller, so you need to be willing to assume these risks in exchange for the premium income:

✔ If the price of the underlying stock rises beyond the point value you received in premium, you lose the opportunity to realize profits in owning the stock. You settle for premium income only. However, when this occurs, your put expires worthless and you are free to sell another and receive additional premium.

✔ If the price of the underlying stock falls significantly, you are required to buy 100 shares at the striking price, which will be above current market value. It might take considerable time for the stock's market value to rebound to the striking price level. Meanwhile, your capital is tied up in stock you bought above current market value.

While the risks of put selling are far more limited than those associated with uncovered call selling, you can also miss opportunities for profits in the event of stock price movement in either direction.

Strategy 4: Writing a Covered Put on Short Stock

While covered puts are not the same as covered calls, there is a corresponding position. If you are short 100 shares of stock, you cover that position by selling one put. (Your put is also defined as covered as long as you have cash in your brokerage account adequate to purchase shares at the striking price.)

In the case of a short put accompanied by a short position in stock, profit is limited to the net difference between striking price of the put and the original price per share in the short position. However, the potential loss is a far more serious problem. If the price of stock were to increase substantially, profits in the put would not be enough to match the resulting loss in the stock. Thus, the covered put does not provide the same definition of "cover" as does the covered call.

Alternative options strategies—such as buying calls—provide better protection for those with short stock positions. In the event the stock were to rise in value, in-the-money calls would match the loss with dollar-for-dollar profits. In comparison, the covered put is too limited to offer any true protection against the worst case outcome.

tax put
a strategy combining the sale of stock at a loss—taken for tax purposes—and the sale of a put at the same time. (The premium received on the put offsets the stock loss; if the put is exercised, the stock is purchased at the striking price.)

Strategy 5: Creating a Tax Put

A fifth reason to sell puts is to create an advantage for tax purposes, which is known as a *tax put*. However, before employing this strategy, you should consult with your tax advisor to determine that you time the transaction properly and legally, and to ensure that the tax rules have not changed. You also need to be able to identify the risks and potential liabilities involved with the tax put.

An investor who has a paper loss position on stock has the right to sell and create a capital loss at any time, even if the timing is intended to reduce income tax liability. Such losses are limited to annual maximums. You can deduct capital losses only up to those maximums and the excess is carried over to future years. By selling puts at the same time that you take a tax loss, you offset part of the loss. The tax put is maximized when the put expiration occurs in the following tax year. (For example, expiration will occur in January or later, but you sell the put in December or earlier.) If your net stock loss is greater than the maximum allowed, the profit on the put is absorbed by that over-the-limit loss. By selling a put as you also sell stock at a loss, one of three possible outcomes will occur:

1. The stock's market value rises and the option expires worthless. The stock loss is deducted in the year stock is sold, but profit on the short put is taxed in the following year, when it expires. This has the effect of enabling you to take stock losses in the current year, but deferring put premium gains until the following year.

2. The stock's market value rises and you close the position in the put, profiting by the premium difference. This creates a short-term capital gain in the year the position is closed.

3. The stock's market value falls below the striking price, and you are assigned the stock. In this case, your basis in the stock is discounted by the amount received for selling the put.

A potential problem arises in the event that the put is exercised within 30 days from the date you sold the shares of stock. Under the wash sale rule, you cannot claim a loss in stock if you repurchase the same stock within 30 days.

The tax put provides you with a twofold advantage: First, you take a current-year loss on stock, reducing your overall tax liability, while deferring tax on the put sale until the following tax year. Second, you profit from selling the put, as shown in Figure 8.2, in the following two ways:

1. The premium income offsets the loss in stock.

2. In the event of exercise, your basis in the stock is discounted by the put premium.

DATE	ACTION	RECEIVED	PAID
Aug. 15	buy 100 shares at $50		$5,000
Dec. 15	sell 100 shares at $47	$4,700	
Dec. 15	sell 1 Feb 50 put at 6	$ 600	
	total	$5,300	$5,000
	net cash	$ 300	

PRICE MOVEMENT	RESULT
stock rises above striking price	$300 profit
	put is bought at a profit
stock falls below striking price	put is exercised at $50, net cost $47 (with $300 profit from tax put)

FIGURE 8.2 Example of tax put.

Example: You bought stock at $38 per share, and it is valued currently at $34. You sell shares in December and take a $400 loss. At the same time, you sell a March 35 put at 6. The $400 loss in stock is offset by a $600 premium from selling the put. If exercised, adjusted basis in the stock is discounted by the put premium. The put is not taxed until exercised, closed, or expired, so this also creates a tax deferral on the option side and a current write-off for loss on the stock side.

Put sellers enjoy an important advantage over call sellers: Their risk is not unlimited because the stock's market value can fall only so far. An example of a put write is described next and illustrated with profit and loss zones in Figure 8.3.

Example: You sold one May 40 put at 3. The outcome of taking this short position will be profitable as long as the stock's market value remains at or above the striking price

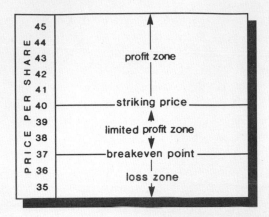

FIGURE 8.3 Example of put write with profit and loss zones.

of $40. If at expiration, the market value is below $40, the put will be exercised and you will buy 100 shares at $40 per share. Losses are limited between striking price and $37 due to the put premium received. If the stock's market value falls below $37, you will take a loss at the point of exercise.

You may look at losses upon exercise of a put as paper losses in one regard: While the premium you receive for the put is yours to keep, you acquire stock above market value and you can wait until the price rebounds. So selling puts does require you to spend money on overpriced shares, but the condition may be a temporary one. You could also absorb the paper loss on acquired stock by selling covered calls against it, further discounting your basis in the stock.

The most dire outcome for put sellers is that stock may become worthless. As remote a possibility as this might be, it remains within the realm of possible outcomes. You mitigate the risk by selecting stocks critically and applying fundamental tests aimed at identifying tangible value, rather than depending on popularity measures and technical—price-related—indicators. The possibility only emphasizes the importance of selecting stock carefully before writing puts. In the event a stock became worthless, your put would be exercised and you would buy 100 shares at the striking price. Current market value would be zero. The more likely true risk level, of course, is book value. Remember, however, that it is always possible for a stock's market value to fall below book value. The fundamental value of a company's equity has little to do with market pricing, especially in the short term. Tangible net worth often is overlooked in the more important factor affecting price—the *perception* of future potential value, which might be positive or negative and certainly will affect current share price. Even when a stock is associated with the fundamental strength of a well-capitalized company, the market might discount that value entirely. Market pricing is far from rational, and every put seller needs to keep that reality in mind.

As with all options strategies, the best stocks to select for put selling are those that tend to experience price movement within a limited trading range. The ideal stock has experienced moderate volatility in the recent past in order to create attractive time value, but that has not had ever-broadening support and resistance ranges and has exhibited unpredictable and sudden price changes. Highly volatile stocks are high-risk alternatives for selling puts, and a loss could require many months, perhaps even years to recover.

Put sellers should always be willing to buy 100 shares at the striking price, recognizing that exercise is always possible when the put is in the money. This is essential because your exercised price will always be above current market value. As long as you believe that striking price is reasonable, short-term price movement does not affect the stock's long-term growth potential. If you have studied thoroughly the company's strength and prospects as a long-term investment, selling puts can be a smart way to increase current income while discounting potential basis in the stock.

In the next chapter, you will see how mixing various buying and selling strategies can be used to decrease (or increase) risks and returns.

Chapter

9

Combined Techniques

*Decision making isn't a matter of arriving at a right or wrong answer;
it's a matter of selecting the most effective course of action from among
less effective courses of action.*
                    —Philip Marvin, *Developing Decisions for Action*, 1971

The richness of possible uses for options makes this one of the most intriguing tools for investors. In this chapter, you will see how to combine the basics in many different ways.

Options traders can employ only four basic strategies: buying calls, selling calls, buying puts, and selling puts. These four approaches can be applied in numerous methods and strategies, as shown in previous chapters. For example, you can modify risks in long positions with offsetting short positions in options.

Your reasons for buying or selling options define the level and degree of risk that you are willing to assume. In that regard, the utilization of options defines another investment, specifically your ownership of stock. Of course, any covered strategy should be secondary to the more important selection of stock. In any discussion of risk elements, a lot of emphasis is placed on option risk or reward, but unfortunately, the stock risk is easily overlooked. Before even considering how or if to employ options, you need to first identify a strategy that helps you select stocks with several objectives in mind, including:

✔ Protecting your capital from catastrophic losses due to stock market volatility.

✔ Avoiding long positions in stocks with severe liquidity or solvency problems.

✔ Selecting companies whose industry position is strong and growing.

This short list defines only the overall importance of selecting stocks as a starting point in your program that may include options as well. The big mistake made by too many investors is to pick stocks for the purpose of covering rich-premium options, and in the process unintentionally filling their portfolios with highly volatile issues. Any downturn in the larger market then is likely to cause a severe loss of capital value in the stock. In that situation, a limited short-term option profit is accompanied by a larger loss in stock value and, potentially, problems recapturing value through a reversal in direction of price movement.

Every investor has to decide individually how much risk exposure is appropriate. Applied to the options market, this definition phase also helps you to decide whether a particular strategy is right for you. Consider, for example, the difference between one investor who wants only to profit from buying and selling options, and another who covers calls with shares of stock in order to maximize returns. The risks are on opposite sides of the spectrum, and the uses of options by each person defines and distinguishes their perceptions of risk and opportunity, their desired outcomes, and even the basic idea about how to operate within the market.

spread
the simultaneous purchase and sale of options on the same underlying stock, with different striking prices or expiration dates, or both.

In moving beyond the four basic options strategies, you may discover that you need to use a variety of combinations for several different reasons. For example, long and short option positions can be engaged in at the same time, so that risks offset one another. Some combined strategies are designed to create profits in the event that the underlying stock moves in either direction; others are designed to create profits if the stock price remains within a specific range. There are three major classifications of advanced strategies.

The first advanced strategy is called a *spread*. This is

the simultaneous opening of both a long position and a short position in options on the same underlying stock. The spread increases potential profits while also reducing risks in the event that the underlying stock behaves in a particular manner, as illustrated shortly.

In order to meet the definition of a spread, the options should have different expiration dates; different striking prices; or both. When the striking prices are different but the expiration dates are the same, it is called a *vertical spread*. This is also referred to as a *money spread*.

vertical spread
a spread involving different striking prices but identical expiration dates.

Example: You buy a 45 call and, at the same time, sell a 40 call. Both expire in February. Because expiration dates are identical, this is a vertical spread.

Example: You buy a 30 put and, at the same time, sell a 35 put. Both expire in December. This is also a vertical spread.

The vertical spread is created using either calls or puts. The spread can have different expiration dates or a *combination* of different striking prices and expiration dates. Spreads can be put together in numerous formations.

money spread
alternative name for the vertical spread.

Spread strategies using short-term options—expiring in six months or less—are, of course, limited in value to that time range. However, spread strategies are far more complex when you combine short-term options with LEAPS. These longer-term options may have a life up to three years, so the offsetting possibilities can be far more complex. Knowing, for example, that time value declines the most during the last two to three months, you "cover" a short-position option with a longer-term LEAPS option. We qualify the term "cover" in this strategy. Although it is widely referred to in that manner, it is in fact more accurately a form of spread.

combination
any purchase or sale of options on one underlying stock, with terms that are not identical.

Example: You purchase a LEAPS 40 call that expires in 36 months. The stock is currently selling at $36 per share. You pay 11 ($1,100). Although time value premium is high due to the long-term nature of this option, you believe that the stock will rise in price during this period and justify your investment. A month later, the stock's market value has risen to $41 per share. You sell a 45 call expiring in four months and receive a premium of 3. Three months later, the stock is selling at $44 per share and the short call is valued at 1. You close the position and take a profit of $200 (minus trading fees). You now are free to sell another call against the LEAPS that expires in 32 months.

This transaction should be evaluated with several points in mind. The LEAPS cost $1,100 and you have already recovered $200 of that cost. The LEAPS is now in the money, so the price movement direction is favorable. This transaction took four months, so you have 32 more months before the long LEAPS call expires. You could repeat the short-term call sell again and again during this period. It is possible that you could recover the entire premium invested in the long position through well-timed short-term call sales—and potentially still profit from the long position as well. This would be an ideal outcome, and you have as long as three years for it to materialize. In comparison to using only short-term calls, you have far greater flexibility using short-term options with long-term LEAPS options.

The second combined strategy is called a *straddle*. This is defined as the simultaneous purchase and sale of an identical number of calls and puts with the same striking price and expiration date. While the spread requires a difference in one or more of the terms, the straddle is distinguished by the fact that the terms of each side are identical. The exception, of course, is that a straddle consists of combining calls on one side, with puts on the other.

 straddle
the simultaneous purchase and sale of the same number of calls and puts with identical striking prices and expiration dates.

The third advanced strategy is the *hedge*, which has been discussed many times throughout this book. For example, you hedge a short sale in stock by purchasing a call. In the event the stock rises, the short seller's losses will be offset by a point-for-point rise in the call. A put also protects a long stock position against a decline in price. So one use of a hedge is to use options as insurance. In some respects, both spreads and straddles contain hedging features, since two dissimilar positions are opened at the same time; price movement reducing the value on one side of the transaction tends to be offset by price increase on the other side.

If you are new to the options market, you will want

to keep your strategies fairly simple at first. If you venture beyond the basic strategies, you will most likely begin with a vertical spread. Other, more advanced strategies are used by more experienced options traders and are included here to explain the full range of possibilities in options trading. However, they often produce minimal profits for each option contract, given the need to pay trading fees upon opening and closing. Such marginal outcomes do not necessarily justify the associated risks, so advanced options traders apply these strategies with large multiples of option contracts. This more advanced use of options is efficient in terms of trading costs. Remember, however, that the multiple of profit opportunity is invariably accompanied by an equal multiple of risk. In addition to greater risks, you also need to be aware of your brokerage requirement for cash or securities deposits required when you use some strategies. When you deal in multiples, the security requirements are increased as well.

Remember, too, that what appears simple and logical on paper does not always work out the way you expect in the real world. Changes in option premium levels are not always logical or predictable as you might hope, and short-term variations can occur for a number of reasons. This is what makes option investing so interesting; such experiences also test your true risk tolerance level. You could discover that your risk tolerance is much different from what you thought, once you begin dabbling in advanced option strategies. The experience of being at risk can be daunting, and it is important that you understand the full range of possible risks and costs before embarking on any advanced strategies.

VERTICAL SPREAD STRATEGIES

Options traders use spreads to take advantage of the predictable course of changes in option time value premium. These changes are predictable because everyone knows what happens to time value as expiration approaches. And when options are in the money, it is reasonable to expect intrinsic value premium to react dollar-for-dollar with movement in the price of the underlying stock. Of course, these values are not entirely predictable any more than stock movement itself, and time value premium can move irrationally (or seemingly irrationally), a condition that presents opportunities for short-term profits. The relationship between intrinsic value and time value is what makes the spread an interesting and challenging strategic tool for the options investor.

> **Smart Investor Tip** As with most option strategies, time value spells the difference between profit and loss in most spreads.

You have an advantage when offsetting long and short positions in the spread. The spread employing standard short-term options is likely to involve one side in the money and the other side out of the money. The in-the-money side will tend to change in value at a different rate from the out-of-the-money side, because it contains intrinsic value—and because when in the money, time value tends to act differently as well. By observing the differences on either side of the striking price, you can anticipate advantages that you gain through the spread strategy, whether the market moves up or down.

Bull Spreads

bull spread
a strategy involving the purchase and sale of calls and puts that will produce maximum profits when the value of the underlying stock rises.

A *bull spread* provides the greatest profit potential if and when the underlying stock's market value rises. With the bull spread, you buy an option with a lower striking price and sell another with a higher striking price. You can employ either puts or calls in the bull spread.

Example: You open a bull spread using calls. You sell one December 55 call and buy one December 50 call, as shown in Figure 9.1. At the time of this transaction, the underlying stock's market value is $49 per share. After you open the spread, the stock's market value rises to $54 per share. When that occurs, the 50 call increases in value point-for-point once it is in the money. The short 55 call does not change in value as it remains out of the money

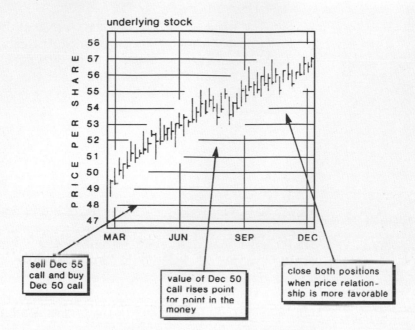

FIGURE 9.1 Example of bull spread.

and, in fact, will drop in value as its time value falls. Because of the advantage the spread creates at the time the stock has reached the $54 per share level, both sides of the spread will be profitable. The long 50 call rises in value and the short 55 call remains out of the money, so it loses time value.

This example describes the ideal situation, in which both sides of the spread are profitable, because the stock's price behaves perfectly to suit the spread. Of course, you have no control over price movement, so this outcome will not always occur. Even when only one side is profitable, however, the strategy works as long as you achieve an overall profit.

Smart Investor Tip The spread is most profitable when the stock's price changes in the desired timing and pattern. Both sides of the spread can work out well. Of course, this would be much easier if stock price movement could be controlled or predicted—which it cannot.

A bull vertical spread is profitable when the underlying stock's price moves in the anticipated direction. For example, a lower-priced call will be profitable if the stock rises in value, whereas the higher-priced short call will not be exercised as long as it remains out of the money, as illustrated previously.

A bull vertical spread, with defined profit and loss zones, is shown in Figure 9.2.

Example: You sell one September 45 call for 2, and buy one September 40 call for 5. The net cost before brokerage fees is $300. When the stock rises between $40 and $45 per share, the September 40 call rises dollar-for-dollar with the stock, while the short September 45 call remains out of the money. Its premium value will decline as time value disappears. As long as the stock remains within this five-point range, both sides can be closed at a profit (as long as closing the positions would exceed your initial cost of $300). If the stock's price rises above $45 per share, the five-point spread in striking prices will be offset by the long and short positions. Both calls will be in the money. So this strategy limits both profits and losses.

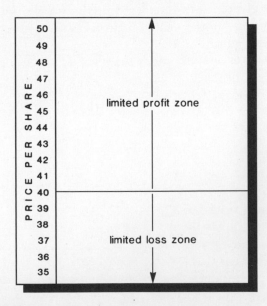

FIGURE 9.2 Bull vertical spread profit and loss zones.

Bear Spreads

Compared to the bull spread, the *bear spread* will produce profits if the stock's market value falls. In this variety of the spread, the higher-value option is always bought, and the lower-value option is always sold.

bear spread
a strategy involving the purchase and sale of calls or puts that will produce maximum profits when the value of the underlying stock falls.

Example: You open a bear spread using calls. You sell one March 35 call and buy one March 40 call. The stock's market value is $37 per share. The premium value of the lower call, which is in the money, will decline point-for-point as the stock's market value falls; if the stock's value does fall, the position can be closed at a profit.

Example: You open a bear spread using puts. As shown in the example in Figure 9.3, you sell one December 50 put and buy one December 55 put. The underlying stock's market value is $55 per share. As the price of the stock moves down, the long 55 put will increase in value point-for-point with the change in stock price. By the time the stock's price moves down to $51, both puts will be

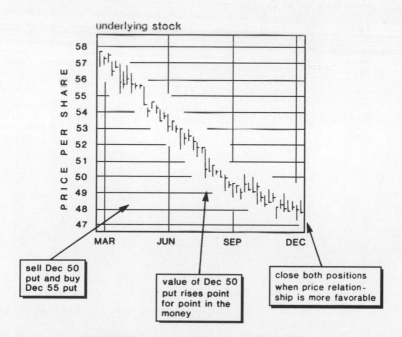

FIGURE 9.3 Example of bear spread.

profitable—the long put from increased intrinsic value, and the short put from lower time value.

Of course, this scenario assumes ideal conditions in which the stock's price moves the desired number of points in the maximized time frame, which enables the bear spread writer to profit. This does not always happen, of course, but it illustrates the ideal outcome you would desire upon using a bear spread. You gain more flexibility in the bear spread if your long position is a LEAPS; this enables you to write several short-term puts against the "covered" longer position. The cost for the long position will be greater due to the time factor, but the potential for profit makes the entire strategy far more interesting as well.

> **Smart Investor Tip** Bear strategies often are overlooked by investors, who tend more often than not to be optimists. Look at *all* of the possibilities. You can make money when the stock goes down in value, too.

A detailed bear spread with defined profit and loss zones is illustrated in Figure 9.4.

Example: You sell one September 40 call for 5 and buy one September 45 call for 2; your net proceeds are $300. As the stock's market value falls below the level of $45 per share, the short 40 call will lose point value matching the stock's decline; the lower long call will not react in the same way, as it remains out of the money. As the $40 per share price level is approached, the spread can be closed with profits on both sides.

Consider how this example would work with puts instead of calls. In the previous scenario, the higher long put would *increase* point-for-point with a decline in the stock's market value.

When the bear spread employs calls, profits are

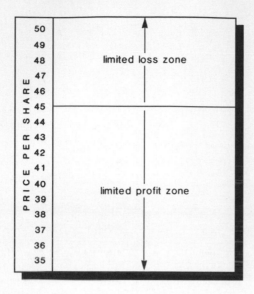

FIGURE 9.4 Bear vertical spread profit and loss zones.

frozen once both sides are in the money, at least to the degree that intrinsic value changes; one side's increase will be offset by the other side's decrease. The only remaining opportunity to increase profits at that point would lie in time value premium remaining in the short position.

In all of these examples, the most significant risk is that the stock will move in the direction opposite that desired. Be prepared to close a spread in that event before the short position increases to value (meaning you will lose). You risk exercise on the short side at any time that option is in the money, and you might need to close to avoid exercise and to reduce potential losses as well. Your maximum risk other than that of exercise is limited to the point difference between the two striking prices (minus net premium received when the position was opened; or plus net premium paid). In the preceding examples, a five-point spread was used, so that maximum point-spread risk is $500. The point-spread risk increases as the gap between striking prices changes, as shown in Table 9.1.

Example: You open a spread. The difference between striking prices on either side is five points. Your

TABLE 9.1   Spread Risk Table

Number of Option Spreads	Striking Price Interval	
	5 Points	10 Points
1	$ 500	$ 1,000
2	1,000	2,000
3	1,500	3,000
4	2,000	4,000
5	2,500	5,000
6	3,000	6,000
7	3,500	7,000
8	4,000	8,000
9	4,500	9,000
10	5,000	10,000

maximum risk is $500 plus brokerage fees, plus net premium paid when you opened the position (or minus net premium received).

Example: You open a spread buying and selling four options on either side. The difference between striking prices is five points. Your maximum risk is $2,000 (modified as in the previous example), because four positions are involved, each with a five-point difference between striking prices.

Box Spreads

box spread
the combination of a bull spread and a bear spread, opened at the same time on the same underlying stock.

When you open a bull spread *and* a bear spread at the same time, using options on the same underlying stock, it is called a *box spread*. This limits risks as well as potential profits, and is designed to produce a profit in one side or the other, regardless of which direction the stock moves.

Example: As illustrated in Figure 9.5, you create a box spread by buying and selling the following option contracts:

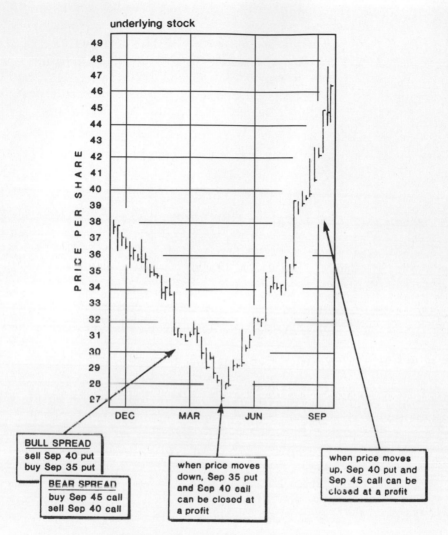

FIGURE 9.5 Example of box spread.

Bull Spread: Sell one September 40 put and buy one September 35 put.

Bear Spread: Buy one September 45 call and sell one September 40 call.

In this example, if the underlying stock's price moves significantly in either direction, portions of the box spread can be closed at a profit. One important reminder: It makes sense to close corresponding long and short positions in the event of a profit opportunity, to avoid the risk of leaving yourself exposed to an uncovered short situation. In the ideal situation, the stock's price will move first in one direction (enabling half the box spread to be closed at a profit) and then in the other (enabling the close of the other half at a profit).

> **Smart Investor Tip**   Remember, when one side of the box spread expires, you might be left exposed on the other side. Keep an eye on the changing situation to avoid unacceptable risks.

The detailed profit and loss zones of a box spread are summarized in Figure 9.6. The net proceeds from this box spread result from the following outcomes:

Bull Spread: Sell one September 45 put for 6 (+$600) and buy one September 40 put for 2 (−$200).

Bear Spread: Sell one December 35 put for 1 (+$100) and buy one December 40 put for 4 (−$400).

If the stock's market price rises between $40 and $45 per share, the bull spread can be closed at a profit. Above that level, the difference in bull spread values will move to the same degree in the money, offsetting one another. If the stock falls to between $35 and $40 per share, the bear spread can be closed at a profit. The long December 40 will be in the money and will change point-for-point with change in the stock's price. Below the level of $35 per share, the long and short position will change in intrinsic value levels, offsetting one another.

> **Smart Investor Tip**   Whenever you close part of a box spread, close both long and short positions to avoid unintended short positions that are not covered or hedged.

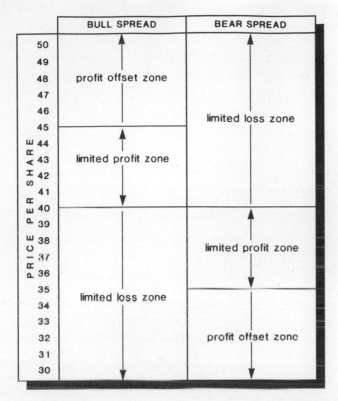

FIGURE 9.6 Box spread profit and loss zones.

Debit and Credit Spreads

The simultaneous opening of long and short positions involves receipt *and* payment of money. When you go short, you receive a premium, and when you go long you are required to pay. While it is always desirable to receive more money than you pay out, it is not always possible. Some strategies will involve making a net payment. When you receive cash when you open a position, that provides you flexibility, because you need less price movement to produce a net profit. When you make a payment to open the position, more profit is required in changes in option premium to offset the amount paid.

A spread in which more cash is received than paid, is called a *credit spread*. When the net outcome requires you to make a payment, it is called a *debit spread*.

 credit spread
any spread in which receipts from short positions are higher than premiums paid for long positions, net of transaction fees.

 debit spread
any spread in which receipts from short positions are lower than premiums paid for long positions, net of transaction fees.

> **Smart Investor Tip**   When a spread involves a net receipt, that broadens your profit potential; a net payment is accompanied by the requirement for greater profits in changed option premium to make up the difference.

HORIZONTAL AND DIAGONAL SPREAD STRATEGIES

In the previous section, the vertical spread was introduced, which involves using options having identical expiration dates but different striking prices. Another variation of spread involves simultaneous option transactions with different expiration months. This is called a *calendar spread*, also called a *time spread*.

> **calendar spread** (also called **time spread**)
> a spread involving the simultaneous purchase or sale of options on the same underlying stock, with different expirations.

The calendar spread can be broken down into two specific variations:

Horizontal Spread: In this variation, options have identical striking prices but different expiration dates.

Diagonal Spread: In this variation, options have different striking prices *and* different expiration dates.

Example: You enter into transactions that create a horizontal calendar spread. You sell one March 40 call for 2; and you buy one June 40 call for 5. Your net cost is $300. Two different expiration months are involved. The earlier, short call expires in March, while the long call does not expire until June. Your loss is limited in two ways: by amount and time. This point is illustrated in Figure 9.7. If, by March expiration, the first call expires worthless, you have a profit in that position and the second phase goes into effect. The short position no longer exists. If the stock rises at least three points above striking price before expiration, the overall position is at breakeven; above that, it will be profitable.

> **horizontal spread**
> a calendar spread in which offsetting long and short positions have identical striking prices but different expiration dates.

Example: You create a diagonal calendar spread. You sell one March 40 call for 2; and you buy one June 45 call for

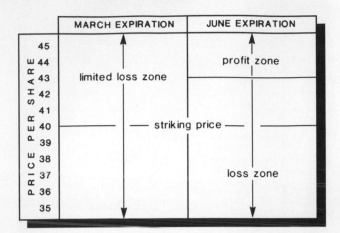

diagonal spread
a calendar spread in which offsetting long and short positions have both different striking prices and different expiration dates.

FIGURE 9.7 Profit and loss zones for an example of horizontal calendar spread.

3. Your net cost is $100. This transaction involves different striking prices *and* expiration months. If the earlier-expiring short position is exercised, the long call can be used to satisfy the call. In other words, as owner of the long position, you can exercise the call when your short position call is exercised. If the earlier call is not exercised, the overall risk is restricted to the net cost of $100. After expiration of the short call, breakeven is equal to the long call's striking price plus the cost of the overall transaction. In this case, the net cost was $100, so $46 is the breakeven price (not allowing for trading costs). This is illustrated in Figure 9.8.

Giving different spread strategies the names "vertical," "horizontal," and "diagonal" helps distinguish them from one another, and to visualize the relationships between expiration and striking prices. These distinctions are summarized in Figure 9.9.

A horizontal spread is an attractive strategy when the premium value between two related options is temporarily distorted, or when the later option's features protect the risks of the earlier-expiring short position.

Example: You open a horizontal spread using calls. You sell a March 40 call for 4, and you buy a June 40 call for 6. Your net cost is $200. If the market value of the

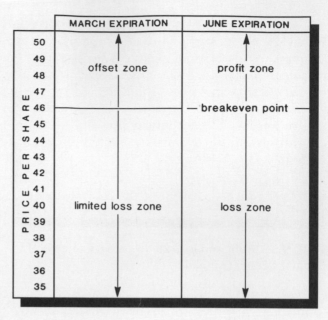

FIGURE 9.8 Profit and loss zones for an example of diagonal calendar spread.

underlying stock rises, the long position protects against the risks of the short position. The risk is no longer unlimited. The maximum risk in this situation is the $200 paid to open the spread. If the stock remains at or below striking price, the short call will lose value and expire worthless; or it can be bought and closed at a profit. For example, if its value fell to 1, you could buy and realize a profit of $300. Compared to the net cost of opening the spread, this puts you $100 ahead overall, but you still own the long call. If the premium value were to rise above the $600 paid for this call, it could be sold at a profit.

VERTICAL

	MAR	JUN	SEP
55			
50	●		
45	●		●
40			●
35			

EXPIRATION DATES — STRIKING PRICE

HORIZONTAL

	MAR	JUN	SEP
55			
50	●	●	
45			
40		●	●
35			

EXPIRATION DATES — STRIKING PRICE

DIAGONAL

	MAR	JUN	SEP
55		●	
50	●		
45			
40		●	
35			●

EXPIRATION DATES — STRIKING PRICE

FIGURE 9.9 Comparison of spread strategies.

A horizontal spread is useful for reducing existing risks when one position is already open. For example, if you previously sold a call and the stock begins to change in value so that you are at risk of exercise, you can reduce that risk by buying an option with a later expiration, which offsets the short position. This may be a less expensive alternative than buying the short position at a loss, because the long position has the potential to increase in value.

Smart Investor Tip Devices like the horizontal spread sometimes come about in stages, and can be used to avoid exercise in a previously established short position.

Example: You sold a covered June 45 call last month. The stock's market value is above striking price. You do not want to close the position because that will create a loss, but you also would like to avoid exercise. By buying a September 45 call, you create a horizontal spread. If the June 45 call is exercised, you will be able to exercise the September 45 call, offsetting the assignment. However, if the call is not exercised, you own a later-expiring call which has its own potential for profit within a time span of an additional three months.

A diagonal spread combines vertical and horizontal features. Long and short positions are opened with different striking prices and expiration dates.

Example: You create a diagonal spread. You sell a March 50 call for 4; and you buy a June 55 call for 1. You receive $300 net for these transactions. If the stock's market value falls, you profit from the decline in premium value on the short position. If the stock's market value rises, the long position call rises as well, offsetting increases in the short call. Maximum risk in this situation is five points; however, because you received net premium of $300, real exposure is limited to two points (five points between striking prices, less three points net premium). If the earlier, short call expires worthless, you continue to own the long call. With its longer term, you continue to enjoy potential profit for three more months.

This variety of spread becomes far more interesting when combining LEAPS options for the long side and shorter-term options for the short side. Because so much time is involved in the LEAPS option—up to three years— you have far more flexibility in designing, modifying, and developing strategies for horizontal and diagonal spreads.

For example, it is likely that by selling short-term options against the longer-term LEAPS, the strategy can be repeated many times. It is likely that enough premium income could be generated by selling such calls to offset the cost of the long-position LEAPS. As the stock moves over time, the corresponding horizontal or diagonal differences can be adjusted as well. The result could be to maximize premium income without risking exercise. Remember, the greatest decline in time value occurs in the last quarter of an option's lifespan. So timing of short positions with higher striking prices (for calls) or lower striking prices (for puts) than the offsetting long positions, enables you to maximize returns.

For example, the box spread using vertical approach is complex; however, when you consider the possibility of a box spread within horizontal or diagonal patterns, it becomes far more interesting. A box spread employing long-position LEAPS and a series of offsetting short-term sales, enables you to modify the range as the stock's price moves in either direction.

ALTERING SPREAD PATTERNS

The vertical, horizontal, and diagonal patterns of the spread can be employed to reduce risks, especially if you keep an eye on relative price patterns, and you see a temporary price distortion. Going beyond reduction of risk, some techniques can be employed in advanced strategies to make the spread even more interesting. Combining LEAPS options with shorter-term expiring options also increases the flexibility in spread strategies. In the best possible outcome, you will be able to profit from spreads *and* on the underlying stock.

Varying the Number of Options

The *ratio calendar spread* involves the employment of a different number of options on each side of the spread, and using different expiration dates as well. The strategy is interesting because it creates two separate profit and loss zone ranges, broadening the opportunity for interim profits.

Example: You enter into a ratio calendar spread by selling four May 50 calls at 5, and buying two August 50 calls at 6. You receive $800 net ($2,000 received less $1,200 paid) before transaction fees are deducted. You hope that between the time you open these positions and expiration, the underlying stock's market value will remain below striking price; that would produce a profit on the short side. Your breakeven is $54 per share.

   If the stock is at $54 at the point of expiration, you break even due to the ratio of four short calls and two long calls. Upon exercise, the two short calls will cost $800—the same amount that you received upon opening the ratio calendar spread. If the price of stock is higher than $54 per share, the loss occurs at the ratio of 4 to 2 (since you sold four calls and bought only two). If the May expiration date were to pass without exercise, the four short positions would be profitable, and you would still own the two August 50 calls.

> **ratio calendar spread** a strategy involving a different number of options on the long side of a transaction from the number on the short side, when the expiration dates for each side are also different. (This strategy creates two separate profit and loss zone ranges, one of which disappears upon the earlier expiration.)

   The profit and loss zones in this example are summarized in Figure 9.10. Note that no consideration is given to transaction costs, time value of the longer-expiration premiums, or the outcome in the event of early exercise.

   Another complete ratio calendar spread strategy with defined profit and loss zones, is summarized in Figure 9.11 and explained in the following example.

Example: You sell five June 40 calls at 5, and buy three September 40 calls at 7. Net proceeds are $400. The short position risk is limited to the first expiration period, with potential losses partially covered by the longer-expiration

sell 4 May 50 calls for 5,
buy 2 Aug 50 calls for 6:
net proceeds $800

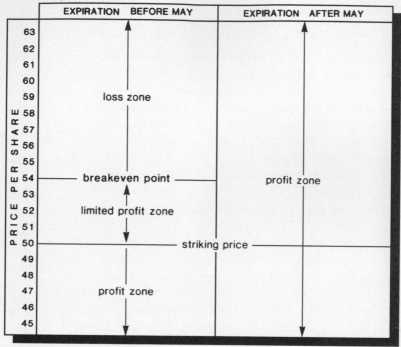

FIGURE 9.10   Example of ratio calendar spread.

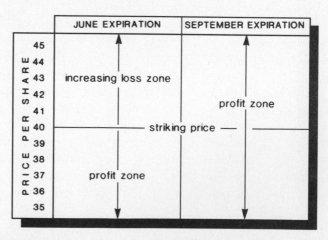

FIGURE 9.11   Ratio calendar spread profit and loss zones.

long calls. As long as the stock's market value does not rise above the striking price of 40, the short calls will expire worthless. However, there are two open, uncovered calls up until the point of the earlier expiration.

Once the June expiration passes, the $400 net represents pure profit, regardless of stock price movement after that date. However, if the stock's market value were to rise above the long calls' striking price, they would increase in value three points for each point of increase in the stock. Of course, the calls can also be sold at any point prior to expiration, to create additional profit.

Table 9.2 shows a summary of the values for this strategy at various stock price levels as of expiration. No time value is considered in this summary. If the stock remains at or below the $40 per share level, the ratio calendar spread will be profitable. However, that profit will be limited as long as all positions remain open.

TABLE 9.2 Profits/Losses for Ratio Calendar Spread Example			
Price	June 40	Sep. 40	Total
$50	−$5,000	+$3,000	−$2,000
49	− 4,500	+ 2,700	− 1,800
48	− 4,000	+ 2,400	− 1,600
47	− 3,500	+ 2,100	− 1,400
46	− 3,000	+ 1,800	− 1,200
45	− 2,500	+ 1,500	− 1,000
44	− 2,000	+ 1,200	− 800
43	− 1,500	+ 900	− 600
42	− 1,000	+ 600	− 400
41	− 500	+ 300	− 200
40	+ 2,500	− 2,100	+ 400
39	+ 2,500	− 2,100	+ 400
38	+ 2,500	− 2,100	+ 400
Lower	+ 2,500	− 2,100	+ 400

Expanding the Ratio

ratio calendar combination spread

a strategy involving both a ratio between purchases and sales and a box spread. (Long and short positions are opened on options with the same underlying stock, in varying numbers and with expiration dates extending over two or more periods. This strategy is designed to produce profits in the event of price increases or decreases in the market value of the underlying stock.)

The ratio calendar spread can be expanded into an even more complex strategy through employment of the *ratio calendar combination spread*. This adds yet another dimension to the ratio calendar spread by adding a box spread to it.

Example: As illustrated in Figure 9.12, you open the following option positions:

Buy one June 30 call at 3 (pay $300).
Sell two March 30 calls at $1^3/_4$ (receive $350).
Buy one September 25 put at $^3/_4$ (pay $75).
Sell two June 25 puts at $^5/_8$ (receive $125).

The post-decimalization values in this list are denoted differently. The value $1^3/_4$ is now expressed as 1.75; $1^3/_4$ is expressed as 0.75; and five-eighths is expressed as 0.625 apiece.

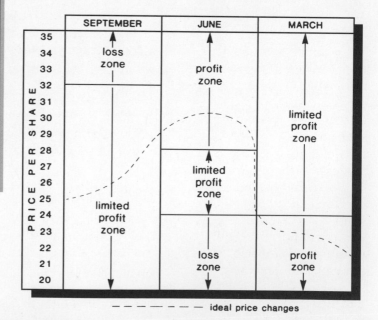

FIGURE 9.12 Example of ratio calendar combination spread.

The net result of these transactions is a receipt of $100, before calculation of trading charges. This complex combination involves 2 to 1 ratios between short and long positions on both sides (two short option positions for each long option position). In the event of unfavorable price movements in either direction, you risk exercise on at least a segment of this overall strategy. The ideal price change pattern would enable you to close parts of the total combination at a profit, while leaving other parts. Ideally, short positions should be closed in advance of long positions, because the long positions provide at least partial coverage against exercise.

> **Smart Investor Tip** You normally will need to close short positions in advance of long positions to avoid unacceptable risk, a point worth remembering when you open the positions at the beginning.

Because trading fees add up quickly, combinations using only a small number of options is a costly strategy. Considering the risk exposure, potential profits would not justify the action in many cases, the previous example is a case in point. However, for the purpose of illustration, this shows how the strategy works. In practice, such actions would be likely to involve much larger numbers of option contracts, thus more money—and more risk exposure.

Exercise risk is reduced by owning shares in the underlying stock, providing full or partial coverage against short call positions. For example, when you are writing two calls and buying one, the risk of a price increase is eliminated if you also own 100 shares. Those shares cover one call, and the other is covered by the long call.

Example: A complete ratio calendar combination spread with defined profit and loss zones is shown in Figure 9.13. In this example, you open the following positions:

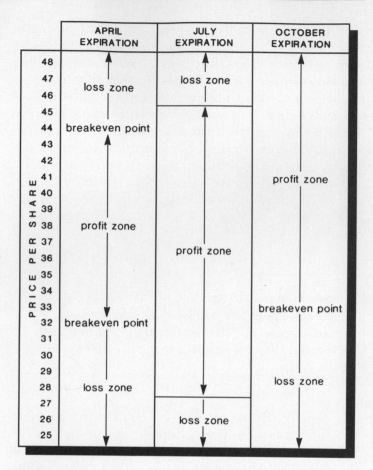

FIGURE 9.13 Ratio calendar combination spread profit and loss zones.

Buy one July 40 call for 6 (−$600).

Sell two April 40 calls for 3 (+$600).

Buy one October 35 put for 1 (−$100).

Sell two July 35 puts for 2 (+$400).

Net proceeds in this example are $300.

This example consists of two separate ratio calendar spreads, boxed together. Profits would occur if the stock's market value were to move in either direction, whereas losses are limited. Three separate expiration dates are involved. One danger in this elaborate strategy is that, as earlier options expire, later open positions become exposed to uncovered losses, so risks are increased. This situation can be reversed—so that chances for profits are greater—by building a combination using later-expiring long positions instead of short positions. Table 9.3 provides a breakdown of profit and loss produced at various price levels based on the example.

TABLE 9.3 Profits/Losses for Ratio Calendar Combination Spread Example

Price	April 40 Call	July 40 Call	July 35 Put	Oct. 35 Put	Total
$47	+$100	−$800	$ 0	+$400	−$300
46	0	− 600	0	+ 400	− 200
45	− 100	− 400	0	+ 400	− 100
44	− 200	− 200	0	+ 400	0
43	− 300	0	0	+ 400	+ 100
42	− 400	+ 200	0	+ 400	+ 200
41	− 500	+ 400	0	+ 400	+ 300
40	− 600	+ 600	0	+ 400	+ 400
39	− 600	+ 600	0	+ 400	+ 400
38	− 600	+ 600	0	+ 400	+ 400
37	− 600	+ 600	0	+ 400	+ 400
36	− 600	+ 600	0	+ 400	+ 400
35	− 600	+ 600	0	+ 400	+ 400
34	− 600	+ 600	0	+ 200	+ 200
33	− 600	+ 600	+ 100	0	+ 100
32	− 600	+ 600	+ 200	− 200	0
31	− 600	+ 600	+ 300	− 400	− 100
30	− 600	+ 600	+ 400	− 600	− 200
29	− 600	+ 600	+ 500	− 800	− 300
28	− 600	+ 600	+ 500	−1,000	− 500
27	− 600	+ 600	+ 500	−1,200	− 700
26	− 600	+ 600	+ 500	−1,400	− 900

A Strategy with a Middle Range

butterfly spread
a strategy involving open options in one striking price range, offset by transactions at higher and lower ranges at the same time.

Another technique calls for the opening of offsetting options in middle striking price ranges, with opposing positions above *and* below. This is known as the *butterfly spread*. It can involve long and short positions, in calls or puts. There are several possible variations of the butterfly spread. For example:

✔ Sell two middle-range puts and buy two calls, one with a striking price above that level and one with a striking price below that level.

✔ Sell two middle-range puts and buy two puts, one with a striking price above that level and one with a striking price below that level.

✔ Buy two middle-range calls and sell two calls, one with a striking price above that level and one with a striking price below that level.

✔ Buy two middle-range puts and sell two puts, one with a striking price above that level and one with a striking price below that level.

Example: You sell two September 50 calls at 5, receiving $1,000. You also buy one September 55 call at 1 and one September 45 call at 7, paying a total of $800. Net proceeds are $200. This is a credit spread, since you received more than you paid. You will profit if the underlying stock's price falls. And no matter how high the stock's price rises, the combined long positions' value will always exceed the values in the two short positions.

Smart Investor Tip Exotic combinations are more often good for studying strategy than for actual use in the market. Trading costs are likely to offset potential limited profits in such strategies.

Butterfly spreads often are created when a single open position is expanded by the addition of other calls or puts, most often to protect a short position when a stock moves in a direction other than anticipated. It is difficult to find situations in which you can create a risk-free combination such as the one in the previous example.

Example: You sold two calls last month with a striking price of 40. The underlying stock's market value has declined to a point that the 35 calls are cheap, so you buy one to partially cover your short position. At the same time, you also buy a 45 call, which is deep out of the money. This series of trades creates a butterfly spread.

The trading fees charged by your brokerage firm make butterfly spreads impractical when you are using a small number of options. A credit spread is even less likely. The potential gain should be evaluated against the potential loss, commission costs, and ongoing exposure to risk.

Butterfly spreads can involve either calls or puts. A bull butterfly spread will be most profitable if the underlying stock's market value rises, and the opposite is true for a bear butterfly spread.

A detailed butterfly spread, with defined profit and loss zones, is shown in Figure 9.14. In this example, the following transactions are involved.

Sell two June 40 calls at 6 (+$1,200).

Buy one June 30 call at 12 (–$1,200).

Buy one June 50 call at 3 (–$300).

The net cost is $300. This butterfly spread with either yield a limited profit or result in a limited loss. In the butterfly spread, the potential yield often does not justify the strategy, since trading costs will not offset the limited potential profit. That is why the butterfly spread is often created in increments rather than all at once.

Table 9.4 summarizes profit and loss status at various prices of the underlying stock, based on the previous example. It is based on values at expiration and including no time value. If the stock's market value rises to $50 or more, the short position losses will be offset by an equal number of long position profits. And if the stock's market value declines, the maximum loss is $300, the net cost of opening these positions.

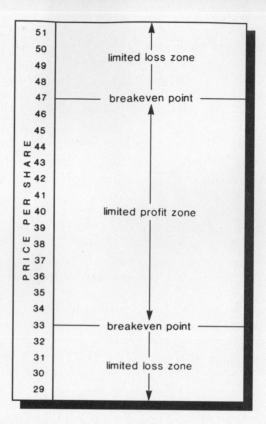

FIGURE 9.14 Butterfly spread profit and loss zones.

 long hedge

the purchase of options as a form of insurance to protect a portfolio position in the event of a price increase, a strategy employed by investors selling stock short and ensuring against a rise in the market value of the stock.

HEDGE STRATEGIES

Whenever options are bought or sold as part of a strategy to protect another open position, the combination of positions represents a hedge.

The Two Types of Hedges

A *long hedge* protects against price increases. A *short hedge* protects against price decreases.

Example of a Long Hedge: You are short on 100 shares of stock. This puts you at risk in the event the market value of that stock were to rise. You buy one call on that stock, which hedges your short stock position.

TABLE 9.4 Profits/Losses for Butterfly Spread Example			
Price	June 30	June 40	June 50	Total
$51	+ $900	−$1,000	−$200	−$300
50	+ 800	− 800	− 300	− 300
49	+ 700	− 600	− 300	− 200
48	+ 600	− 400	− 300	− 100
47	+ 500	− 200	− 300	0
46	+ 400	0	− 300	+ 100
45	+ 300	+ 200	− 300	+ 200
44	+ 200	+ 400	300	+ 300
43	+ 100	+ 600	− 300	+ 400
42	0	+ 800	− 300	+ 500
41	− 100	+ 1,000	− 300	+ 600
40	− 200	+ 1,200	− 300	+ 700
39	− 300	+ 1,200	− 300	+ 600
38	− 400	+ 1,200	− 300	+ 500
37	− 500	+ 1,200	− 300	+ 400
36	− 600	+ 1,200	300	300
35	− 700	+ 1,200	− 300	+ 200
34	− 800	+ 1,200	− 300	+ 100
33	− 900	+ 1,200	− 300	0
32	−1,000	+ 1,200	− 300	− 100
31	−1,100	+ 1,200	− 300	− 200
30	−1,200	+ 1,200	− 300	− 300
29	−1,200	+ 1,200	− 300	− 300
Lower	−1,200	+ 1,200	− 300	− 300

short hedge the purchase of options as a form of insurance to protect a portfolio position in the event of a price decrease, a strategy employed by investors in long positions and insuring against a decline in the market value of the stock.

A *short hedge* protects against price decreases.

Example of a Short Hedge: You own 100 shares of stock and, due to recent negative news, you are concerned that the market value could drop. You do not want to sell the shares, however. To hedge against the risk of lost market value, you have two choices: Buy one put or sell one call. Both positions hedge the 100 shares. The put provides unlimited protection because it would increase in value for each point lost in the stock's value. The call provides limited downside protection, only to the extent of the points received in premium.

An expanded example of a long hedge, with defined profit and loss zones, is shown in Figure 9.15. In this example of a long hedge, you sold short 100 shares of stock at $43, and hedged that position with a May 40 call bought at 2. The cost of hedging your short position reduces potential profits by $200, but protects you against potentially greater losses without requiring that you close the position. The risk is eliminated until the call expires. At that point, there are three choices:

1. Close the short position to eliminate risk.
2. Replace the call with another, later-expiring one.
3. Do nothing since perception of the risk might have changed.

In this example, if the underlying stock's market value increases, then profit potential is limited to the offsetting price gap between the stock's market value and the call's premium value. If the stock's market value falls, the

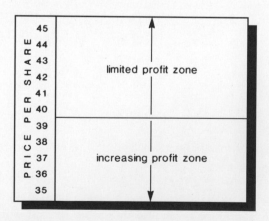

FIGURE 9.15   Long hedge profit and loss zones.

short stock position will be profitable, with profits reduced by two points for the call premium you paid.

Table 9.5 summarizes this hedged position's overall value at various stock price levels.

Hedging beyond Coverage

One of the disadvantages of the hedge when matched precisely is that potential profits may be limited. A solution is to modify the hedge to increase profit potential, while still minimizing the risk of loss.

A *reverse hedge* involves providing more protection than needed just to cover another position. For example, if you are short on 100 shares of stock, you need to purchase only one call to hedge the position. In a reverse hedge strategy, you buy more than one call, providing protection for the short position *and* potential for addition profits that would outpace adverse movement in the stock's price. With two calls, the call profits would outpace stock losses 2 to 1, for example; with three calls, the ratio would be 3 to 1.

An expanded example of a reverse hedge with defined profit and loss zones, is shown in Figure 9.16. In

 reverse hedge an extension of a long or short hedge in which more options are opened than the number needed to cover the stock position; this increases profit potential in the event of unfavorable movement in the market value of the underlying stock.

TABLE 9.5 Profits/Losses from the Long Hedge Example			
Price	Stock	Call	Total
$45	−$200	+$300	+$100
44	− 100	+ 200	+ 100
43	0	+ 100	+ 100
42	+ 100	0	+ 100
41	+ 200	− 100	+ 100
40	+ 300	− 200	+ 100
39	+ 400	− 200	+ 200
38	+ 500	− 200	+ 300
37	+ 600	− 200	+ 400
36	+ 700	− 200	+ 500
35	+ 800	− 200	+ 600

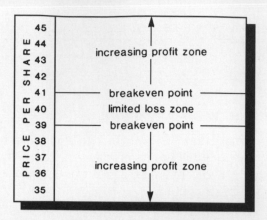

FIGURE 9.16 Reverse hedge profit and loss zones.

this example, you sold short 100 shares of stock at $43 per share, and the value now has declined to $39. To protect the profit in the short position and to insure against losses in the event the price rises, you bought two May 40 calls at 2.

This reverse hedge solves the problem of risk in the short stock position, while also providing the potential for additional gain in the calls. In order for this profit to materialize, the stock's value would have to increase enough points to offset your cost in buying the calls. This hedge creates two advantages: First, it protects the short position in the event of unwanted price increase in the stock. Second, the 2-to-1 ratio from calls to stock means that if the price were to increase in the stock, the calls would become profitable.

Smart Investor Tip The reverse hedge protects an exposed position while adding the potential for additional profits (or losses). This makes the hedge more than a form of insurance.

Table 9.6 summarizes this position's value as of expiration at various stock prices.

TABLE 9.6 Profits/Losses from Reverse Hedge Example			
Price	Stock	Call	Total
$45	–$200	+$600	+$400
44	– 100	+ 400	+ 300
43	0	+ 200	+ 200
42	+ 100	0	+ 100
41	+ 200	– 200	0
40	+ 300	– 400	– 100
39	+ 400	– 400	0
38	+ 500	– 400	+ 100
37	+ 600	– 400	+ 200
36	+ 700	– 400	+ 300
35	+ 800	– 400	+ 400

The reverse hedge works in the opposite direction as well. For example, you may own 100 shares of stock that has risen in value. To protect against a decline in value, you may buy two puts, a reverse hedge that would produce 2-to-1 profits in calls over decline in the stock's value. You may also sell two calls for the same reason. One would be covered while the other would be uncovered. Or, looking at this another way, the hedged position would be one-half covered overall. If the stock's market value were to fall, the calls would lose value, providing downside protection to the extent of the total premium received. However, if the stock were to rise, profits in the stock would be reduced by losses in the calls.

Hedging Option Positions

Hedging can protect a long or short position in an underlying stock, or it can reduce or eliminate risks in other option positions. Hedging is achieved with various forms of spreads and combinations. By varying the number of options on one side or the other, you create a *variable hedge*, which is a hedge involving both long and short positions.

 variable hedge
a hedge involving a long position and a short position in related options, when one side contains a greater number of options than the other. (The desired result is reduction of risks or potentially greater profits.)

However, one side will contain a greater number of options than the other.

Example: You buy three May 40 calls and sell one May 55 call. This variable hedge creates the potential for profits while completely eliminating the risk of selling an uncovered call. If the underlying stock's market value were to increase above the level of $55 per share, your three long positions would increase in value by three points for every point in the short position. If the stock's market value were to decrease, the short position would lose value and could be closed at a profit.

This particular situation would be difficult to create all at once with a credit, because the lower-striking-price calls would tend to cost more than the higher-priced short position call. However, the variable hedge may be created at different times, when a singular position needs to be protected due to future price changes in the underlying stock.

Long and short variable hedge strategies, with defined profit and loss zones, are shown in Figure 9.17. In the long variable hedge example, you buy three June 65 calls for 1, paying $300; and you sell one June 60 call for 5. Net proceeds are $200. This long variable hedge strat-

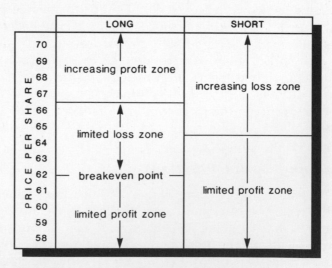

FIGURE 9.17 Variable hedge profit and loss zones.

egy achieves maximum profits if the underlying stock's market value rises. Above the striking price of 65, long call values would increase three points for every point increase in the underlying stock. If the stock's market value decreases, all of the calls lose value and the net $200 proceeds will be all profit.

Table 9.7 summarizes this position's value as of expiration at various stock price levels. The problem in this strategy is that the short positions expire later than the long positions; in most circumstances, this is the most likely way to create a credit in a variable hedge. So you need to experience price movement that creates an acceptable profit before expiration of the long position options, or be prepared to close out the short positions once the long ones expire, to avoid exposure to the risk of exercise.

The previously discussed Figure 9.17 also shows an increasing loss zone and limited profit zone in the example of a *short* hedge. In that example, you sold five June 60 calls for 5, receiving $2,500; and you bought three June 65 calls for 1, paying $300; net proceeds were $2,200. This short variable hedge strategy is a more aggressive variation

TABLE 9.7 Profits/Losses from the Long Variable Hedge Example			
Price	Stock	Call	Total
$70	+$1,200	-$500	+$700
69	+ 900	- 400	+ 500
68	+ 600	- 300	+ 300
67	+ 300	- 200	+ 100
66	0	- 100	- 100
65	- 300	0	- 300
64	- 300	+ 100	- 200
63	- 300	+ 200	- 100
62	- 300	+ 300	0
61	- 300	+ 400	+ 100
60	- 300	+ 500	+ 200
59	- 300	+ 500	+ 200
58	- 300	+ 500	+ 200

than the long example, with more proceeds up front and a corresponding higher risk level overall. When the offsetting call positions are eliminated, two of the calls remain uncovered. A decline in the value of the underlying stock would create a profit. However, an increase in the stock's market value creates an increasing level of losses. Beyond striking price, the loss is two points for every point of movement in the stock's price. Outcomes for this short hedge at various price levels of the stock are summarized in Table 9.8.

Partial Coverage Strategies

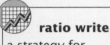 **ratio write**
a strategy for partially covering one position with another for partial rather than full coverage. (A portion of risk is eliminated, so that ratio writes can be used to reduce overall risk levels.)

Another variation of hedging involves cutting partial losses through partial coverage. This strategy is known as a *ratio write*. When you sell one call for every 100 shares owned, you have provided a one-to-one coverage. A ratio write exists when the relationship between long and short positions is not identical. The ratio can be greater on either the long side or the short side. See Table 9.9.

TABLE 9.8 Profits/Losses from the Short Variable Hedge Example			
Price	*Stock*	*Call*	*Total*
$70	−$2,500	+$500	−$2,000
69	− 2,000	+ 400	− 1,600
68	− 1,500	+ 300	− 1,200
67	− 1,000	+ 200	− 800
66	− 500	0	− 500
65	0	− 300	− 300
64	+ 500	− 300	+ 200
63	+ 1,000	− 300	+ 700
62	+ 1,500	− 300	+ 1,200
61	+ 2,000	− 300	+ 1,700
60	+ 2,500	− 300	+ 2,200
59	+ 2,500	− 300	+ 2,200
58	+ 2,500	− 300	+ 2,200

TABLE 9.9 Ratio Writes			
Calls Sold	Shares Owned	Percent Coverage	Ratio
1	75	75%	1 to ¾
2	150	75	2 to 1½
3	200	67	3 to 2
4	300	75	4 to 3
5	300	60	5 to 3
5	400	80	5 to 4

Example: You own 75 shares of stock and you sell one call. Because some of your shares are not covered, this position actually consists of two separate positions: 75 shares of stock are long, and one call is short. In practice, however, in the event of exercise, your 75 shares would satisfy three-quarters of the assignment. You would need to buy 25 shares at the striking price. Your short position is 75 percent covered. The ratio write is 1 to ³/₄.

Example: You own 300 shares of stock and you recently sold four calls. You have two positions here: 300 shares that are associated with covered calls; and one uncovered short call. In practice, however, you have a 4 to 3 ratio write.

Smart Investor Tip The ratio write is appropriate when you are willing to accept some of the risk. Consider ratio writes when you think the chances of loss are minimal.

An expanded example of the ratio write, with defined profit and loss zones, is shown in Figure 9.18.

In this example, you buy 50 shares of stock at $38 per share and you sell one September 40 call for 3. This creates a partially covered call. Half of the risk in the short call position is offset by the 50 shares. The other half of

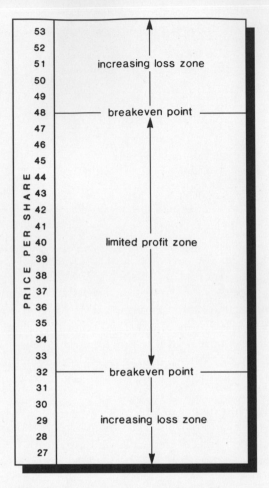

FIGURE 9.18 Ratio write profit and loss zones.

the risk is uncovered. If the value of the underlying stock rises, the risk is cut in half in the event of exercise. However, if the stock's market value falls, a loss in the stock will be offset by premium received from selling the call. A summary of this strategy is shown at various prices of the stock at expiration in Table 9.10.

STRADDLE STRATEGIES

While spreads involve buying and selling options with different terms, straddles are the simultaneous purchase

TABLE 9.10 Profits/Losses from the Ratio Write Example

Price	50 Shares of Stock	Sept. 40 Call	Total
$50	+$600	−$700	−$100
49	+ 550	− 600	− 50
48	+ 500	− 500	0
47	+ 450	− 400	+ 50
46	+ 400	− 300	+ 100
45	+ 350	− 200	+ 150
44	+ 300	− 100	+ 200
43	+ 250	0	+ 250
42	+ 200	⌐ 100	+ 300
41	+ 150	+ 200	+ 350
40	+ 100	+ 300	+ 400
39	+ 50	+ 300	+ 350
38	0	+ 300	+ 300
37	− 50	+ 300	+ 250
36	− 100	+ 300	+ 200
35	− 150	+ 300	+ 150
34	− 200	+ 300	+ 100
33	− 250	+ 300	+ 50
32	− 300	+ 300	0
31	− 350	+ 300	− 50
30	− 400	+ 300	− 100

and sale of options with the same striking price and expiration date.

Middle Loss Zones

A *long straddle* involves the purchase of calls and puts at the same striking price and expiration date. Because you pay to create the long positions, the result is a middle-zone loss range above and below the striking price; and profit zones above and below that zone.

 long straddle the purchase of an identical number of calls and puts with identical striking prices and expiration dates, designed to produce profits in the event of price movement of the underlying stock in either direction adequate to surpass the cost of opening the position.

Example: You open a long straddle. You buy one February 40 call for 2; and you buy one February 40 put for 1. Your total cost is $300. If the underlying stock's value remains within three points above or below the striking price, the straddle will lose money. If the stock's market value moves higher or lower by more than three points from striking price, then the long straddle will be profitable.

Another example of a long straddle is summarized with defined profit and loss zones in Figure 9.19. In this example, you buy one July 40 call for 3 and one July 40 put for 1; total cost is $400. The long straddle strategy will be profitable if the underlying stock's market price exceeds the four-point range on either side of the striking price.

The four points required on either side of the striking price point out the most important fact about long straddles: The more you pay in overall premium, the greater the required stock point movement away from striking price. It does not matter which direction the price moves, as long as its total point value exceeds the amount paid to open the position. Table 9.11 summarizes the outcome of this example at various stock price levels.

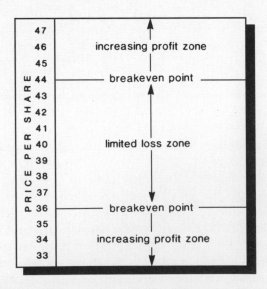

FIGURE 9.19 Long straddle profit and loss zones.

TABLE 9.11	Profits/Losses from the Long Straddle Example		
Price	50 Shares of Stock	Sept. 40 Call	Total
$47	+$400	–$100	+$300
46	+ 300	– 100	+ 200
45	+ 200	– 100	+ 100
44	+ 100	– 100	0
43	0	– 100	– 100
42	– 100	– 100	– 200
41	– 200	– 100	– 300
40	– 300	– 100	– 400
39	300	0	– 300
38	– 300	+ 100	– 200
37	– 300	+ 200	– 100
36	– 300	+ 300	0
35	– 300	+ 400	+ 100
34	– 300	+ 500	+ 200
33	– 300	+ 600	I 300

You have some flexibility in the long straddle. Since both sides are long, you are free to sell off one portion at a profit while holding onto the other. In the ideal situation, the stock will move in one direction and produce a profit on one side; and then it will move in the opposite direction, enabling you to profit on the other side. A long straddle may be most profitable in highly volatile stocks, but of course, premium value of the options will tend to be greater as well in that situation. To show how the price swing can help to double profit potential, let's say that the stock's price moves up two points above striking price. The call can then be sold at a profit. If the stock's market value later falls three points below striking price, the put can also be sold at a profit. The strategy loses if the stock remains within the narrow loss range and time value premium offsets any minor price movements. In other words, time works against you as a buyer; and when you buy both calls and puts, you have a time value premium problem on both sides of the transaction.

Middle Profit Zones

short straddle
the sale of an identical number of calls and puts with identical striking prices and expiration dates, designed to produce profits in the event of price movement of the underlying stock within a limited range.

In the previous example, two related long positions were opened, creating a middle loss zone on either side of the striking price. The opposite situation—a middle profit zone—is created through opening a *short straddle*. This involves selling an identical number of calls and puts on the same underlying stock, with the same striking price and expiration date. If the stock's market price moves beyond the middle profit zone in either direction, this position would result in a loss. Short straddles offer the potential for profits when stocks do not move in an overly broad trading range, and when time value premium is higher than average. Of course, less volatile stocks also tend to contain lower time value, whereas more volatile stocks have higher time value and higher risks with short straddles. Because time value decreases as expiration approaches, the advantage in this position is the same for sellers of calls and puts—time works for the short seller.

Example: You open a short straddle. You sell one March 50 call for 2 and one March 50 put for 1; total proceeds are $300. As long as the underlying stock's market value remains within three points of the striking price—on either side—any intrinsic value in one option is offset by the other side. But if current market value of the stock exceeds the three-point range, the short straddle will produce a loss.

The problem with the short straddle is that one side or the other is always at or in the money, so the risk of exercise is constant. And the preceding example does not allow for the transaction costs. In a practical application, the profit zone would be smaller for single options. The best outcome for this strategy, assuming that exercise does not take place, is that both sides will lose enough time value so that they can both be closed at a profit. Considering that the profit margin will be slim and risks are considerable, you need to evaluate whether this two-sided short position would be worth the risk. As with other examples of advanced strategies, the short straddle might be the result of opening one position and later adding the other.

> **Smart Investor Tip**   For each and every strategy with limited profit potential, always ask the critical question: Is it worth the risk?

An example of a short straddle with defined profit and loss zones is shown in Figure 9.20. In this example, you sell one July 40 call at 3, and one July 40 put at 1; total proceeds are $400. This creates a four-point profit zone on either side of the striking price.

The short straddle in this example creates a middle profit zone extending four points in both directions from the striking price. Unless the stock's market value is at the money at the point of expiration, the likelihood of exercise of one side or the other is high. Table 9.12 summarizes the outcome of this short straddle at various stock price levels.

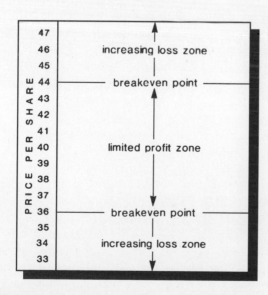

FIGURE 9.20   Short straddle profit and loss zones.

TABLE 9.12 Profits/Losses from the Short Straddle Example

Price	July 40 Call	July 40 Put	Total
$47	−$400	+$100	−$300
46	− 300	+ 100	− 200
45	− 200	+ 100	− 100
44	− 100	+ 100	0
43	0	+ 100	+ 100
42	+ 100	+ 100	+ 200
41	+ 200	+ 100	+ 300
40	+ 300	+ 100	+ 400
39	+ 300	0	+ 300
38	+ 300	− 100	+ 200
37	+ 300	− 200	+ 100
36	+ 300	− 300	0
35	+ 300	− 400	− 100
34	+ 300	− 500	− 200
33	+ 300	− 600	− 300

Actual profits and losses have to be adjusted to allow for trading costs on both sides of any position. So a thin margin of profit can be entirely wiped out by those fees, making more elaborate option strategies less than practical, notably when using only single options on either side. To compare outcomes of long and short straddles, refer to Figure 9.21, which shows profit and loss zones in a side-by-side format for each strategy.

THEORY AND PRACTICE OF COMBINED TECHNIQUES

Advanced option strategies expose you to the risk of loss, which could be significant especially when short positions are involved. If you do decide to employ any of these strategies, remember the following seven critical points:

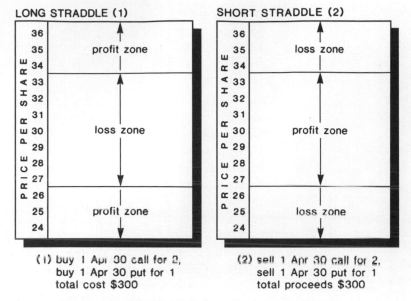

FIGURE 9.21 Comparison of long and short straddle strategies.

1. *Brokerage fees are part of the equation.* Transaction fees reduce profit margins significantly, especially when you are dealing in single-option increments. The more contracts involved, the lower the transaction fees per contract—and the greater your risks. A marginal potential profit could be wiped out by fees, so approach advanced strategies from a practical point of view. Remember that profits could be minimal, but risks could be high.

2. *Early exercise can change everything.* Buyers have the right of exercise at any time, so whenever your short positions are in the money, you could face early exercise. It is easy to forget this point and to assume that exercise is only a risk at the point of expiration. What seems a straightforward, easy strategy can be thrown into complete disarray by early exercise. In evaluating combined strategies, be sure to consider the possibility of exercise and study what its effects would be on the position.

3. *Potential profit and risk are always related directly to one another.* Many options traders tend to pay

attention only to potential profits, while over-looking potential risks. Remember that the greater the possibility of profit, the higher the potential for losses. The relationship between risk and return is inescapable.

4. *Your degree of risk will be limited by your brokerage firm.* You may devise a complex series of trades that, in your opinion, limit your risks while providing potential for significant gains. However, remember that as long as your strategy includes short positions, your brokerage firm will restrict your exposure to risk—because if you cannot meet assignment obligations, the firm will be stuck with them. The brokerage firm might not be willing to view the coverage you provide in offsetting positions, but is more likely to look at your short positions on their own merit, recognizing that you can always close long positions and be left with significant risk exposure.

5. *You need to thoroughly understand a strategy before opening positions.* Never employ any strategy before you understand how it will work out, given all possible outcomes. You need to evaluate risks carefully, not only for the most likely results but for the worst-case possibilities as well. You will need to know what to do if and when price movement happens that you were not expecting, whether the result is positive or negative in its effect on your strategy. You will not have time to think it through in every case, because changes happen quickly in the options market. You need to know how to react to every possible situation.

6. *Using LEAPS options vastly increases the flexibility of combinations.* You can always limit combinations to standardized options, ensuring that risk exposure stays within the typical six-month range. However, combination strategies can also be designed to avoid exercise risk or naked option writing risk, by employing longer-term LEAPS options. Although the long position cost is going to be higher because of extended time values, a debit position could be transformed into

a credit position with repeated short position sales over as long a period as three years. However, it is always true that higher profit potential also means greater risk. A strategy for combinations involving LEAPS has to include the same cautions as those applying to shorter-term combination strategies. The potential profits have to justify the risk exposure.

7. *It doesn't always work out the way it was planned on paper.* When you are working out an option strategy on paper, it is easy to convince yourself that a particular strategy cannot fail, or that failure is only a remote possibility. However, once you enter into a transaction, prices may not move as you expect. Remember that option premium changes are not completely predictable, and neither are stock prices. Risk is only fully understood once it is experienced directly, and only experience can demonstrate the difference between theory and practice. Sudden changes in market value of an underlying stock, or in the market as a whole, could throw a paper model into disarray.

Options add a new dimension to your portfolio. You can protect existing positions, ensure profits, and take advantage of momentary opportunities. However, every potential profit is associated with an offsetting risk. The market is efficient at least in that regard. Pricing of options reflects the risk level, so while a price is an opportunity, it also reflects exposure to the inherent risk in opening a position. Only through evaluation and analysis can you identify strategies that make sense for you, that protect your stock positions, and that you believe have a reasonable chance of producing profits at risk levels you are willing to undertake.

The next chapter explains why each investor needs to develop a personalized, individual strategy. No one approach is a proper fit for everyone.

Chapter

10

Choosing Your Own Strategy

Happiness, wealth, and success are byproducts of goal setting; they cannot be the goals themselves.
—Denis Waitley and Remi L. Witt, *The Joy of Working*, 1985

A tremendous opportunity awaits anyone who considers including options in their portfolio. Of course, that opportunity comes with degrees of risk. However, when you review the broad range of possible uses for options, it becomes clear that they can serve the interests of a wide spectrum of investors.

You will ultimately decide to employ options in your portfolio only if you conclude that they are appropriate in your particular circumstances. If your personal risk tolerance and goals dictate that you should *not* employ options at any level, then you should avoid them altogether. Keep in mind, however, that there are a broad range of reasons to use options—some high risk and others very conservative.

Your success as an investor depends on how well you are able and willing to set policies based on your long-term goals, and then identify appropriate strategies and investment choices to achieve those goals. Every investor, and particularly those using options, needs to be able to establish standards and then follow the rules they set for themselves, ignoring the temptation to deviate from a preestablished course.

With options, perhaps more than with most other forms of investing, the establishment of firm policies is critical. There are so many variations on the use of options that you need to examine with great care what you need and what you can afford. Most important in the mix of analyzing your portfolio requirements and long-term goals is the identification of what will be considered an acceptable risk. Your personal risk standards identify and define which forms of option investing—if any—fit with your profile and long-term goals. Perhaps they fit today but will not fit tomorrow. Or perhaps the reverse is true. Your personal investment requirements do not remain stationary. Your financial environment is dynamic, and it changes as your circumstances change. Along with changing long-term goals, your risk standards change with time, age, and experience.

Options might provide you with a convenient form of diversification, protection, or income—or all of these in various combinations. First, though, you need to decide what type of investor you are today and what type of investor you expect to be in the future. For so many people, the process of definition and goal-setting involves setting down ways to accumulate wealth. Along the way, the accumulation needs to be protected, altered, and properly invested so that it increases rather than remains at the same level or shrinks. Wise investors are aware not only of the need to accumulate wealth, but also to offset the double effect of taxation and inflation which, together, can erode an overly conservative and low-yielding portfolio. The loss of buying power can be as damaging in the long term as failing to plan altogether.

Option investing contains many traps, making it one of the more challenging specialties you can find. It has a complex and specialized language; it changes rapidly; and it requires a high degree of comfort with mathematics. Thus, it is easy for people to become lost in terminology, to fail to act quickly enough to take advantage of the momentary situation, or to become confused by the calculations required to assess risk and potential profit. It is also easy to become distracted by the theoretical profit of options, ignoring the associated risks, the result being taking on risks that in fact are unacceptable. Novice options traders often fail to realize how important it is to monitor the market regularly and to look for action points in their open positions.

ESTABLISHING YOUR OWN PLAN

To properly determine what risks are acceptable to you, the first step is to arrive at a series of definitions. What kinds of risks can you take? If you are a speculator, you will seek short-term income and you will have little interest in long-term growth potential. You will be willing to take exceptionally high risks while seeking higher than average profits. Selling uncovered calls or buying near-expiration options will appeal to you. You may also gravitate toward the more exotic spreads and straddles for maximum profit with limited loss exposure. If you also speculate in your stock portfolio, you will be interested in using options along with highly volatile stocks, or for coverage of short positions. The big danger for speculators is that they tend to be attracted to exotic strategies not always because they are appropriate, but because they are exotic.

Smart Investor Tip   Speculators should be certain that they use a complex strategy because it makes sense, and not just because it is complex.

If you are conservative investor and you seek long-term growth more than immediate income, your primary interest will be in the proper selection of stocks. However, even in this situation, options can supplement your portfolio. You can sell puts as one means for acquiring stocks that you consider well-priced at a particular striking price. Covered calls can be used to supplement dividend income and capital gains. And puts can be bought for temporary insurance against downside movement in the stock's price, especially during market corrections.

Many investors diversify their portfolios so that options do not jeopardize longer-term plans. You may set aside a small portion of your investment capital to use in option speculation—for example, to take advantage of short-term market price movement. Or the fund can be used to provide insurance against downside corrections when a stock's price has gone up in what you consider an overreaction to current news. Since such changes in price often are corrected in the short term, buying puts at such times could be a wise move. The opposite is true as well. If the price of stock falls, buying puts in anticipation of an upward correction could produce short-term profits in the speculative side of your portfolio.

The use of longer-terms LEAPS options opens up an even wider range of option uses. All of the popular option strategies have to be reviewed in light of the longer life-span of the LEAPS option. Time value premium changes on a different course, premium levels are higher, and the uses of LEAPS with shorter-term cover strategies is most interesting. Some features will appeal to buyers, others to sellers; certain strategies are designed to combine buying and selling together. LEAPS may also serve as a contingent purchasing plan. So many investors want to be invested for the long term but are understandably worried about the next two to three years. By buying a LEAPS option instead of 100 shares of stock, you have the right to acquire (to sell) 100 shares at a fixed price as far out as three years; but you do not have to place capital at risk. So if it turns out that the timing was bad, losses are limited to the LEAPS premium paid—which can also be reduced by selling short-term options against the longer-term expiration. The LEAPS strategies expand the entire range of possible options plays, helping you to expand profits while leveraging capital and keeping risks at a minimum.

All of the investment decisions you make depend on definition, whether involving stock, options, or both. The definition of yourself as a speculator or conservative investor is only the beginning of the process. You also need to define the long-term purpose in investing. Young families plan for the purchase of a home or saving for their child's college education. Some people want to accumulate a fund to start their own business, or to supplement retirement income. All of these long-term goals define the kinds of risks you can take. Of course, all situations require a more comprehensive planning point of view than investments. Most people need various forms of insurance (life, health, homeowners, disability); and virtually everyone needs an emergency reserve, a fund of easily accessible money they can use for emergencies. How much to set up in a reserve depends on your situation. For example, if you have a line of credit secured by your home or available through credit cards, you may not need to put a large sum of cash in a low-yielding savings account.

In the past, much has been made of financial planning. An entire industry offers to help people define their goals, usually for a fee. The financial plan might involve a written document that carefully defines your risk tolerance, long-term goals, and identification of investments that are appropriate for you. A problem with most financial planners is that they are compensated through commissions. So their investment recommendations often are self-serving. For example, a financial planner will invariably recommend a load mutual fund over a no-load fund, because the latter does not pay a commission. However, there are no significant differences in market performance between load and no-load funds, so it makes no sense to pay a commission to a financial planner. If you are comfortable enough and knowledgeable enough to be thinking about employing options in your portfolio, you probably are well beyond the need for financial planning advice. In addition, it is important to make a distinction between "planning" and "investing," and the differences often are obscured. The plan is the long-range goal and purpose to the investment program, risk identification, finding the right kind of insurance, and involves an overview of all of your personal investing needs. The investments are the means for executing the plan. Financial planners usually do not have direct access to a trading floor, so it is impractical to operate a stock portfolio through a commission-paid or fee-based planner. If you do need planning help, you probably need to separate these two aspects. Pay the planner a fee for general advice but make your own investment decisions.

Even if you think you will get valuable advice from a planner, you still need to ask the right questions. All too often, individuals representing themselves as planners or advisors are functioning only as salespeople. Thus, you need to protect yourself by ensuring that you are getting objective advice. If you hire a planner, make sure that he or she is properly licensed by the state, and qualified by education and experience to make recommendations. A Certified Financial Planner (CFP) has the proper training and experience to understand investing—which does not necessarily mean the individual understands *all* of the investment choices available to you.

> **Smart Investor Tip** Before hiring anyone, check them out thoroughly. Check the CFP website for more information, at http://www.cfp-board.org. Also check to see if the individual belongs to the Financial Planning Association (FPA), whose website is http://www.fpanet.org.

If you are considering using options as part of your portfolio, it is unlikely that you will find a planner or advisor who is knowledgeable in this area. It is even less likely that such a person will be willing to help you set up a program for options trading. The commissions simply will not be high enough to make it practical for the planner. In practical application, a financial planner often is not justified. If you plan to use options as part of your investment program, you are probably sophisticated enough about the stock market without the additional guidance, and you are able to make your own decisions.

By the same argument, you are not going to benefit by using a full-commission brokerage firm. One of the dozens of discount brokerage firms is adequate for the execution of your trades. If you believe that you can trade in options but also need a broker's advice, it might not be a practical route to take just yet. The low-cost trading services widely available on the Internet are rapidly making the older, more traditional forms of brokerage obsolete.

Select a trading service based not only on price, but also on level of service. How easy is it to get connected to the website, and how fast or slow is it? Ask for referrals from friends and locate the service offering reasonable price and excellent service. Remember, the cheapest trading cost is not necessarily going to be the best source. You should seek out a combination of reasonable service and fast online response time.

You will operate most effectively as an options trader without any outside help or interference. You do not need a financial planner or a stockbroker for advice. As an options trader, you will need to develop your confidence and knowledge to the point that you are able to make decisions on your own. One of the myths about the stock market is that professional help is necessary to make wise decisions. More often than not, the help you get from paying a professional is not any better than decisions you make on your own. Successful investors recognize that no matter how much professional help they pay for, they are responsible for their own profits or losses. Many people have discovered at great expense that no one will care for their money as much as they do. As an options investor—or as an experienced investor employing any strategy—you do not need to pay for advice from a market professional.

Smart Investor Tip Options traders, because of the type of market, do not serve themselves well by paying someone else for advice.

If you subscribe to any outside service, be sure it provides you with value for its cost. The options and stock analysis services provided by ValueLine and S&P are both excellent, especially if you want to get a large volume of good fundamental and technical analysis quickly and efficiently. If you are thinking about using the research services of one of the big Wall Street firms, be careful. Recent events have demonstrated that the Wall Street analysts have had serious conflicts of interest concerning their firms' investment banking operations, so many questions should be raised: Is the analyst skilled in accounting? On what basis do they make recommendations? What is their track record?

The most significant problem for analysts is a misdirected tendency to emphasize price targets and earnings projections. The price of the stock in the next few months should be of no value nor interest to the serious long-term investor; it is a guessing game at best. Predicting earnings is similarly shortsighted and often based on what management has told the analyst. Perhaps the most scandalous aspect of the broad-ranging Wall Street problems revealed in recent years is the lack of value in analysts' advice—and the concerted effort among Wall Street firms themselves to artificially inflate the value of useless predictions.

Anyone using options is operating at a level of skill and expertise so that they do not need the help of a Wall Street research department. Indeed, recent history has shown, again and again, that the advice has been poor and that those taking it have lost *more* than the average investor.

IDENTIFYING THE RANGE OF RISK

In any discussion of risk, a starting point should be a discussion of *information* risk. Are you getting valid information? If you have listened to analysts in the past, or have followed the crowd in deciding when to buy or sell, then you have been operating with the wrong information. But if you have picked stocks carefully and for the right reasons, identified option opportunities, and found ways to use options to reduce other risks, then you are on the right track.

Beyond the problems associated with information risk, you have to remain vigilant and watch for the whole range of risks you face whenever you are in the market. Options serve the entire spectrum of risk profiles, and can be used in combinations of ways to supplement income, insure other positions, leverage future long positions, or modify exposure to loss. To determine how to use options in your portfolio, first go through these three steps:

1. *Study the full range of possible option strategies.* Before opening any positions in options, prepare hypothetical variations and track the market to see how you would have done. Track options through the Internet, which provides ongoing

quotations free of charge, usually with only a 20-minute delay. Watch how values change from day to day and pay special attention to the course of time value. Note how time value decreases over time and how that rate of change is affected when stock market prices are at different levels in relation to striking prices. In other words, become familiar with valuation and changes in valuation by watching a particular series of options over time.

2. *Identify your personal risk tolerance levels.* Before picking an option strategy, first determine what levels of risk you can afford to take. Set standards and then follow them. Limit your market activities to only those strategies that fit your risk profile, and avoid the temptation to open the more exotic positions—at least when you are starting out. Also remember that your investing goals *and* risk tolerance will change over time, based on changes in your financial position, experience, and age. Be prepared to abandon outdated ideas and perceptions of risk, and continually refresh your outlook based on current information. Avoid the mistake of assuming that you can set down your entire lifetime's investing goals today, because these will change over time.

3. *Identify and understand all of the risks associated with options trading.* Consider every possible risk, including the risk that a stock's market price will not move as you expect, or that a short position could be exercised early. Anticipate even the most remote possibility, because in the options market, that possibility could materialize without warning. Remember that it is easy to be distracted by the most obvious or most likely outcome, and to overlook the complexity of the market. Develop a deeper sense of the market by tracking it and, ultimately, by experiencing it directly. In most forms of investing, perceptions about risk tend to be fixed. In option investing, it all depends on the position you assume. For example, when you are a buyer, time is the enemy; and when you are a seller, time defines your profit potential.

The obvious risk in each and every option position is that the underlying stock will do one of two things. It may move in a direction you didn't expect or want; or it will fail to move enough for a position to be profitable. Always identify and make a graph of the profit and loss zones before opening positions. The visualization of these zones helps you to identify when strategies make sense, and when the potential profit does not justify the risk.

Beyond this, be aware of the other forms of risk that are going to be involved when you trade in options.

Margin and Collateral Risks

Most investors think of margin investing as buying stock on credit. That is the most familiar and common form. In the options market, margin requirements are different and margin is used in a different way. Your brokerage firm will require that short positions be protected, at least partially, through collateral. The preferred form of collateral is owning 100 shares of stock for each call sold; in other situations, your maximum exposure will be limited by the brokerage firm.

Whenever you open uncovered short positions in options, cash or securities will have to be placed on deposit or otherwise committed to protect the brokerage firm's position. The level required is established by minimum legal requirements, subject to increases by individual brokerage firms' policies. Any balance owed above the deposit represents risk, both for the brokerage firm and for you. If the stock moves in a direction you do not desire, the margin requirement goes up as well. In that respect, margin risk could be defined as leverage risk.

The margin requirement limits your freedom to be involved in short option positions. The amount of capital available to you defines the maximum scope of participation you can enjoy in the options market, as a short seller. Before entering any uncovered short positions, you will need to determine the policies of the brokerage firm, and ensure that you will be able to meet them. If you cannot, you could be required to close positions at a loss before you want to. For positions like spreads and straddles, the brokerage firm may view each position separately, and not in combination. So a short position may be seen as representing full exposure, and the margin requirement could be significant.

If you have to pledge securities to cover option positions, you lose the flexibility to sell those securities whenever you wish. Typing up your portfolio to cover option contracts could be a smart move or a mistake. For example, if potential profit is relatively limited, does it make sense to freeze your entire portfolio because of possible losses? Evaluate the situation before opening option positions requiring you to tie up other securities or cash.

Personal Goal Risks

Successful investors always establish goals. Putting it another way, they always know what they want and where they stand; they also know what they need to do in every possible change in their investment positions. For example, if you establish a goal that you will invest no more than 15 percent of your total portfolio in option speculation, it is important to stay with that goal. This requires constant review. Sudden market changes can mean sudden and unexpected losses, especially when you buy options and when you sell short. Getting away from the maximum goal you set is all too easy.

Your goal should also include identification of the point at which you will close positions, either to take profits or to limit losses. Avoid breaking your own rules by delaying, hoping for favorable changes in the near-term future. This is tempting, but often leads to unacceptable losses or missing a profit opportunity. Establish two price points in every option position: *minimum gain* and *maximum loss*. When either point is reached, close the position.

Smart Investor Tip   Options traders, like gamblers, can succeed if they know when to fold. If they don't fold when they should, they will lose.

Unavailability of Market Risks

One of the least talked about risks in any investment is the potential that you will not be able to buy or sell when you want to. The discussion of options strategies is based on the basic idea that you will be able to place orders whenever you want to, without problems or delays.

The reality is quite different in some situations. When market volume is especially heavy, it is difficult and sometimes impossible to place orders when you want to. In an exceptionally large market correction, volume will be exceptionally heavy as investors try to cut losses. So if you trade by telephone, your broker's lines will be overloaded and those who do get through will experience longer than usual delays—because so much business is taking place at the same time. If you trade online, the same problem will occur. You will not be able to get through to the online brokerage website if it is already overloaded with traders placing orders. In these extreme situations, your need to place orders will be greater than normal, as it is with all other investors. So at such times, the market is unavailable to you.

Current rules require that the markets shut down when large downside losses take place, protecting you to a degree. However, this still represents the unavailability of the market. The most desirable price level for a particular strategy might come and go in moments and if the market is unavailable to you—because of high traffic or a programmed shutdown—that opportunity will be gone and might never return. This problem is rare, but the risk is very real.

Disruption in Trading Risks

Another risk you face as an options trader is that trading could be halted in the underlying stock. For example, if rumors about a company are affecting the stock's market price, the exchange may halt trading for a day or more. When stock is halted, all related option trading is halted as well. For example, a company might be rumored as a takeover candidate. If the rumors affecting price are true, when the trading halt is lifted, the stock may open at a much higher or lower price than before. As an options investor, you are exposed to potentially significant risks, perhaps even preventing you from being able to limit your exposure to loss by offsetting the exposed side of the transaction. You will be required to wait until trading re-opens, and by then it might be too late. The cost of protecting your position might be too high, or you might be subjected to automatic exercise.

Brokerage Risks

As with all other institutions, brokerage firms can become insolvent and go out of business. As a general rule, a type of industry self-insurance protects most positions if and when a particular firm were to go out of business. This rare occurrence would not necessarily affect you, because the Options Clearing Corporation (OCC) would normally cover all of the open positions. However, in a particularly severe situation involving thousands of open positions, the risk—as remote as it is—does exist.

A more severe potential risk is the individual action of your broker. If you use a discount brokerage, you are not exposed to this risk, because the role of the broker is to place orders as you direct. However, if you are using a broker for advice on options trading, you are exposed to the risk that a broker will use his or her discretion, even if you have not granted that right. Never grant unlimited discretion to someone else, no matter how much trust you have. As an options trader, you need to know it is highly questionable that using a broker's advice makes sense; however, you need to ensure that the broker follows your instructions and does not exceed the authority you grant. In this fast-moving market, it is difficult for a broker with many clients to pay attention to your options trades to the degree required. In fact, with online free quotations widely available, you really do not need a full-commission broker at all. In the Internet environment with a lot of free information services and low-cost trading, commission-based brokerage is becoming increasingly obsolete.

Yet another risk, even with online brokerage accounts, is that mistakes will be made in placing orders. Fortunately, online trading is easily traced and documented. However, it is still possible that a "buy" order goes in as a "sale," or vice versa. Such mistakes can be disastrous for you as an options trader. If you trade by telephone or in person, the risk is increased just due to human error. If you trade online, check your order carefully before sending it.

Trading Cost Risks

A calculated profit zone has to be reduced, or a loss zone increased, to allow for the cost of placing trades. Brokerage trading fees apply to both sides of every transaction. If you trade in single-option contracts, the cost is high on a per-option basis. Trading in higher increments is economical because the cost of trading is lower on a per-option basis.

This book uses examples for single contracts in most cases to make outcomes clear; in practice, such trading is not practical because the trading fees require more profit just to break even in many circumstances. A thin margin of profit will evaporate quickly when trading costs are added into the mix.

Every investor needs to shop for the most economical brokerage arrangement, given the need for high-quality service. With online competition, trading fees are reasonable and, in most instances, lower than in the past. However, be sure to compare option fees as well as other features of online trading. Seek a high service level combined with competitive option trading fees to minimize the cost of trading.

In cases where you buy and then exercise an option, or you sell and the option is exercised by the buyer or the exchange, you not only pay the option trading fee; you also have to pay for the cost of transacting the shares of stock, a point to remember in calculating overall return. It is possible that if you're operating on a thin profit margin, it could be taken up entirely by trading fees on both sides of the transaction; so that cost has to be calculated beforehand. As a general observation, single-contract trades involve about one-half point for the combined cost of opening and then closing the option position; so you need to add a half-point cushion to allow for that. The calculation changes as you deal in multiple contracts, in which trading costs on a per-contract basis are going to be far lower.

Lost Opportunity Risks

One of the more troubling aspects of options trading involves lost opportunity. This arises in several ways, the most obvious being that experienced by covered call sellers. You risk the loss of stock profits in the event of price increase and exercise. Your profit is locked in at the striking price. Covered call writers accept the certainly of a consistent, better-than-average return and, in exchange, they lose the occasional larger capital gain on their stock.

Opportunity risks arise in other ways, too. For example, if you are involved in exotic combinations including long and short positions, your margin requirements may prevent you from being able to take advantage of other investment opportunities. Most investors find themselves existing in an environment of moderate scarcity, so that not every opportunity may be seized. With this in mind, it is important that before committing yourself to an open position in options, you recognize how that could limit you in other choices.

All stock investors have to be concerned with the lost opportunity associated with the timing of buying stock. Some opportunities come up after prices have fallen to bargain levels; but at those times, you don't really know if the stock will rebound quickly or take years. This type of lost opportunity can be overcome using LEAPS. You can purchase the right to buy (or sell) shares up to three years out, and as any investor knows, a lot can happen in three years. Using LEAPS helps you to tie in striking prices and control 100 shares without risking the whole amount you would need to buy 100 shares. So the LEAPS strategy not only leverages your portfolio; it also helps you diversify and place control over several different stocks rather than placing a larger sum into a single issue.

EVALUATING YOUR RISK TOLERANCE

Every investor has a specific level of risk tolerance—the ability and willingness to accept risk. This trait is not fixed, however, but changes over time. Your personal risk tolerance is affected by several factors:

✔ *Investment capital.* How much money do you have available to invest? How much do you have committed to long-term growth, and how much can you spare for more adventurous alternatives? Obviously, those with a large amount of what is called "disposable income" can afford to dispose of it, more than those who cannot afford to lose at all.

✔ *Personal factors.* Your risk tolerance is significantly affected by your age, income, debt level, economic status, job, and job security. It changes drastically with major life events such as marriage, birth of a child, divorce, or death of a family member.

✔ *Your investing experience.* How experienced are you as an investor? Confident investors are going to be more likely to willingly undertake option investing without the advice of a broker, and less experienced investors will hesitate to go on their own. The length of time you have been investing is also a factor. No matter how much you study investing in theory, you do not really gain market experience until you place real money at risk.

✔ *Type of account.* Your risk tolerance depends on how and why you invest, and the type of account involved. For example, if you use options as part of a self-directed retirement plan, you will be limited in most cases to covered call writing. Because the portfolio is long term, you will tend to pick stocks with good growth potential. If you invest in your personal account, you will have greater flexibility and could take a broader range of strategic risks.

✔ *Your personal goals.* Every investor's goals ultimately determine how much risk is acceptable. You may wish to conserve capital, hedge against inflation, maximize short-term income, attain a consistent rate of return, accumulate capital for retirement, or a combination of these and other goals. Remember that definition of personal goals should dictate how you invest. It is easy to invest in ways that are contrary to your goals, so definition has to be applied in the market as well.

Smart Investor Tip   Risk tolerance is reflected in the way you invest. You will have a better chance of succeeding if you ensure that the risks you take are risks you can afford.

As you develop your risk tolerance profile, use that profile to determine how to invest. Many investors find themselves making decisions based on rumor or unsubstantiated opinion or suggestions from others. They fail to check out information for themselves; more to the point, they do not apply the basic test to determine if a particular action fits with their own risk profiles. Your tolerance for risk should be the guiding force for all investment decisions you make. Select fundamental and technical indicators that not only provide information about trends in the company and its stock, but also identify specific risk factors that should affect your decision to take one of the four basic market actions: buy, hold, sell, or stay away.

The best investment decisions invariably are made as the result of thorough evaluation of the essential features of an investment or strategy, the most important being risk. By putting down on paper the various types of options trades in which you can engage and studying possible outcomes—including the visualized graph of profit and loss zones—you will gain a clear view of how options fit—or don't fit—into your overall plan. Of equal importance, you will discover which strategies clearly are inappropriate for you, and those can be abandoned. The evaluation process helps you to avoid mistakes and focus attention on what will be beneficial, given your risk tolerance level. The risk evaluation worksheet for option investing in Table 10.1 will help you to classify options by degrees of risk.

Applying Limits

Awareness of your personal limits is important as a guide for option investing. Whenever you have open positions in options, you need to know what your immediate goals are—when or if you will close those positions, for example, on either the profit or loss side. Establishing a target rate of return or maximum bailout loss position clearly defines your policies as an options trader.

To define these limits, identify option trades you will make defined by rate of return and other features of the option: time until expiration, time value level, distance between current market value of the stock and striking price of the option, premium level, volatility of the stock,

TABLE 10.1   Risk Evaluation Worksheet

Lowest Possible Risk

____ Covered call writing

____ Put purchase for insurance (long position)

____ Call purchase for insurance (short position)

Medium Risk

____ Ratio writing

____ Combined strategies

     ____ Long   ____ Short

High Risk

____ Uncovered call writing

____ Combined strategies

     ____ Long   ____ Short

____ Call purchases for income

____ Put purchases for Income

overall market conditions, and the potential for rolling forward to avoid exercise. In the case of covered calls, also identify potential rates of return if the stock is unchanged versus return if exercised. You improve your chances of success by narrowing down your choices with these four points in mind:

1. _Maximum time value._ As a buyer, avoid purchasing options with a high level of time value. Remember that time works against you, and the more time value, the lower your prospects for profit. As a seller, apply the opposite advice. Look for options containing maximum time value premium. Time works _for_ you as seller, so the higher the time value premium, the greater your profit potential and the higher your protection against increasing premium in the option.

2. _Time until expiration._ Buyers of very short-term options will be fortunate to earn a profit. These options tend to be very cheap as long as they are at the money or out of the money; however,

you will depend on movement in the stock's market value in a short period of time. Novice options traders easily overlook the fact that time value premium declines as expiration approaches, but it rarely increases. Sellers benefit from short-term trading in options for the same reasons, but they expose themselves to risk of exercise for relatively low premium income. As a general observation, it takes time for the buyer's option to build intrinsic value; and it also takes time for the seller's option to lose time value. How much time is ideal will depend on the option, current status, and volatility of the underlying stock, and the relationship between the stock's current market value and the option's striking price.

3. *The number of option contracts.* How many options should you trade at one time? You do not have to limit yourself to a single contract when it makes more sense and costs less in trading costs to use several contracts. Of course, while this increases your profit potential, it also exposes you to higher risks. You will also be limited in terms of uncovered short positions by the degree to which your brokerage firm is willing to let you face exposure to exercise; and by the regulations governing coverage of short positions.

4. *Target rate of return.* Enter every option trade with a specific target return in mind, either in terms of rate of return or dollars of profit. Remember that if more than one outcome is possible, you need to define your target with each outcome in mind. For example, you might determine that an open long position will be closed when you double your money or lose half.

By identifying all of the features that you consider acceptable in order to employ a specific option strategy, you define your risk tolerance level. You can then select options and strategies that fit within your self-defined limits. If your limits are unrealistic, you will soon discover that no options meet your criteria.

Example: You have set a policy for yourself that incorporates several features. You desire to buy options. First, the time value should not exceed 25 percent of total premium. Second, they must have at least four months to go until expiration. Third, they must be in the money. However, when you try to apply this set of rules, you cannot locate any options meeting your list of rules. Adjustments are necessary.

When considering an option strategy of any nature, first calculate potential profits in the event of expiration or exercise, and then set criteria for other features: maximum time value, time until expiration, the number of contracts involved in the transaction, target rate of return, and the price range at which you will close. Obviously, these criteria will be drastically different for buyers than for sellers, and for covered versus uncovered option writing.

Use the option limits worksheet in Table 10.2 to set your personal limits. Then always use these limits as rules, and follow your rules to guide your option trading activity. If you discover that your standards are unrealistic, adjust them so that profit opportunities are not lost. By deciding in advance the characteristics of your option investments, and by knowing when you will close an open position, you will avoid the most common problem faced by option investors: making decisions in a void. Many have invested well in the beginning, only to fail later by not knowing when to take profits; or by falling into the second common trap: impatience.

LOOKING TO THE FUTURE

Besides setting immediate standards and goals for option strategies in your portfolio, set long-term investing policies for yourself. Then fit option strategies that conform to those policies.

It is a mistake to open option positions on the advice of a broker or friend, without first considering how it fits into your long-term investing policy and how the move fits with your risk profile. Options, like all other investments, should always be used in the context of your individual plans. This is one of the long-term problems with

TABLE 10.2   Option Limits

Covered Call Sale Criteria

Rate of Return If Unchanged

Dividends	$____		
Call premium	____	Total	$____
		Cost of stock	$____
		Gain	____%

Rate of Return If Exercised

Dividends	$____		
Call premium	____		
Stock gain	____	Total	$____
		Cost of stock	$____
		Gain	____%

Option Purchase Criteria

Maximum time value: ____%

Time until expiration: ____ months

Number of options: ____ contracts

Target rate of return: ____%

Sell level: increase to $____ or decrease to $____

taking advice from individuals whose compensation depends on generating trades: They tend to think in terms of volume rather than starting from the point of view of what works for the client.

Example: You have written down your personal investing goals, and have identified what you hope to achieve in the intermediate and long-term future. You are willing to assume risks in a low to moderate range, so all of your capital is invested in shares of blue-chip companies. In order to increase portfolio value, you consider one of the following two possible strategies:

Strategy 1: Hold shares of stock as long-term investments. Aim for appreciation and continuing dividend income.

Strategy 2: Increase the value of your portfolio by purchasing shares as in the first strategy and waiting for a moderate increase in value; then begin writing covered calls. As long as your minimum rate of return if exercised or unchanged will always exceed 35 percent, you will write a call, and then avoid exercise through rolling techniques. If a call is exercised and stock is called away, you plan to reinvest the proceeds in additional purchases of other blue-chip company shares.

In this comparison, the rate of return from the second strategy will always be higher than the first, due to the yield from writing covered calls. A 35 percent rate of return is not unreasonable, because it includes the capital gain from selling shares in the event of exercise; and because calls can be closed and replaced several times per year. So an annualized double-digit rate is not only possible, it is likely under this strategy. In addition to providing impressive returns, writing covered calls also provides downside protection by discounting your basis in shares of stock.

An interesting point to remember about the covered call strategy, especially as described in strategy 2: The common argument *against* writing covered calls is that you may lose future profits in the event the stock's price rises dramatically, because your striking price locks you in. It is true that, were the stock's market value to climb dramatically, you would experience exercise and "lose" those profits. However, remember that well-selected stocks will also tend to be less volatile than average, so that the chances of such increases—while they can happen—are lower than average. In addition, covered call writers take their double-digit returns consistently in exchange for the occasional lost paper profit. The goal of long-term growth is not inconsistent with writing covered calls, as long as you have a plan and stick to it; and as long as exercised shares are replaced with other shares of equal growth potential.

The long-term goal of building a portfolio can be achieved while also using options in appropriate ways. Covered call writing is a conservative strategy that yields exceptionally high returns when done correctly, especially for the patient investor who is willing to build some profit into the basis before embarking on a covered call writing program. The impatient investor is constantly tempted to take unacceptable risks, and ultimately will lose, not because a strategy is wrong but because such an investor sabotages his or her own plans. A smart approach is to first create and build a portfolio of strong growth-oriented stocks, wait for some price appreciation, and then embark on a program of income enhancement through covered call writing. For example, you might decide that you need a stock's market value to grow by five points or 10 percent above your basis, before you will begin writing covered calls. With that policy, exercise ensures profits with properly selected calls.

You can employ options to provide downside protection for stocks you are holding for the long term, an especially valuable feature in a volatile market. As reforms take place in the way the corporations report to stockholders and even do their accounting, we may also experience greater fundamental volatility. This will concern many investors who prefer predictability. However, it is better in the long run to get reliable, accurate, and honest reports from companies, without any manipulation of the results. The fundamental volatility problem will settle down and be absorbed in the market culture just as other important changes have done. All investors need to adjust their expectations, however. Predictability in results is not a realistic goal, and to some degree, the corporate scandals were fed in part by pressure to meet or beat predictions made by analysts. In the real world of finance, predicting future profits should serve as a corporate target and monitoring tool, and not as a deciding point for whether a company's stock is good or bad for investors.

Being aware of the limitations in reporting, technical, and fundamental volatility, and the likelihood of unsettled conditions for many years to come, options investors face a great opportunity. You can profit from the volatility that is so unsettling, just by employing options to insure your portfolio, speculate on temporary price movement, or hedge other portfolio positions. The use of LEAPS to leverage your capital enables you to make potential profits whether the market trend is up or down.

All forms of investing contain their own set of opportunities and risks. Investors who lose money consistently in options tend to share many characteristics: They do not set goals, so they do not have a preestablished plan for closing positions profitably. They do not select strategies in their own best interests, often describing themselves as conservative while using options in a highly speculative manner. They believe in the fundamentals but they follow only technical indicators. They have not taken the time to define their risk tolerance level, so they do not know when the risks they are taking are too high. A popular maxim in the investing community is If you don't know where you're going, any road will get you there. This is as true for option investors as for anyone else.

Successful investors are focused. They take the time to define their goals carefully, and they narrow down their risk tolerance with great care. In other words, they define themselves in terms of what works for them, and what doesn't work. This enables them to use strategies that make sense, *and* to resist temptation when they receive advice from others. They also tend to be patient, and are willing to wait for the right opportunities rather than taking chances even when conditions are not right for them.

To succeed in the market, place yourself in the second group of investors. Work from clear definition of goals and risk tolerance levels, avoid the temptation to chase fast profits; start by selecting stocks wisely and waiting for the right opportunities to use options to enhance your portfolio. Also study option terminology and trading rules so that you are completely comfortable with the market before risking your money. Success does not come to the unprepared—a cliché to be sure, but still an unavoidable truth. Success with options can be both predictable and controllable. If you gain knowledge, learn the rules of the playing field, research stocks thoroughly, and stay disciplined in your decisions; then you will succeed.

To some extent, you may also need to experiment, to try out a strategy to find out whether you are comfortable in a particular risk profile; and to see how you react when markets move in the opposite direction from what you expected. You cannot really know your risk tolerance until you have placed money at risk—no matter how much time you spend on the theory of the market. There is no substitute for experience.

Devising a personal, individualized strategy is a rewarding experience. Seeing clearly what you need to do and then executing the strategy successfully gives you a well-deserved sense of achievement and competence, not to mention control. You will profit from devising and applying options strategies based on calculation and observation. You will also benefit from the satisfaction that comes from mastering a complex investment field, and from finding yourself completely and totally in control.

Glossary

The most bloodthirsty language in the newspapers today is not found in the international pages. It's found in the business pages.
—Al Ries and Jack Trout, *Marketing Warfare*, 1986

after-tax breakeven point   the point level at which you will break even on an option trade, considering the taxes due on short-term capital gains you will be required to pay for trading options.

American-style option   an option that can be exercised at any time before expiration. All equity options and some index options are American-style.

annualized basis   a method for comparing rates of return for holdings of varying periods, in which all returns are expressed as though investments had been held over a full year. (It involves dividing the holding period by the number of months the positions were open, and multiplying the result by 12.)

assignment   the act of exercise against a seller, done on a random basis or in accordance with orderly procedures developed by the Options Clearing Corporation and brokerage firms.

at the money   the status of an option when the underlying stock's value is identical to the option's striking price.

auction market   the public exchanges in which stocks, bonds, options, and other products are traded publicly; and in which values are established by ever-changing supply and demand on the part of buyers and sellers.

automatic exercise   action taken by the Options Clearing Corporation at the time of expiration, when an in-the-money option has not been otherwise exercised or canceled.

average down   a strategy involving the purchase of stock when its market value is decreasing. (The average cost of shares bought in this manner is consistently higher than current market value, so a portion of the paper loss on declining stock value is absorbed, enabling covered call writers to sell calls and profit even when the stock's market value has declined.) (See Figure G.1.)

average up   a strategy involving the purchase of stock when its market value is increasing. (The average cost of shares bought in this manner is consistently lower than current market value, enabling covered call writers to sell in the money when the basis is below the striking price.) (See Figure G.2.)

bear spread   a strategy involving the purchase and sale of calls or puts that will produce maximum profits when the value of the underlying stock falls.

beta   a measurement of relative volatility of a stock, made by comparing the degree of price movement in comparison to a larger index of stock prices.

book value   the actual value of a company, more accurately called "book value per share"; the value of a company's capital (assets less liabilities), divided by the number of outstanding shares of stock.

box spread   the combination of a bull spread and a bear spread, opened at the same time on the same underlying stock.

breakeven price (also called the **breakeven point**)   the price of the underlying stock at which the option investor breaks even. (For call buyers, this price is the number of points above striking price equal to the call premium cost; for put buyers, this price is the number of points below striking price equal to the put premium cost.)

breakout   the movement of a stock's price below support level or above resistance level.

bull spread   a strategy involving the purchase and sale of calls or puts that will produce maximum profits when the value of the underlying stock rises.

buy 100 shares per month

MONTH	PRICE	AVERAGE
Jan	$40	$40
Feb	38	39
Mar	36	38
Apr	34	37
May	27	35
Jun	29	34

FIGURE G.1   Average down.

buy 100 shares per month

MONTH	PRICE	AVERAGE
Jan	$40	$40
Feb	44	42
Mar	45	43
Apr	47	44
May	54	46
Jun	52	47

FIGURE G.2   Average up.

butterfly spread   a strategy involving open options in one striking price range, offset by transactions at higher and lower ranges at the same time.

buyer   an investor who purchases a call or a put option; the buyer realizes a profit if the value of stock moves above the specified price (call) or below the specified price (put).

calendar spread   (also called **time spread**) a spread involving the simultaneous purchase or sale of options on the same underlying stock, with different expirations.

call   an option acquired by a buyer or granted by a seller to buy 100 shares of stock at a fixed price.

called away   the result of having stock assigned. (Upon exercise, 100 shares of the seller's stock are called away at the striking price.)

chartist   an analyst who studies charts of a stock's price movement in the belief that recent patterns can be used to predict upcoming price changes and directions.

class   all options traded on a single underlying security, including different striking prices and expiration dates.

closing purchase transaction   a transaction to close a short position, executed by buying an option previously sold, canceling it out.

closing sale transaction   a transaction to close a long position, executed by selling an option previously bought, closing it out.

combination   any purchase or sale of options on one underlying stock, with terms that are not identical.

contract   a single option, the agreement providing a buyer with the rights the option grants. (Those rights include identification of the stock, the cost of the option, the date the option will expire, and the fixed price per share of the stock to be bought or sold under the right of the option.)

conversion   the process of moving assigned stock from the seller of a call option or to the seller of a put option.

core earnings   as defined by Standard & Poors, the after-tax earnings generated from a corporation's principal business.

cover   to protect oneself by owning 100 shares of the underlying stock for each call sold. (The risk in the short position in the call is covered by ownership of 100 shares.)

covered call   a call sold to create an open short position, when the seller also owns 100 shares of stock for each call sold.

credit spread   any spread in which receipts from short positions are higher than premiums paid for long positions, net of transaction fees.

current market value   the market value of stock at any given time.

cycle   the pattern of expiration dates of options for a particular underlying stock. (The three cycles occur in four-month intervals and are described by month abbreviations. They are (1) January, April, July, and October, or JAJO; (2) February, May, August, and November, or FMAN; and (3) March, June, September, and December, or MJSD.)

debit spread   any spread in which receipts from short positions are lower than premiums paid for long positions, net of transaction fees.

debt investment   an investment in the form of a loan made to earn interest, such as the purchase of a bond.

deep in   condition when the underlying stock's current market value is five points or more above the striking price of the call or below the striking price of the put. (See Figure G.3.)

deep out   condition when the underlying stock's current market value is five points or more below the striking price of the call or above the striking price of the put. (See Figure G.3.)

delivery   the movement of stock ownership from one owner to another. (In the case of exercised options, shares are registered to the new owner upon receipt of payment.)

delta   the degree of change in option premium, in relation to changes in the underlying stock. (If the call option's degree of change exceeds the change in the underlying stock, it is called an "up delta"; when the change is less than the underlying stock, it is called a "down delta." The reverse terminology is applied to puts.) (See Figure G.4.)

	CALLS	PUTS
48 47 46	deep in	deep out
45 44 43 42	in the money	out of the money
41 40 39	───── striking price ─────	
38 37 36	out of the money	in the money
35 34 33 32	deep out	deep in

FIGURE G.3   Deep in/deep out.

stock price change	OPTION PREMIUM CHANGE			
	1 point	2 points	3 points	4 points
1	1.00	2.00	3.00	4.00
2	0.50	1.00	1.50	2.00
3	0.33	0.67	1.00	1.33
4	0.25	0.50	0.75	1.00
5	0.20	0.40	0.60	0.80

FIGURE G.4   Delta.

diagonal spread a calendar spread in which offsetting long and short positions have both different striking prices and different expiration dates.

discount to reduce the true price of the stock by the amount of premium received. (A benefit in selling covered calls, the discount provides downside protection and protects long positions.)

dividend yield dividends paid per share of common stock, computed by dividing dividends paid per share by the current market value of the stock.

dollar cost averaging a strategy for investing over time, either buying a fixed number of shares or investing a fixed dollar amount, in regular intervals. (The result is an averaging of overall price. If market value increases, average cost is always lower than current market value; if market value decreases, average cost is always higher than current market value.)

downside protection a strategy involving the purchase of one put for every 100 shares of the underlying stock that you own. (This insures you against losses to some degree. For every in-the-money point the stock falls, the put will increase in value by one point. Before exercise, you may sell the put and take a profit offsetting stock losses, or exercise the put and sell the shares at the striking price.)

Dow Theory a theory that market trends are predictable based on changes in market averages.

early exercise the act of exercising an option prior to expiration date.

earnings per share a commonly used method for reporting profits. Net profits for a year or other period are divided by the number of shares of common stock outstanding as of the ending date of the financial report. (The result is expressed as a dollar value.)

EBITDA a popular measurement of cash flow, which stands for earnings before interest, taxes, depreciation, and amortization.

efficient market hypothesis a theory stating that current stock prices reflect all information publicly known about a company.

equity investment an investment in the form of part ownership, such as the purchase of shares of stock in a corporation.

European-style option an option than can be exercised only during a specified period of time immediately preceding expiration. Some index options are European-style.

exercise the act of buying stock under the terms of the call option or selling stock under the terms of the put option, at the specified price per share in the option contract.

expiration date the date on which an option becomes worthless, which is specified in the option contract.

expiration time the latest possible time to place an order for cancellation or exercise of an option, which may vary depending on the brokerage firm executing the order and on the option itself.

fundamental analysis a study of financial information and attributes of a company's management and competitive position, as a means for selecting stocks.

fundamental volatility the tendency for a company's sales and profits to change from one period to the next, with more erratic change representing higher volatility.

GAAP acronym for Generally Accepted Accounting Principles, the rules and standards for reporting financial results among companies and auditing firms.

hedge a strategy involving the use of one position to protect another. (For example, stock is purchased in the belief it will rise in value, and a put is purchased on the same stock to protect against the risk that market value will decline.)

horizontal spread a calendar spread in which offsetting long and short positions have identical striking prices but different expiration dates.

incremental return a technique for avoiding exercise while increasing profits with written calls. (When the value of the underlying stock rises, a single call is closed at a loss and replaced with two or more call writes with later expiration dates, producing cash and a profit in the exchange.)

in the money the status of a call option when the underlying stock's market value is higher than the option's striking price, or of a put option when the underlying stock's market value is lower than the option's striking price. (See Figure G.5.)

intrinsic value that portion of an option's current value equal to the number of points that it is in the money. ("Points" equals the number of dollars of value per share, so 35 points equals $35 per share.) (See Figure G.6.)

know your customer a rule for brokers requiring the broker to be aware of the risk and capital profile of each client, designed to ensure that recommendations are suitable for each individual.

last trading day the Friday preceding the third Saturday of the expiration month of an option.

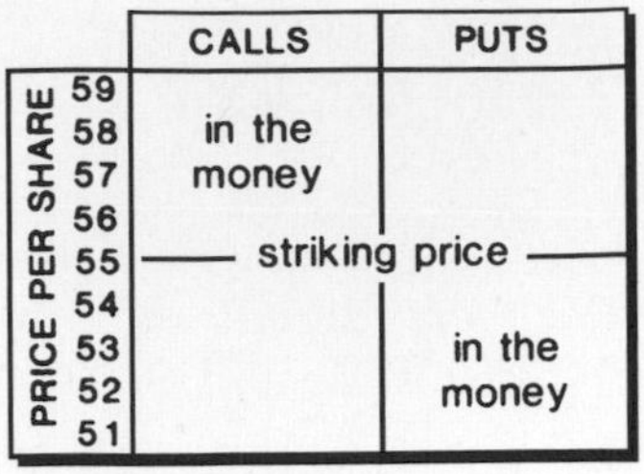

	CALLS	PUTS
59	in the	
58	money	
57		
56		
55	—— striking price ——	
54		
53		in the
52		money
51		

PRICE PER SHARE

FIGURE G.5 In the money.

STOCK VALUE	STRIKING PRICE	INTRINSIC VALUE
$38	$35	$3
43	45	0
41	40	1
65	65	0
21	20	1

FIGURE G.6 Intrinsic value.

LEAPS Long-term Equity AnticiPation Securities, long-term option contracts that work just like standardized options, but with expiration up to three years.

leverage the use of investment capital in a way that a relatively small amount of money enables the investor to control a relatively large value. (This is achieved through borrowing—for example, using borrowed money to purchase stocks or bonds—or through the purchase of options, which exist for only a short period of time but enable the option buyer to control 100 shares of stock. As a general rule, the use of leverage increases potential for profit as well as for loss.)

listed option an option traded on a public exchange and listed in the published reports in the financial press.

lock in to freeze the price of the underlying stock when the investor has sold a corresponding short call. (As long as the call position is open, the writer is locked into a striking price, regardless of current market value of the stock. In the event of exercise, the stock is delivered at that locked-in price.)

long hedge the purchase of options as a form of insurance to protect a portfolio position in the event of a price increase, a strategy employed by investors selling stock short and ensuring against a rise in the market value of the stock.

long position the status assumed by investors when they enter a buy order in advance of entering a sell order. (The long position is closed by later entering a sell order, or through expiration.)

long straddle the purchase of an identical number of calls and puts with identical striking prices and expiration dates, designed to produce profits in the event of price movement of the underlying stock in either direction adequate to surpass the cost of opening the position.

loss zone the price range of the underlying stock in which the option investor loses. (A limited loss exists for options buyers, since the premium cost is the maximum loss that can be realized.)

margin   an account with a brokerage firm containing a minimum level of cash and securities to provide collateral for short positions or for purchases for which payment has not yet been made.

market value   the value of an investment at any given time or date; the amount a buyer is willing to pay to acquire an investment and what a seller is also willing to receive to transfer the same investment.

married put   the status of a put used to hedge a long position. (Each put owned protects 100 shares of the underlying stock held in the portfolio. If the stock declines in value, the put's value will increase and offset the loss.)

money spread   alternative name for the vertical spread.

naked option   an option sold in an opening sale transaction when the seller (writer) does not own 100 shares of the underlying stock. (See Figure G.7.)

naked position   status for investors when they assume short positions in calls without also owning 100 shares of the underlying stock for each call written.

odd lot   a lot of shares that is fewer than the more typical round lot trading unit of 100 shares.

open interest   the number of open contracts of a particular option at any given time, which can be used to measure market interest.

open position   the status of a transaction when a purchase (a long position) or a sale (a short position) has been made, and before cancellation, exercise, or expiration.

opening purchase transaction   an initial transaction to buy, also known as the action of "going long."

opening sale transaction   an initial transaction to sell, also known as the action of "going short."

option   the right to buy or to sell 100 shares of stock at a specified, fixed price and by a specified date in the future.

orderly settlement   the smooth process of buying and selling, in full confidence that the terms and conditions of options contracts will be honored in a timely manner.

out of the money   the status of a call option when the underlying stock's market value is lower than the option's striking price, or of a put option when the underlying stock's market value is higher than the option's striking price. (See Figure G.8.)

paper profits (also called **unrealized profits**)   values existing only on paper but not taken at the time; paper profits (or paper losses) become realized only if a closing transaction is executed.

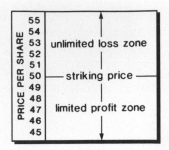

55		
54		
53	unlimited loss zone	
52		
51		
50	— striking price —	
49		
48		
47	limited profit zone	
46		
45		

(PRICE PER SHARE)

FIGURE G.7 Naked option.

	CALLS	PUTS
59		
58		out of the
57		money
56		
55	— striking price —	
54		
53	out of the	
52	money	
51		

(PRICE PER SHARE)

FIGURE G.8 Out of the money.

parity   the condition of an option at expiration, when the total premium consists of intrinsic value and no time value.

premium   the current price of an option, which a buyer pays and a seller receives at the time of the transaction. (The amount of premium is expressed as the dollar value of the option, but without dollar signs; for example, stating that an option is "at 3" means its current market value is $300.)

price/earnings ratio   a popular indicator used by stock market investors to rate and compare stocks. The current market value of the stock is divided by the most recent earnings per share to arrive at the P/E ratio.

profit margin   the most commonly used measurement of corporate operations, computed by dividing net profits by gross sales.

profit on invested capital   a fundamental test showing the yield to equity investors, computed by dividing net profits by the dollar value of outstanding capital.

profit zone   the price range of the underlying stock in which the option investor realizes a profit. (For the call buyer, the profit zone extends upward from the breakeven price. For the put buyer, the profit zone extends downward from the breakeven price.)

prospectus   a document designed to disclose all of the risk characteristics associated with a particular investment.

put   an option acquired by a buyer or granted by a seller to sell 100 shares of stock at a fixed price.

put to seller   action of exercising a put and requiring the seller to purchase 100 shares of stock at the fixed striking price.

quality of earnings   the real value of earnings as reported, which should include nonrecurring earnings, revenues from acquisitions, earnings resulting in changes in accounting methods, pro forma estimated earnings that depend on future performance, and other nonpermanent items; and including recurring earnings from primary lines of business, adjusted for bad debts.

random walk a theory about market pricing, stating that prices of stocks cannot be predicted because price movement is entirely random.

rate of return the yield from investing, calculated by dividing net cash profit upon sale by the amount spent at purchase.

ratio calendar combination spread a strategy involving both a ratio between purchases and sales and a box spread. (Long and short positions are opened on options with the same underlying stock, in varying numbers and with expiration dates extending over two or more periods. This strategy is designed to produce profits in the event of price increases or decreases in the market value of the underlying stock.)

ratio calendar spread a strategy involving a different number of options on the long side of a transaction from the number on the short side, when the expiration dates for each side are also different. (This strategy creates two separate profit and loss zone ranges, one of which disappears upon the earlier expiration.)

ratio write a strategy for partially covering one position with another for partial rather than full coverage. (A portion of risk is eliminated, so that ratio writes can be used to reduce overall risk levels.)

ready market a liquid market, one in which buyers can easily sell their holdings, or in which sellers can easily find buyers, at current market prices.

realized profits profits taken at the time a position is closed.

resistance level the price for a stock identifying the highest likely trading price under present conditions, above which the price of the stock is not likely to rise.

return if exercised the estimated rate of return option sellers will earn in the event the buyer exercises the option. (The calculation includes profit or loss in the underlying stock, dividends earned, and premium received for selling the option.) (See Figure G.9.)

return if unchanged the estimated rate of return options sellers will earn in the event the buyer does not exercise the option. (The calculation includes dividends earned on the underlying stock, and the premium received for selling the option.) (See Figure G.10.)

reverse hedge an extension of a long or short hedge in which more options are opened than the number needed to cover the stock position; this increases profit potential in the event of unfavorable movement in the market value of the underlying stock.

exercise price 40
purchase price 38
May 40 call sold for 3
dividends earned $80

call premium	$300
dividend income	80
capital gain	200
return	$580
	15.3%

basis in stock $3,800

sold May 40 call	$300
dividends earned	80
total	$380
return	10.0%

FIGURE G.9   Return if exercised.   **FIGURE G.10**   Return if unchanged.

risk tolerance   the amount of risk that an investor is able and willing to take.

roll down   the replacement of one written call with another that has a lower striking price.

roll forward   the replacement of one written call with another with the same striking price, but a later expiration date.

roll up   the replacement of one written call with another that has a higher striking price.

round lot   a lot of 100 shares of stock or of higher numbers divisible by 100, the usual trading unit on the public exchanges.

seller   an investor who grants a right in an option to someone else; the seller realizes a profit if the value of the stock moves below the specified price (call) or above the specified price (put).

series   a group of options sharing identical terms.

settlement date   the date on which a buyer is required to pay for purchases, or on which a seller is entitled to receive payment. (For stocks, settlement date is three business days after the transaction. For options, settlement date is one business day from the date of the transaction.)

share   a unit of ownership in the capital of a corporation.

short hedge   the purchase of options as a form of insurance to protect a portfolio position in the event of a price decrease, a strategy employed by investors in long positions and insuring against a decline in the market value of the stock.

short position   the status assumed by investors when they enter a sell order in advance of entering a buy order. (The short position is closed by later entering a buy order, or through expiration.)

short selling   a strategy in the stock market in which shares of stock are first sold, creating a short position for the investor, and later bought in a closing purchase transaction.

short straddle   the sale of an identical number of calls and puts with identical striking prices and expiration dates, designed to produce profits in the event of price movement of the underlying stock only within a limited range.

speculation   the use of money to assume risks for short-term profit, in the knowledge that substantial or total losses are one possible outcome. (Buying calls for leverage is one form of speculation. The buyer may earn a very large profit in a matter of days, or could lose the entire amount invested.)

spread   the simultaneous purchase and sale of options on the same underlying stock, with different striking prices or expiration dates, or both.

straddle   the simultaneous purchase and sale of the same number of calls and puts with identical striking prices and expiration dates.

striking price   the fixed price to be paid for 100 shares of stock specified in the option contract, which will be paid or received by the owner of the option contract upon exercise, regardless of the current market value of the stock.

suitability   a standard by which a particular investment or market strategy is judged. (The investor's knowledge and experience with options represent important suitability standards. Strategies are appropriate only if the investor understands the market and can afford to take the risks involved.)

supply and demand   the market forces that determine the current value for stocks. A growing number of buyers represent demand for shares, and a growing number of sellers represent supply. The price of stocks rises as demand increases, and falls as supply increases.

support level   the price for a stock identifying the lowest likely trading price under present conditions, below which the price of the stock is not likely to fall.

tax put   a strategy combining the sale of stock at a loss—taken for tax purposes—and the sale of a put at the same time. (The premium received on the put offsets the stock loss; if the put is exercised, the stock is purchased at the striking price.)

technical analysis   a study of trends and patterns of price movement in stocks, including price per share, the shape of price movements on charts, high and low ranges, and trends in pricing over time.

terms (also called **standardized terms**)   the attributes that describe an option, including the striking price, expiration month, type of option (call or put), and the underlying security.

time value   that portion of an option's current value above intrinsic value. (See Figure G.11.)

total return   the combined return including income from selling a call, capital gain from profit on selling the stock, and dividends earned and received. (Total return may be calculated in two ways: return if the option is exercised, and return if the option expires worthless.) (See Figure G.12.)

uncovered option   the same as a naked option—the sale of an option not covered, or protected, by the ownership of 100 shares of the underlying stock.

underlying stock   the stock on which the option grants the right to buy or sell, which is specified in every option contract.

variable hedge   a hedge involving a long position and a short position in related options, when one side contains a greater number of options than the other. (The desired result is reduction of risks or potentially greater profits.)

vertical spread   a spread involving different striking prices but identical expiration dates.

volatility   a measure of the degree of change in a stock's market value, measured over a 12-month period and stated as a percentage. (To measure volatility, subtract the lowest 12-month price from the highest 12-month price, and divide the answer by the 12-month lowest price.) (See Figure G.13.)

TOTAL PREMIUM	INTRINSIC VALUE	TIME VALUE
$4	$3	$1
2	0	2
4	1	3
1	0	1
3	1	2

FIGURE G.11   Time value.

stock exercised at $40 (basis $34), held for 13 months

option premium	$ 800
dividends	110
capital gain	600
total	$1,510
13 months	44.4%
annualized	41.0%

FIGURE G.12   Total return.

$$\frac{\text{high} - \text{low}}{\text{low}}$$

ANNUAL HIGH	ANNUAL LOW	PERCENT
$ 65	$ 43	51%
37	34	9
45	41	10
35	25	4
84	62	35
71	68	4
118	101	17
154	112	38

FIGURE G.13 Volatility.

volume   the level of trading activity in a stock, an option, or the market as a whole.

wasting asset   any asset that declines in value over time. (An option is an example of a wasting asset because it exists only until expiration, after which it becomes worthless.)

writer   the individual who sells (writes) a call (or a put).

Index